DEATH TRAP

"A chilling tale of a sociopathic wife and mother . . . a compelling journey from the inside of this woman's mind to final justice in a court of law. For three days I did little else but read this book."

> —**Harry N. MacLean**, *New York Times* best-selling author of *In Broad Daylight*

I'LL BE WATCHING YOU

"Phelps has an unrelenting sense for detail that affirms his place, book by book, as one of our most engaging crime journalists."

> —**Katherine Ramsland**

IF LOOKS COULD KILL

"M. William Phelps, one of America's finest true-crime writers, has written a compelling and gripping book about an intriguing murder mystery. Readers of this genre will thoroughly enjoy this book."

> —**Vincent Bugliosi**

"Starts quickly and doesn't slow down. . . . Phelps consistently ratchets up the dramatic tension, hooking readers. His thorough research and interviews give the book complexity, richness of character, and urgency."

> —**Stephen Singular**

MURDER IN THE HEARTLAND

"Drawing on interviews with law officers and relatives, the author has done significant research. His facile writing pulls the reader along."

> —*St. Louis Post-Dispatch*

"Phelps expertly reminds us that when the darkest form of evil invades the quiet and safe outposts of rural America, the tragedy is greatly magnified. Get ready for some sleepless nights."

> —**Carlton Stowers**

"This is the most disturbing and moving look at murder in rural America since Capote's *In Cold Blood*."

—**Gregg Olsen**

SLEEP IN HEAVENLY PEACE

"An exceptional book by an exceptional true-crime writer. Phelps exposes long-hidden secrets and reveals disquieting truths."

—**Kathryn Casey**

EVERY MOVE YOU MAKE

"An insightful and fast-paced examination of the inner workings of a good cop and his bad informant, culminating in an unforgettable truth-is-stranger-than-fiction climax."

—**Michael M. Baden, M.D.**

"M. William Phelps is the rising star of the nonfiction crime genre, and his true tales of murder are scary-as-hell thrill rides into the dark heart of the inhuman condition."

—**Douglas Clegg**

LETHAL GUARDIAN

"An intense roller-coaster of a crime story . . . complex, with twists and turns worthy of any great detective mystery . . . reads more like a novel than your standard non-fiction crime book."

—**Steve Jackson**

PERFECT POISON

"True crime at its best—compelling, gripping, an edge-of-the-seat thriller. Phelps packs wallops of delight with his skillful ability to narrate a suspenseful story."

—**Harvey Rachlin**

"A compelling account of terror . . . the author dedicates himself to unmasking the psychopath with facts, insight and the other proven methods of journalistic leg work."

—**Lowell Cauffiel**

Also By M. William Phelps

Perfect Poison
Lethal Guardian
Every Move You Make
Sleep in Heavenly Peace
Murder in the Heartland
Because You Loved Me
If Looks Could Kill
I'll Be Watching You
Deadly Secrets
Cruel Death
Death Trap
Kill For Me
Love Her to Death
Too Young to Kill
Never See Them Again
Kiss of the She-Devil
Bad Girls
Obsessed
The Killing Kind
She Survived: Melissa (e-book)
She Survived: Jane (e-book)
I'd Kill For You
To Love and To Kill

ONE BREATH AWAY

M. WILLIAM PHELPS

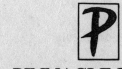

PINNACLE BOOKS
Kensington Publishing Corp.
http://www.kensingtonbooks.com

PINNACLE BOOKS are published by

Kensington Publishing Corp.
119 West 40th Street
New York, NY 10018

All Kensington Titles, Imprints, and Distributed Lines are available at special quantity discounts for bulk purchases for sales promotions, premiums, fund-raising, and educational or institutional use. Special book excerpts or customized printings can also be created to fit specific needs. For details, write or phone the office of the Kensington special sales manager: Kensington Publishing Corp., 119 West 40th Street, New York, NY 10018, attn: Special Sales Department, Phone: 1-800-221-2647.

Pinnacle and the P logo Reg. U.S. Pat. & TM Off.

ISBN-13: 978-0-7860-3501-4
ISBN-10: 0-7860-3501-3
First Kensington Mass Market Edition: March 2016

eISBN-13: 978-0-7860-3502-1
eISBN-10: 0-7860-3502-1
Kensington Electronic Edition: March 2016

10 9 8 7 6 5 4 3 2 1

Printed in the United States of America

This book is dedicated to: Tim Samaras, Mindy McCready, Jenni Rivera, Russell Armstrong, Gia Allemand, Phil Harris, Shain Gandee, Roy Garber, Rodney King, Joey Kovar, Julien Hug, Jennifer Lyon, Frankie Abernathy, Anna Nicole Smith, Pedro Zamora, Mark Balelo, Cheryl Kosewicz, Joe Cerniglia, Mitchell Guist, Najai Turpin, Nathan Clutter, Rachel Brown, Bobbi Kristina Brown, and Tobias Strebel.

All reality stars.

All dead.

Many from suicide.

I knew none of them personally.

Was there a limit to what he could endure? It seemed not. He was more vulnerable to suffering—and at the same time, paradoxically, he had a greater capacity for it. . . .

—Charles Jackson, *The Lost Weekend*

PART ONE

CHAPTER 1

IT WAS ONE of those telephone calls in the middle of the night we all fear. The kind that jolts your heart, puts a pit in your gut, and startles you awake—your adrenaline pumping the moment you open your eyes.

Somebody's dead!

Quickly roused from REM sleep by a voice calling out, letting her know there was someone on the phone, Rachel Robidoux had no idea that everything in life, as she knew it, was about to change. Nor would her life, or that of one of her children, ever be the same again.

She got out of bed and put the phone to her ear: "Hello? What is it?" Rachel could barely get the words out.

That time of night, hell, you'd *expect* bad news on the other end of the line.

The day preceding the telephone call, however, had started out like any other Sunday in forty-year-old Rachel Robidoux's life.

Rachel woke up at her usual 5 A.M. hour to get ready for work. It was October 24, 2010, the weather rather balmy for this time of the year in St. Petersburg, Florida.

As Rachel opened the door to leave, a wall of humid, almost wet, tropical, 75-degree morning air hit her in the face.

Within Pinellas County, St. Petersburg is a rather large city, a population of about a quarter million, give or take. With Tropicana Field downtown, home to Major League Baseball's Tampa Bay Rays, St. Pete, as locals call it, still holds on to that resort-town feel its founder had intended back in 1888 when the city was born.

Rachel Robidoux worked at Denny's on Thirty-Fourth Street North, downtown. She'd been there for well over a decade. Normally, on Sundays, Rachel worked the day shift: seven to four. To this mother of five, although she'd gotten used to it by now, St. Pete might as well have been New York City. Rachel had been born and raised (mostly) in a one-stop-sign, one-intersection, everybody-knows-everybody, small New England town.

As the end of her shift on that Sunday approached, Rachel took a call from one of her five daughters, Ashley McCauley, who had turned seventeen that past April.

"You want to go to Crescent Lake Park with Grandma after you get out?"

This sounded like a good time, Rachel thought. "I'll pick you two up soon," she said.

Crescent Lake Park is in an area of St. Pete where families and lovers and kids hang out on those seemingly endless, perfect Florida days, with skies that warm color of robin's-egg blue. People flock there and enjoy the ducks and geese and swans, as well as the company they keep. Rachel needed this comforting space in her life. Not that things had been chaotic or all that difficult lately, having been through some rather extremely tough times in her life, same as just about every working-class family in the country. However, she'd had some issues over the past few years with her oldest daughter, Jennifer Mee. Jen had turned nineteen in July. Her life, as Rachel later put it, had not gone along a trajectory Rachel and her husband, Chris, Jennifer's stepfather, would have liked. Jen was Rachel's firstborn, a child from a failed relationship when Rachel was twenty-one. In fact, Jen was just eighteen months old when Rachel met Chris, Ashley three months old—their other children, Kayla, Destiny and McKenzie, Rachel and Chris had together. As far as the oldest girls were concerned, however, Chris Robidoux had always considered himself their father.

A little over a year ago, some weeks before her eighteenth birthday, Jennifer had moved out of the house and was out on her own. Before that, she had one foot out, anyway, often staying with one friend for a month, or babysitting, or staying with other friends for a few weeks here and there, maybe at a motel or even on a park bench. All this happened after Jennifer had garnered international fame in the days beyond January 23, 2007, for experiencing a bout with the hiccups that lasted for about five weeks. Still, with Jennifer moving out and "changing," as Rachel liked to say, it wasn't a major problem between Rachel and her daughter. For Rachel, it was more about the people who had flocked to Jennifer after her star rose—on top of the guys Jennifer had been dating for what was about four years.

"Thugs," Rachel called them.

Although Rachel and Jennifer spoke as much as two to three times per week, their conversations weren't like they used to be. It was definitely not the personal talk that mothers and daughters have. These days, Rachel understood (though she later admitted some denial on her part) that Jennifer was shielding parts of herself and her chosen lifestyle. Just a look at Jennifer's Myspace page, back when that gulf between mom and daughter had begun to grow, had given Rachel and Chris an idea of where Jen was headed: *My love is nt a game im real n dnt wnt a fake lien cheaten azz nigga.*

"I guess I should have known with the signs," Rachel recalled. "But I didn't. Jen was into some 'activities' and later she [said she] was ashamed of it all."

Rachel had no idea to what extent Jen had become involved in that street life, ripping and running with a group of hard-boiled, seasoned ruffians and tough street kids her own age. Jen had become somebody she had actually once said she despised. Maybe some naiveté existed on Rachel's part, or perhaps it was just a mother struggling to keep up with a middle-class lifestyle while still having three young kids at home. Whatever the reason, Rachel lost that close touch with Jen. As they drifted apart, Rachel felt her daughter was old enough to begin carving out her own life, make her own mistakes, and take responsibility. Besides that, Chris and Jen had been at odds for a long time now, butting heads like rams. Both Rachel and Chris knew they couldn't change Jennifer, or tell her how to live. They had been through so much during Jen's hiccup period. Both were tired, frustrated, and ready to move on.

CHAPTER 2

DOWN AT CRESCENT Lake Park, after Rachel stopped and picked up her mother and Ashley, they sat and enjoyed the early evening. They fed the ducks, talked, and caught up on each other's lives. That early-morning humidity and warmth had turned into a scorching afternoon sun. During the week, Rachel lived at her mother's house just outside downtown St. Pete. Rachel and Chris and the kids had a house about ninety minutes out of town in the north, so it was more feasible and less expensive if Rachel stayed with her mother and father during the workweek. Chris collected disability—a stay-at-home dad, watching the kids, tending to the household chores. He had suffered several ailments, some psychological, others medical. The situation of Chris being home with the kids had been by design, in some ways, Rachel said. It happened after an incident some years back that greatly disturbed the entire family's trust in anyone else being around their children.

Throughout that afternoon at the park, Rachel had called Jennifer several times. She hadn't been able to reach her. Rachel, of course, wanted Jen to join them, but Jen wasn't responding to her phone calls, texts, or voice mails. And although Jen had changed and lived what Rachel and Chris saw as an unhealthy and dangerous lifestyle, they were not estranged from one another. They disagreed about things, but they always talked and tried to see each other when they could. Jen not answering her phone and not calling back was out of character.

"I was actually upset that I couldn't get hold of Jennifer on that day," Rachel remembered.

Where the heck is she?

Something happened during Rachel's break at work earlier that morning that had upset her, especially now as she thought back on it later in the day.

Jennifer had called. "Mom?"

"Yeah . . . ? Jennifer, hi. How are you?"

Jennifer knew her mother had had surgery for a recurring cyst a few weeks prior and had been in a lot of pain. She was taking powerful pain medication for it.

"Do you have any pain pills left from your operation?" Jennifer asked.

Rachel was alarmed. "Pain pills? Why would you need *pain* pills, Jennifer?"

"Mom, listen. . . . Lamont got hurt. He's in a lot of pain." Lamont "Mont" Newton was Jennifer's most recent boyfriend; she had been dating the twenty-two-year-old St. Pete native for the past several months. Lamont seemed like a "nice guy," Rachel said. He was five-nine, and in great physical shape at 165 pounds. Lamont sported Bob Marley–type dreads down across his shoulders, had bushy eyebrows and clean-shaven facial skin, and generally had a calm disposition. He was polite. As Rachel saw it, Lamont was an excellent alternative and the polar opposite to Jen's previous boyfriend, a pants-down-to-his-knees, boxer-shorts-showing, ball cap tipped to one side, "yo" this/"yo" that, spot-on "thug" and violent abuser—a man who had beaten Jen on more than one occasion. In contrast, at least on the surface, Lamont came across as a guy who was entirely into Jennifer as a partner. Not what he could get from her.

"We wanted her to date within her own race," Rachel explained at the risk of coming across bigoted, claiming she and her husband were anything but racists. "Yet, Jen said she had chosen colored men to date because she had lost faith in—and wanted nothing to do with—white men altogether." Her decision stemmed specifically from a difficult period in her life when Jen was a child.

"No," Rachel said to the request for pain pills. "Tell him to go to the hospital, Jennifer. I need my medication."

Jennifer didn't sound frantic or dazed. "She didn't sound normal, either," Rachel was quick to point out. "More anxious—I felt like something was wrong, but I was clueless."

That request had come from Jen as though she was simply calling and asking her mother for some pain meds to help her boyfriend work through a back issue. And when she couldn't get the pills, well, that was it. The pair said their good-byes, promised to talk to one another later, and hung up.

But something was indeed wrong with Jennifer. Rachel had no idea that within a few hours after that phone call, their lives would take a turn none of them ever saw coming.

CHAPTER 3

RACHEL CALLED JENNIFER again as they prepared to leave Crescent Lake Park on October 24, 2010, somewhere around six in the evening.

Still, no answer.

Damn, what's going on? Rachel asked herself.

Now she was truly concerned for her daughter.

On the way to drop off Ashley at her apartment—Ashley lived on her own in the city—Rachel asked Ashley what she thought Jennifer was up to, and if Ashley knew of any recent problems Jen might have, especially ones that Rachel should know about. Ashley and Jen had been tight once, but not so much anymore. Ashley did not approve of the way Jennifer had been living her life.

It was probably nothing, they decided after talking it through. Jen was likely just being herself and secretive for no apparent reason. Jen had a "diagnosed learning disability," Rachel said. She had not graduated high school, partly because of her learning difficulties and the aftermath of her quasi-celebrity while becoming known around the world as the "Hiccup Girl" after a five-week bout with the hiccups. Some of the examinations Rachel had brought her daughter to had classified Jennifer as having the intelligence of a fifth or sixth grader, according to Rachel. Jennifer wasn't stupid by any means. Yet, she did not have a lot of common sense and was often involved in things before she knew what she was getting into, or how deep the water was.

When Rachel got back to her parents' place, she

had dinner with her mother and father, called Chris to say she loved him and to check in with the younger kids still at home. They talked a little bit about the day and night. After that, totally wiped out, Rachel retired to bed by about 9:30 P.M.

As she lay in bed, thinking about her day, Rachel was worried about Jennifer, and what her daughter might be up to weighed heavily on the mind of the mother of five. Why hadn't they been able to get hold of her all day and night? Where had she gone? It was unlike Jennifer to go off without talking to her mother. Not answer a text or call back? Jen might have hidden things from the family, but she wasn't a daughter who disappeared off the radar.

By ten o'clock, Rachel fell asleep—and it was not an hour later when the phone call that would change everything rang throughout the dark stillness of her mother and father's house, rustling them awake.

CHAPTER 4

AFTER THE COUNTY jail computer operator went through the various options for the man on the other end of the telephone, Jennifer Mee came on the line and said, "Is Mommy up?"

Jen's grandfather, Rachel's father, had answered the phone. Rachel was asleep. "No, she went to bed. . . . How you doing?" the grandfather said before asking why Jennifer was calling from jail.

"I got charged with murder . . . first-degree . . . ," Jen

uttered in a casual manner, as if it was just another day. She came across unfazed by this alarming revelation, even as it came out of her own mouth.

"What'd you do?"

"Murder in the first degree," Jen reiterated.

"Murder? First degree?" the grandfather asked, stunned by the comment.

Rather plainly, maybe even calmly, Jennifer said, "Yes, sir." It was almost as if she herself did not understand what was happening, where she was, or how serious the charges she faced were.

There was silence. Then, "Well . . . who did you kill?" Jen's grandfather asked.

"Um, I didn't do nothing. I was just there at the wrong time, the wrong place. I got caught up in it all."

"When did all of this happen?"

"It took place last night and the police found me and arrested me today."

That must have been the reason why Rachel had sensed something in Jen's voice earlier that morning. She'd been involved in an incident where someone was murdered the previous night and yet she hadn't mentioned it to Rachel during that phone call. Why hadn't she shared this information with her mother when she had the opportunity while trying to pry those pills out of Rachel?

Jen's grandfather told her he was going to wake up her mother.

Rachel sounded groggy and still half asleep when she came on the phone. "Hello . . . ?"

"Hi, Momma."

"Jennifer, what's going on?" Rachel asked, right away

thinking, *Drugs. She's been arrested on drug charges, along with all of those derelicts she hangs out and now lives with.*

"I'm in jail."

"*Why* are you in jail?"

"Um, first degree . . . um, murder in the first degree." Jennifer sounded a little more humbled now, even a bit scared.

"Who'd you kill?"

"I ain't kill nobody."

"Well, then, how are they charging you with . . . murder?"

"Because I set everything up."

There was a brief moment of quiet between them after that.

Then Jennifer continued: "It all went wrong, Momma. Shit just went downhill after everything happened, Mom." She was crying now, maybe realizing for the first time how serious a turn her life had just taken.

"Who were you trying to kill, Jennifer?"

"Nobody," she said through tears and anguish, the weight of it all hitting her very hard. "It wasn't even supposed to happen like that, Mom—"

Rachel cut her off: "Well, something happened, obviously, Jennifer, if you're in jail."

"Okay," Jennifer said. "Me, Laron, and Lamont, all right . . . A dude . . . was talking about he wanted a half, right, so I told him to come meet me at the park where I . . . and the boys run him into a little alley thing. . . . Then Lamont pulled a gun out on him. The guy went to go reach for the gun and pulled the barrel and . . ." As Jennifer tried to continue, voices could be heard in the background. Jennifer said she had to get off the phone. "Mom?"

"What?"

"I'll call you when I can, because I have to go." She broke down. "Mommy, try to visit me. Please."

Rachel asked how.

Jen told her to call the jail in the morning and sort it out.

"Where you at, Clearwater Jail?" Rachel asked.

"Yes, ma'am," Jennifer answered.

"All right, Jennifer. I love you."

"I love you, too, Mom."

"Bye."

CHAPTER 5

HOW DOES A parent hang up the phone with a child in tears, sounding desperate and somewhat confused about what is happening to her, all in the context of a murder charge, and then go back to bed?

Doesn't happen.

Rachel sat down at the dining-room table, rubbed her face, and took a deep breath.

Murder?

This was the last phone call she had ever expected to receive.

Jennifer arrested for first-degree murder? What in the hell?

The call was likely recorded, Rachel thought as she tried to figure out her next move and how she could help Jennifer. *There must be some mistake here,* Rachel told herself. *Jennifer, a murderer?* It didn't sound right.

"*Because I set everything up,*" Rachel heard Jennifer

say. That was the reason why she had been arrested, Jennifer had told her mother.

"Because I set everything up."

Set what up? A drug deal? Or was the drug deal a ruse to rob some dude and kill him?

None of it made sense. Rachel knew her daughter. Jennifer was a lot of things, but a murderer? No parent wanted to think his or her child could commit a morally corrupt, morally reprehensible act as murder. Further, Rachel believed Jennifer did not have that type of malevolence within her soul, nor had she enough intelligence, essentially, to pull it off. In addition, Jennifer had been raised under a strict Christian upbringing. She understood there was a price to pay eternally for breaking one of the Commandments and committing an act of evil, such as murder.

As Rachel sat, thinking about what her daughter was being accused of, the phone rang.

Jennifer?

Caller ID said it was the jail.

Jennifer!

Maybe it was *all some sort of misunderstanding?*

"Yes?" Rachel said eagerly.

A female guard was on the other end. "Listen," she said, "if I had a daughter eighteen, nineteen years old, and I had just been given that kind of news, I would want more details than she was able to give you in the very short phone call you two just had."

"Thank you," Rachel responded.

Indeed. What in the world had happened?

The guard began by explaining why Jennifer had been brought in and booked.

"Come to find out," Rachel explained later, "the guard got a lot of the details wrong, but I was able to get the gist of why Jennifer was locked up. [The guard] told me a drug deal had been set up and a girl was murdered."

That murdered "girl" was actually Shannon (pronounced SH-NON) Griffin, a twenty-two-year-old male Florida transplant from Hurricane Katrina–ravaged Petal, Mississippi. Shannon was part of a migration of people on the move after the storm devastated the southern coast, and those left without homes had nowhere to set their pillows. Shannon's much older cousin had brought him to St. Pete and set him up with a job at Walmart, where Shannon had just recently celebrated his first-year anniversary with his first paid weeklong vacation. Shannon, a good-looking kid with short-cropped hair and a glowing smile everyone noticed, was planning to go to college. He wanted to get out of Florida eventually and travel. To Shannon, Florida seemed so confining. It was also a place where things happened to people that would, otherwise, never happen anywhere else.

A family member later said Shannon was humble and understood what he had because he'd come from a poverty-stricken community in Mississippi, where there was nothing to do and no work. As he integrated himself into the St. Pete community, where he was living, Shannon realized opportunity was all around him.

"From all aspects of his life," said one person closely connected to this case, "Shannon Griffin seemed like a really, *really* nice person."

Shannon's cousin Doug Bolden later explained that after he was given the news "nobody should ever have to receive," which informed him that Shannon had been murdered, he wondered what could have happened and where things could have gone wrong? It didn't seem possible the way people were saying. Doug described Shannon as a "loner" and the type of young adult who stayed inside, surfed the Internet mostly, and then went to work. He wasn't some gangbanger wannabe hanging around the street corners of St. Pete, looking for trouble.

For one, Walmart and drug use generally didn't fall within the same category. Like other major retail corporations, Walmart conducted random drug tests after an initial hiring drug screen on all employees, no exemptions. Why would Shannon be out buying drugs if he knew he'd eventually lose his job? Furthermore, Shannon was a recluse—why would he even be out at night?

Family members in St. Pete were dumbfounded by the accusation that Shannon was out cruising for dope. It didn't sound like him at all.

Rachel found out from that same guard that Jennifer was somehow the "bait" to get Shannon Griffin to show up at a park, but the guard couldn't really say much else about that aspect of the crime.

Bait? What does she mean by that?

After the phone call, Rachel went to her room and sat on the edge of the bed. Heavy stuff. The Robidoux family wasn't used to this type of distress. They weren't people in and out of court, always in trouble with the law or family services. For the most part, their lives had been somewhat "normal" since Jennifer's bout with the hiccups landed them on NBC's *Today*, not to mention *Inside Edition,* and news outlets from Florida to Russia, along with hundreds of thousands of Internet links. At one time, Hiccup Girl was a worldwide nickname associated with Jennifer Mee. Everyone had seen and heard Jennifer's story, and most had felt compassion and empathy for her condition.

"I was trying to wake up from a nightmare I literally felt like I was walking around in," Rachel explained.

Those moments after the call were so surreal, Rachel concluded, she hoped to watch the sun rise and realize it *was* a dream.

"And then I could have a good laugh."

CHAPTER 6

AFTER TOSSING AND turning throughout the night, Rachel called her boss. She didn't know how she was going to make it into work after what had happened.

"I don't know what time or even if I'll be in tomorrow," she said, explaining what was going on, saying how she needed to focus on her daughter and find an attorney.

"Look, Rachel," her boss said, "I need you to come in until I can find someone to cover for you."

Great.

Rachel forced herself to wake up and drive into work like a disciplined soldier. She was exhausted, of course. As her morning went on, the local media picked up on the story, which was gaining plenty of traction considering Jennifer had become an international, fifteen-minute celebrity for having those hiccups. The hiccups, Rachel and Jennifer had learned since her star rose and fell, had actually been a symptom of a more serious, underlying medical condition.

As she went about her day, Rachel didn't realize how tight a grip the story had taken on pop culture because she had not paid attention to the television or radio as she worked. Her mind was focused on her kid. What were they going to do? They did not have the funds or the assets to hire an expensive, high-profile attorney who could get Jennifer out of jail on bond (if the court allowed it).

A disc jockey for one of the local radio stations out of Tampa who had spoken to Jennifer back when she had the hiccups called Rachel at work. She didn't know it, Rachel later alleged, but the station recorded the conversation with her that day and put it on air. The quote that was played and replayed all day long, and would continue to be in the weeks and months that followed, was Rachel saying: "I don't think she knew what was going to happen because that's not Jennifer. She's not out to hurt anyone. She is a lovable, sweet little girl who wouldn't hurt a fly."

The problem now, however, was that as Jennifer's life was being dissected by journalists and bloggers, the same "sweet little girl who wouldn't hurt a fly" had recently described herself on her Myspace page as the "female version of a hustla."

Jennifer, it appeared, was one person to her mother and family, and quite another out in her world of "hustling." The media was picking up on the "bad girl" side of Jennifer and running with it. Many assumed that the innocent fifteen-year-old who had battled intractable hiccups, and whom the world had felt sorry for, was a very different person now.

CHAPTER 7

JENNIFER MEE WAS a confused, mixed-up, under-educated problem child with learning disabilities and health concerns. There can be no denying those facts. In early 2014, Jennifer wrote to me and talked about how her life back then had changed so suddenly, literally overnight, from the time she became America's hiccupping sweetheart—and someone to feel sorry for—to one of the most hated, debated, and ridiculed pop culture celebrities Americans have seen since "celebrity" and "reality" have become engrained in society.

Life had not started out for Jennifer with all of these problems. She had always lived a quiet existence, devoid of much trouble, controversy, major problems, or issues other than her own educational challenges and health concerns. Jennifer actually dreamed of one day "playing in the WNBA," professional women's basketball. This, mind you, coming from a girl who is five feet tall, 145 pounds—not your typical starting forward or guard on the court in women's basketball. A second dream she had, if basketball fell out of her reach, was to own a hair salon.

Jennifer had long, brownish black hair—thick,

healthy hair—bushy eyebrows (for which she was actually ridiculed after becoming a celebrity, with one website seemingly devoted to pointing out that her only crime was having a "disastrous battle zone" over her eyes), brown eyes (constantly darting left to right), pudgy cheeks, and a fair-skinned, white complexion (for a Floridian). Jen and Rachel, despite the mom being much taller, shared similar features and could have, at one time, passed for sisters.

"I'm a very hands-on type of person," Jennifer explained to me. "I've always seen my life going into doing *big* things."

Moving out of the house, away from Rachel and her sisters, Jennifer said, was something she did because staying at home made her feel "like an outcast," as though she didn't belong or fit in. She and her stepfather, Chris Robidoux, at the time Jennifer moved out in the months before her eighteenth birthday, could not stand to be in the same room together.

"I felt like I couldn't make anyone happy," Jennifer recalled of that period when things came to a head and she left home.

According to others, during the time Jennifer's star had completely fallen (mid-2007, after the hiccup popularity subsided, and when she was arrested on murder charges in 2010), she led a "transient" lifestyle, hopping from one motel room to another, one friend's apartment to the next, with nowhere truly to call home. And that transitory way of life was going to hurt Jennifer as she went before a judge for the first time.

CHAPTER 8

AFTER SHE TALKED to that radio station, and the interview she gave went viral in Tampa and the surrounding communities outside St. Pete, the media became like a growth on Rachel's skin, now infected and bleeding, more irritating by the moment.

This story exemplified the fact that in this country, whether we want to admit or dismiss it, we love nothing better than to see a star dissolve in the sky as it falls, crashing and burning before our eyes. We prop people up, knock them down, and turn the fall into entertainment.

Rachel was a nervous wreck at work and couldn't do her job after the radio interview and subsequent satellite truck invasion moving into St. Pete.

"I have to sit in the office," Rachel told her boss.

"Go ahead."

"I almost felt as if I was outside of my body," Rachel recalled. "I had so much stress."

The massive movement to report on this story began to twist Rachel's insides out. It was as if, Rachel explained, zombies attacked the restaurant. Media were unyielding. Reporters began badgering her: phone calls, texts, e-mails. They'd had her contact information because of the hiccup story. Now they all wanted the exclusive with Rachel. What was the mother of the Hiccup Girl thinking? How was she feeling? How was Jennifer handling jail? Was she still hiccupping?

This was so much more than going to the next-door neighbor— *"She was a quiet kid. You'd never expect it from her"*—and getting that proverbial clichéd sound bite for the nightly news. Quite the opposite, Rachel was the mother of the Hiccup Girl, whom everyone had come to know so well after Rachel had made all those appearances with Jennifer. How did she feel about her daughter allegedly being involved in a brutal murder? And what happened, anyway? What was Jennifer saying about her involvement?

In any other place, at any other time, with any other suspect, this sort of murder would have been a blip on page A-24 of the local newspapers, a little article mentioning what happened, and that would be all. It would have been forgotten. No television media whatsoever. It's a sad testament to what we value as news in today's world, but it's the truth that an inner-city crime isn't as interesting to news watchers as the wealthy socialite knocking off her husband in Palm Beach. We want our murder stories packaged one way—and this case would not have been considered newsworthy had Jennifer Mee not been a part of it.

The feel of the first stories published about Jennifer's arrest was that the media members were hoping and wishing like hell she were guilty. It would be a much bigger story if Jennifer had pulled the trigger and had turned into some type of villainous murderer in the years since her hiccup celebrity had risen and fallen. Already, within a day, Jennifer's Myspace pages were being pillaged and quoted by media, the emphasis on her "gangsta" lifestyle, as if this had been a clear indication that Jennifer had turned to deadly means to sort out her problems in life. As it was, none of the facts surrounding twenty-two-year-old Shannon Griffin's murder had been made public yet.

Not one media outlet had looked into the background of this girl and where she had come from— there was an assumption that her life had spiraled out of control because she was once famous and, after losing all of that fame, became bitter and self-centered and needed that fame in order to exist.

My name is jennifer, im almost 19, she had posted on her Myspace months before her arrest, *but dont let the age fool you, the struggles ive been through has made me grown up so much. . . .*

Jennifer explained to me that her life growing up "with four younger sisters" was "okay": "My mother always worked to make ends meet."

But something happened early in life, Rachel and Jennifer later claimed, and it changed everything.

"I was raped at an early age," Jennifer said, ". . . and after that happened, I became very depressed. I felt like it was my fault." The alleged perpatrators were white, which became the reason, Jennifer claimed, she wound up depising white men and dating just African-American males.

CHAPTER 9

RACHEL NEEDED TO get out of Denny's, into her car, and move the hell away from the mob of media, with the calls, texts, and e-mails, and find a lawyer who could take Jennifer's case. For her own sake, Rachel needed to find out what had happened. Before she had the facts to contend with, Rachel didn't want to start judging people and those Jennifer hung around. (After all, Rachel knew Jennifer was no Girl Scout.) If

Jennifer was involved, there was an explanation and they'd deal with it. However, they couldn't do that without a lawyer—a damn good one, too. Rachel worried that Florida had become a ground zero over the past ten years for super-high-profile court cases seen around the world. Jennifer's was now slated to be next in a line that included William Kennedy Smith, Casey Anthony, and soon George Zimmerman—all of whom had been, or would eventually be, acquitted.

Rachel took a call from the radio station after the interview aired, according to Rachel's recollection, and the disc jockey felt bad, he said, about airing the interview without Rachel knowing. Rachel was careening off the walls, her mind a mishmash of possibilities, none of them good.

"I know a lawyer you can call," the disc jockey said. "He's waiting for you to phone him."

"Yeah, who?"

"John Trevena. He's out of Largo."

Trevena was a well-respected litigator, who had represented some high-profile defendants and won. As a Board Certified Criminal Trial Lawyer, Trevena brought to the courtroom a wide swath of experience as a former police officer, former assistant state's attorney (ASA), not to mention his more than twenty-five years in criminal and related civil rights matters. Big and burly, at times donning a Burl Ives goatee or just the mustache half of it, Trevena's career, as what he once called an "effective litigator," spoke for itself. His core message was one that included the thoughts of a lawyer who understood "what is at stake" for his clients on a personal level. Trevena wasn't a guy collecting a check to sit next to some newsworthy criminal and go through the motions; he promoted himself as a guy who deeply cared about justice and its place in a free society. Incredibly, he did not think murder cases were the toughest to fight inside a courtroom. He once told a reporter, "In my experience, I would say that DUI manslaughter cases are the most complex, because sometimes you are representing people who have no criminal history, but are facing a double-digit prison sentence. . . ."

He further explained that representing "professionals or mothers who are not alcoholics or frequent drinkers," but still face the sledgehammer of a judge and years behind bars for a "single mistake," takes an incredible amount of defensive tact and legal knowledge to support properly. In addition, Trevena knew that plea deals had never been easier to negotiate, mainly because the court system, at least in Florida, cannot deal with the flood of criminals and potential long-term court proceedings it faces: "I believe that the system does not have the financial ability to sustain the number of defendants entitled to a jury trial. If everyone were to exercise their right to a jury trial, the system wouldn't be able to function."[1]

Still, could Rachel afford such a lawyer? With that kind of experience came a second mortgage and debt.

"No way," she said.

"Pro bono," her radio guy advised. "Call him!"

It appeared John Trevena had expressed some interest in representing Jennifer without a fee.

CHAPTER 10

RACHEL AND CHRIS Robidoux had always been, as Rachel later put it, "more country-living kind of people" than the city dwellers they became after moving to Florida. Whereas Florida is a winter mecca for snowbirds flying south to escape the cold New England winters, Rachel and Chris left their home state of Vermont and wound up in St. Pete after several extended family members got together and made the decision to relocate. Thus, after Rachel's daughter, Ashley McCauley (Rachel's maiden name), moved out at seventeen (Jennifer following shortly after), Rachel and Chris responded to that country blood pumping through their veins and moved to Spring Hill, Florida, a ninety-minute drive from St. Pete.

"Chris and I believed it was better to live in Spring Hill and raise the [younger] kids there, away from the city," Rachel explained.

Spring Hill was closer to their roots. Rachel and Chris had grown up in different New England states as children: Rachel in Connecticut; Chris in Vermont. They had actually met for the first time on a class field trip to Old Sturbridge Village, Massachusetts, in the fifth grade. That was 1981. Rachel was eleven, Chris one month older.

Fast-forward to 1993. Rachel and Chris were introduced by Rachel's girlfriend. This was after Rachel and her family moved to Rutland, Vermont, from East Hartford, Connecticut, and Rachel made the decision to stay in Rutland after her family moved back to Connecticut. Rachel and Chris had no idea they had hung out on that field trip so many years earlier, until one day after they started dating and began chatting about it. When she met Chris, Rachel had two young children from different fathers to take care of already and was in her early twenties.

Rachel had been in a "long-term relationship" with Jennifer's father before she met Chris, "but that didn't work out," she said. Jennifer was just eighteen months old, and Ashley three months, when Rachel and Chris fell in love. And over the next several years, as they built a home in Rutland, living just outside the town seat, they had three children together: Kayla, Destiny, and McKenzie. Chris and Rachel now had five girls to raise.

"By 2004, my parents, who were living in New Jersey with my brother," Rachel recalled, "were retired and wanting to move to Florida." And after several conversations between everyone, it was agreed that they'd all make the move to St. Pete.

Jennifer was the oldest when they moved; she had just turned thirteen. The principal culture shock to Jennifer was the transition from a "very small school and town," Rachel made a point of saying. "K through eight [grades] were in the same building, one stop sign in the center of town back home." This, on top of all those other small-town New England clichés you might find in a Stephen King novel. On top of that, Jennifer had grown accustomed to the intimacy and personal connection between student and teacher that the New England school system offered. It seemed as if it happened overnight that Jennifer was thrust into the hustle, bustle, and absolute disconnected school environment most of Florida has experienced, where classrooms can run into the forty to fifty students, with some forced to sit at desks in the hallways. Yet, as large as Florida's education system is, within all of that, Florida has still managed to post rankings in the top ten and twenty of the nation (2012). When Jennifer entered Florida's school system, it was ranked thirty-fourth. At the time of her arrest, it was eighth.

"The school Jen went to when we first got to Florida," Rachel explained, "had an elevator—and it was just a middle school."

Additionally, Jen had friends in Vermont she had left behind, and she was now forced, essentially, to integrate herself into a mixture of classes and cultures that she had not been used to or had ever interacted with before.

"Not an excuse," Rachel noted, "but just the fact that her life changed so remarkably."

"We had never even seen black people in Vermont," one family member later said.

During their first week in Florida, Rachel had a scare. Jen usually got off the bus at the same time, same location (nearly in front of the house), every day she had gone to school since they had been in Florida. But just a few days into this new routine, Rachel waited, but Jen never showed up.

Rachel thought at first that the bus was late or had broken down. She soon found out, however, the bus had dropped off other kids in the neighborhood on time.

Her heart raced.

Where's Jennifer? Oh, my . . . she's gone.

"My daughter is missing," Rachel said after phoning the police. "She hasn't come home from school. I have no idea where she is."

The school confirmed Jennifer got on a bus.

Rachel panicked. She was frantic.

It got real when the police showed up and asked for a "recent photograph" of Jennifer, along with any information regarding where Jennifer might have gone off to, or if she could have run away.

After taking a report, the cop said, "Come with us."

Rachel got into the cruiser and off they went in search of Jen.

Jen had unintentionally gotten on the wrong bus and was dropped off at a stop where she had no idea how to get home, so she started walking.

As Rachel and the cop drove around, there she was, a few miles from the house, trying to navigate her way home.

A mother saw her firstborn and breathed a tremendous sigh of relief.

Welcome to Florida, Rachel thought.

CHAPTER 11

AS RACHEL WONDERED whether the high-profile attorney she had been introduced to, John Trevena, could actually help, a bit of hope began to dawn over the horizon. Still, after hearing that Trevena wanted to take on the case, Rachel had a hard time getting a grasp on the severity of the situation and what was happening. Everything seemed so surreal—maybe even unreal, as if events were happening to someone else, at some other time. Running on pure adrenaline, Rachel still held on to that out-of-body sensation, wondering when reality would finally sink in.

"Not sure I ever did understand what was going on," Rachel said years later as she looked back. "I had a hard time accepting that it was all as bad as it was—I mean, my daughter was being charged with first-degree *murder.*"

Trevena told Rachel what time to come in for their meeting, while adding one caveat: "Come in through the back."

The local media had found out that Trevena might be taking on the "Hiccup Girl Case" and reporters had stormed his offices. Besides that one statement to the radio station, Rachel had not come out and said much of anything. The media, which had grown accustomed to unfettered access to Rachel and Jennifer during the hiccup phase, desperately wanted that exclusive, local take on the case from Jennifer's mother. The way Rachel explained their constant badgering, she felt as if the local media thought they deserved the story because of how much exposure they had given Jennifer during her hiccup phase.

Rachel brought along her mother—Jen's grandmother—for support. They were escorted up through the back, ushered into Trevena's office, and told to have a seat.

By now, Rachel was in tears, surely beginning to feel the weight of this escalating, unfolding situation. Here she was sitting in an attorney's office discussing her daughter—who was sitting in jail on felony murder charges—and not really having any idea what had happened.

Most of what Trevena initially asked was in regard to Rachel and Chris's finances.

Rachel made it clear they could not afford any sort of retainer. They just didn't have the assets or the capital. Neither did her parents. If Trevena was looking for a big payday out of this, he was speaking to the wrong family.

Undoubtedly seeing the marketing potential and extraordinary notoriety he could obtain for his law firm for taking on the case, Trevena agreed to represent Jennifer pro bono. It might sound self-serving, or maybe a fifteen-minutes-of-fame ride on the media wave, but attorneys like Trevena take on these cases free of charge for several reasons, and it is hardly for the fame or notoriety. Sure, who could blame a guy for wanting to expand his business? But Trevena had a track record of taking on high-profile cases and getting people off—or at least getting sweet plea deals. He wanted to help this family. He said he was going to do everything in his power to first get Jennifer out of jail on bond. Then they could find out what in the name of Florida oranges had happened and deal with it from there.

"What can you tell me about what she's done? What do you know?" Trevena asked. He was a well-groomed, well-dressed man in a fitted suit, with a silk tie. His office was modest; awards and citations and graduate certificates hung on the walls. There were plants and a watercooler, along with velvety, plush carpeting. It smelled of air freshener.

Rachel explained all she had been told thus far, which wasn't much.

"How is Jennifer as a person?" Trevena wanted to know.

That was easy. Rachel said her daughter had always been good-natured and good-hearted overall. "She's had problems. She's done some things I am not proud of. And she might be a lot of things, but I can tell you she is *not* a murderer."

It was clear that Rachel did not know the extent to which Jennifer had been involved with Lamont Newton, her boyfriend, and the "empire," as one source later put it, Lamont and Jennifer were supposedly building together.

As they talked, Rachel explained that she knew Jennifer had been smoking weed on occasion, acting badass and street tough, as though she was some sort of hustler online and around her friends, but she was mainly being influenced by that crowd, Rachel assumed. Jennifer had been through so much, over such a short period of time, and did not have the educational or psychological abilities to deal with it all. She probably did not realize what was going on around her, even though she was part of it.

Trevena said he understood. They'd get to the bottom of everything as soon as possible. He then got up from his desk, walked over to Rachel and her mother, told them he was taking over now. "I'll do what I can."

He handed Rachel "a few hundred" business cards.

"If anybody tries to contact you, you hand them my card and have them call me. Listen," Trevena said next, quite sincerely, "do not speak to anybody directly yourself. Don't worry about this. I will take care of everything."

No sooner had Rachel and her mother reached her car in Trevena's parking lot after the meeting than the local media descended upon them, sticking microphones and cameras in their faces, pestering them for comments. This was going to be a huge story, not just locally, but nationally and internationally as well. The Hiccup Girl had gone down in flames. The local celebrity had taken a bite out of a rotten apple and was now on her way from Eden to eternal damnation. Was there a better story from a pop culture perspective? It was going to be the lead story all over Florida. *Inside Edition* would pick it up. *Good Morning America,* the *Today* show, and several other gossipy-type print publications and television shows would be waiting. Nancy Grace was going to have a field day with the Hiccup Girl. Anderson Cooper would surely lead off *360* with the hiccup headline. FOX News would run with it, as would all the others: HICCUP GIRL CHARGED WITH MURDER AFTER ALLEGEDLY LURING MAN INTO TRAP.

There was that damn word: "allegedly." Rachel knew enough about the media to know that they could wrap any accusation they wanted around that adverb and paint any picture they wanted to of her daughter, as long as they qualified it with *allegedly.*

And why weren't they reporting the story as Jennifer Mee? Why the Hiccup Girl?

"Ratings grab," Rachel said. "The Hiccup Girl was a name."

One local reporter asked Rachel, as she tried to get into her car, "How do you feel now that your daughter is a murderer?"

Rachel was overwhelmed by this question. How dare the woman! Nothing had been proven. Nothing in the form of evidence or statements from the police had yet been released. There was no confession Rachel or Trevena knew of, but here was Jennifer being called a murderer!

Does Jen even have a chance? Rachel wondered.

"I did not know it at the time, even with all we had been through with the hiccups, but the media, that's what they do—they try to bait you into showing emotion."

"No comment," Rachel told the woman. "I am *not* going to be talking."

Rachel was struggling to get into her car as a reporter actually positioned her body in between the door and Rachel, so Rachel couldn't get in.

"Excuse me," Rachel said. "Please. Leave us alone."

Just then, according to Rachel's recollection, her mother came over from around the other side of the vehicle and pushed the female reporter out of the way so Rachel could get in.

"Don't you dare lay your hands on me, I'll have you arrested," the reporter said to Rachel's mom.

Rachel got into the driver's seat. Her mother went around and hopped into the passenger side. Sitting, starting the vehicle, Rachel wanted to scream and bang her hands on the steering wheel. Let it all out. Have a good, long tantrum. However, she pressed forward, switching the shifter into DRIVE and taking off.

At home that night, Rachel had no idea where to turn or what to do next. Was she doing everything she could for her daughter? Was Jennifer okay? What would happen to her after fellow inmates found out who she was? Would she be ridiculed and beaten? The fear of the unknown asphyxiated Rachel. She was choking on a feeling of helplessness.

As she sat crying, her mother came over. She was comforting and consoling. "We'll figure it out, honey. It's going to be okay."

While thinking through things, the telephone rang. It was a producer from *Today*. Rachel and Jennifer had told the world Jennifer's hiccup story on that morning program three years prior. Here was the same producer wanting Rachel's exclusive story about what had happened to Jennifer.

Rachel explained that she couldn't do or say anything without John Trevena's stamp of approval, but she didn't think it was a good time right now to go on television and talk, anyway.

"We've already spoken to him and he wants you and him to come on as soon as you can get to New York."

"I'll get back to you."

Rachel hung up, sat down on the edge of her bed, ran her hands through her hair, and took a long, deep breath. Maybe if she went on *Today* and explained to the world that Jennifer was that same girl who'd had the hiccups back in 2007, only somewhat mixed-up now as her life had taken a downward spiral after the hiccups ended, people would understand and sympathize. Maybe they would see Jennifer wasn't some cold-blooded killer. She was a mixed-up young girl whose star had fallen and had turned to numbing agents to lessen the pain of life. Since Jennifer's battle with the hiccups, she had been diagnosed with Tourette's syndrome.[2] Notably, in Jennifer's case, children who suffer from Tourette's generally experience more serious medical conditions as early as seven to ten years old, and as they age into adulthood, too. Among these are ADHD, OCD, impulse control disorder, and severe depression—all of which could be applied to Jennifer at various times of her life.

After speaking with Trevena, and under his guidance, Rachel agreed to fly to New York, with her mother supporting her. Rachel would appear on *Today* and talk about how she felt. While this was occurring, the

St. Petersburg Police Department (SPPD) prepared to hit the airwaves themselves, ready to give its version of the events leading up to the murder of Shannon Griffin.

CHAPTER 12

IF THERE WAS any aspect of Jennifer Mee's character she might have hidden from her mother during those days leading up to her arrest for murder, it would have to be the *entirety* of the life she led on her own. Rachel knew some things, but definitely not all. This life Jennifer led included a routine she had not been built for—and, consequently, was unprepared for, emotionally or otherwise. Jennifer had fallen in with several serious players totally plugged into the streets, a type of hustler whom Jennifer believed she would become one day. For one, Jennifer's first boyfriend in Florida, a man Jennifer had claimed to have loved like no other boy she knew, was into things Jennifer had no experience with whatsoever. It's clear from what she wrote on her Myspace pages during the latter part of 2009 that Jennifer had become someone completely different from that young, naïve, friendly girly-girl from Vermont whom friends and family had always known:

Im always havin fun chillin or vibbin to some gucci:) im a down ass chick and all the others will never compare so dont try me like im the next hoe. Ive lived in florida for a while now but my heart is still in vermont? im trying to better myself and just move on in life. Im single& not lookin but if a real nigga comes along then im here:) hit me up if you need to kno anymore . . .

Roberts Recreation Center on Fiftieth Avenue North, downtown St. Pete, was a popular place for Jennifer to hang out and meet new people as she got used to life in Florida. Alongside the recreation center was a park, where Jennifer would go and watch the kids play hoops, where she would meet and befriend new people. Allison Baldwin (pseudonym) was there one day. She and Jennifer hit it off.

"I basically became part of her family, and she became part of mine," Allison recalled with a degree of disappointment and concern.

Allison and Jennifer were both in their early teens when they met. The two girls soon became like sisters as the hiccup fame engulfed Jennifer and she quit high school, began collecting state assistance, and moved out of the family house and into an efficiency apartment by herself.

Allison witnessed firsthand the life Jennifer led on her own and wanted no part of it. She encouraged Jennifer to get away from Lamont Newton, especially, and also nineteen-year-old Laron Raiford and Jennifer "Jenni" Charron, the couple Jen had moved in with at 610 Fifth Avenue in St. Pete after Jennifer and Lamont were tossed from her efficiency. This was definitely not a clique of people, Allison knew, that were going to steer Jen in the right direction. These weren't high-school kids going through some phase. They were a few years older and definitely were more in touch with how to hustle and work the street.

To Allison, back in those days when they hung around Roberts Park and spoke of all the things young girls chat about when their parents aren't around, Jennifer was "always happy." She gave Allison the sense that she'd had a good life, despite a few traumatic bumps along the way. She routinely discussed growing up in Vermont and the contrast she noticed now to her life in Florida. "She talked a lot about her family. She loved them."

Not that Jennifer's life was a Disney channel sitcom, but Jennifer expressed to Allison that she understood those tough times had built character. You became who you were based on the way you were brought up and how you chose to deal with the failures and misfortunes you met along your path—whether you forgave and loved, or harbored resentment and hated.

"The one thing about Jennifer," Allison explained, "she was not an angry person—never, *ever* angry."

The darkest part of her life, Jennifer had explained to Allison one day as a somber effect took over the conversation, came when two males repeatedly "raped" Jennifer and "took advantage of her at such a young age." The alleged crime and the subsequent trauma that followed defined Jennifer and she spoke about it often to those in her close inner circle. It was something she never worked through entirely, many of those same friends later believed. Jennifer got kind of stuck in that traumatic moment of her life. As much as she had wanted to forgive and move on, the repeated sexual assaults dictated the path she later chose to take, proving for her that forgiveness and moving forward from the trauma was easier said than done.

"It would be every day," Allison explained, referring to the rape and how often Jennifer said it occurred.

"Her attackers [were close to her], so they would rape her *every* day."[3]

From Jennifer's point of view, the hardest part of it all was that when she began to talk about it, nobody, at first, believed her, Jennifer told Allison. It couldn't be true. Her attackers were from a seemingly strict, solid Christian background. Jennifer claimed she was made to feel as though she was lying about it all. And this, Allison believed when she later looked back, was the beginning of the end for Jennifer and how her life later turned out. Jennifer saw everything through the prism of those assaults and believed her lack of self-esteem to be directly tied to the victimization and then not being believed.

"She told me her parents finally caught on to the rape, which occurred for a few years. . . ."

Allison and Jennifer often discussed the ramifications of the rape and how it affected Jennifer as she made her way through the rigors of life in Florida.

"It totally changed who she was," Allison said. "And Jennifer knew that."

Seeking attention and the way Jennifer viewed romantic relationships and her role in them became the main consequence Jennifer dealt with. Jennifer's self-worth dissolved over time. She never expected to be treated properly by a man. She expected to be let down, to be ridiculed and punished, and so she went out and found those types of relationships that would allow her to have those experiences because she felt she deserved no better. Maybe not consciously, but definitely as an unconscious way of dealing with the sexual trauma she supposedly endured.

"Bad guys," Allison said. "That's who Jennifer went after. She never dated good guys. She always dated people who took advantage of her. And I believe one hundred percent that it was a decision on her part because of the rape."

Jennifer felt comfortable being taken advantage of—and Allison was there on the sidelines to witness it all as she watched Jennifer date her first love and then Lamont Newton. In fact, what Chris and Rachel Robidoux didn't know was that at the time Jennifer and Lamont moved in with Laron Raiford and Jennifer Charron, Lamont frequented a place called Bottom to Top Club, which billed itself as a "bikini bar." To the rest of the modern world, it was known as a strip club. The city had a nude ordinance, which did not allow full nudity. Just about four months before Jennifer's arrest, in June 2010, police raided the Bottom to the Top Club and shut it down after six "dancers" were cited for violating the ordinance—i.e., dancing naked. The disc jockey in the club was arrested for carrying a concealed weapon. Others were charged on the same night with resisting arrest and obstruction. SPPD spokesman Bill Proffitt told the *Tampa Bay Times* that "officers had also received complaints about drug dealing and prostitution at the club. . . ."

Not a good situation to be around. Either for Lamont or Jennifer, but this was Lamont's comfort zone, according to several who knew him personally. Lamont thrived in this type of environment and came off as a player while cruising the club, handing the girls dollar bills, drinking, setting up deals.

The club and the area of the city where it was located was what cops described as "rough." Not a place where you'd want to spend a quiet night in St. Pete. It had become, though, one of Lamont's top hangouts, and he'd bring Jen with him. Yet, according to a source within the group, Lamont wouldn't allow Jen into the club, and not because she was underage. Jennifer Mee, instead, would disappear out into the night around this same superseedy, very dangerous neighborhood to shill crack cocaine and other drugs.

Jennifer was a streetwalking dope peddler. And according to her and Lamont, she did this on her own. Lamont never pushed her to do it, and she had been dealing hard-core drugs far before ever meeting Lamont.

Jennifer was attached to Lamont's youngest child and would often take care of him with great affection whenever Lamont had the child for visitations.

"She loved that baby as though it was her own," a friend said.

Lamont had mixed feelings for Jennifer. This was clear to everyone in that St. Pete circle, except for maybe Jennifer. Some said he did not love her. Yet, all he needed to do was say, "Baby, come on, do this for me. . . . You know I love you," and Jennifer was like his trained puppy. She'd do whatever Lamont wanted.

A lot of this behavior on Jennifer's part, said a friend (with Jennifer's mother and several others later agreeing), was centered on Jennifer's hatred toward white males because her attackers were both white. Jennifer had always said she would date only black guys because she believed they would not hurt her in the same manner as her attackers had.

"You see, [her attackers] were supposed to take care of her, but they, instead, took advantage of her and raped her," a source explained. "And that right there poisoned Jennifer's entire outlook and turned her right around to date black boys only."

Apparently not only date, but to do other things, too—which had made many people wonder as Jennifer's case became the lead story everywhere: did Jennifer's loyalty to Lamont and the others include murder?

CHAPTER 13

A LARGE, HEAVYSET man, with short-cropped, steely gray hair and a mustache, walked up and stood in front of a green-and-yellow banner reading, ST. PETERSBURG POLICE DEPARTMENT. An American flag stood tall and proud over his right shoulder. Embroidered on the right side of the banner was an eagle making its landing atop three words: LOYALTY, INTEGRITY, FIDELITY—the SPPD's core value slogan.

The man at the microphone was Chief of Police Charles Harmon. It was October 25, 2010. Standing next to the chief was another cop, whom some would later confuse with the lead detective in the case, Dave Wawrzynski. But this man was not Detective Wawrzynski; the man standing near the chief was Major Michael Kovacsev, who wore a charcoal-gray suit, light-colored gray tie, and soft peach shirt.

Kovacsev had walked over and dropped some paperwork on a small table next to the lectern, where both men stood. The two police officers were there to announce, as the fact sheet accompanying the press conference stated, "Jennifer Mee [had been] arrested for homicide." Not Lamont Newton and Laron Raiford, both of whom had also been arrested, but this meeting with the media, with the chief of police holding court, had been called to announce that Jennifer Mee, the infamous Hiccup Girl, was in custody on felony murder charges.

"There had been so many media inquiries after [it had been] learned that Miss Mee was involved," one law enforcement source told me, "that the chief and major had no choice but to hold a press conference."

Seemed reasonable enough.

The oak-finished lectern was not as crowded as one might expect with microphones sticking up into the chief's face like lollipops, yet all of the local affiliates had a presence. NBC's microphone, with that boxed-in, recognizable peacock logo just under the ball, stood front and center. The press conference had been set up to give the media some details surrounding the murder of Shannon Griffin and the arrests the SPPD had made. The SPPD had not been accustomed to holding press conferences to announce these types of inner-city crimes and arrests in the past. Some would question why they were doing it now, but it was a simple decision based on the amount of media badgering the department. People were interested, so the SPPD wanted to oblige the media. By doing so, they would likely stop the phone in the public information officer's office from ringing off the hook.

With his protruding stomach stretching and tightening his gray chief's shirt, three gold stars perfectly set on each triangle of his collar, Chief Harmon opened by saying that his officers had responded to 511 Seventh Street North, downtown, just after eleven o'clock on the previous Saturday night, October 23, 2010. As those officers arrived, they were under the impression, based on a 911 call dispatch had taken minutes before, that a homeless man was either sleeping or passed out drunk behind a newly renovated vacant residence up for sale.

That "someone" whom the chief mentioned was Shannon Andre Griffin—but Shannon wasn't sleeping. He was dead. Murdered in cold blood "from multiple gunshot wounds," the first-responder SPPD officers knew right away from looking at him—fatal wounds that the SPPD believed then to have been "received at that particular location," the chief added.

As the press conference continued, Chief Harmon said it was "apparent that the weapon was left at the scene and there was some clothes left at the scene . . . and it looked like the possibility that robbery was the motive."

From the way the chief described the scene and the crime, it felt fairly straightforward and sadly all too common, however disturbing. Somebody surprised Shannon, shot him several times, and took his money and possessions. Though the chief never said anything more regarding how his officers had drawn those conclusions based on what he had described as clothing and a weapon found near the victim, it was clear that the SPPD had additional evidence it was holding back and not releasing publicly at this time.

"What we have since learned is that our victim, Mr. Griffin, had a dialogue with a Jennifer Ann Mee"—he pronounced her name as MAY first, but then corrected himself—"that had started within the last week."

Jennifer and Shannon, the chief went on, had exchanged several Internet messages during the week of the murder via social networking, each of which precipitated a series of phone calls between them. The chief did not say the SPPD had recovered the phone Jennifer used or a computer and gotten the information from those electronics, but one had to assume they were speaking from a place of authority and investigatory confidence.

And probably the most important statement made at the press conference regarding Jennifer's arrest came next: "She enticed him to come down and meet with her at this particular address," the chief stated.

In that one declaration, the SPPD accused Jennifer Mee of luring Shannon Griffin to his death. Shannon, the SPPD gave the impression, believed he was meeting Jennifer for a night out. A simple, innocent date.

Wearing a black tie and black slacks, the chief explained how the exact location where Shannon had been found was a vacant house in a somewhat desolate neighborhood. Jennifer lived with Laron, Lamont, and Jennifer Charron about three hundred feet, or a one-minute walk, from the crime scene, just around the corner on 610 Fifth Avenue. It was fairly clear that Shannon's killer or killers knew the location well and, perhaps most important, felt comfortable there.

"Mr. Griffin," the SPPD was now comfortable in saying for the first time, "told his family that he was leaving his house to go meet a female at about ten o'clock [on] that particular night."

Thus far, what the SPPD was willing to divulge included how Shannon had left his Dr. Martin Luther King Jr. Street apartment on a scooter under the impression that he was meeting a girl. Nothing more. The apartment Shannon lived in with Doug Bolden, his older cousin, was in the Pinellas Park area of St. Pete, to the north of where Jennifer and the others lived. It was a straight drive, about six miles or twenty-five minutes south, down Fourth Street, the gorgeous Tampa Bay to your left, the Gulf of Mexico on your right. At that time of the night on a Saturday, Fourth Street would have been bustling with people and vehicles.

"He drove to this location," the chief said, "and we determined that he was probably met by the female out in front of the residence and they walked in back of the residence, where he was then accosted by two other individuals." He stopped briefly to look at the paperwork in front of him. Then: "A Laron Raiford and Lamont Newton . . ."

The image everyone saw was Jennifer standing out in front of that house, Lamont and Laron hiding around back. As Shannon pulled up and started chatting with Jennifer, she invited him to follow her, and then out of the shadows came the muscle of the operation. What happened after that, the SPPD was uncomfortable revealing at this point.

"The female—Jennifer Mee—was obviously the setup person in this scenario, probably." He then mentioned how Shannon "apparently struggled" with his killers. And as the SPPD began to "backtrack" in its investigation and look at some of the telephone calls and e-mails and online chats Shannon had had throughout that week, it was clear as cellophane that three people were involved in Shannon's murder: Jennifer Mee, Lamont Newton, Laron Raiford. There was "another female," the chief mentioned here, they were not prepared to identify, who was also involved on some level, but her name would be kept out of any of the SPPD's reporting "because she is a witness in this case."

They were talking about Jennifer Charron, Jennifer's roommate, Laron's girlfriend.

"We determined that the one female"—Jennifer Charron—"didn't have anything to do with the case, at this point," but that Jennifer Mee, Laron and Lamont, by late afternoon on Sunday, "had made several admissions . . . that this was a setup, that this was a robbery, and it was a robbery gone awry."

The way the SPPD's case was laid out during this press conference gave everyone the impression that the investigation had been straightforward and clear-cut for these experienced cops: victim, suspects, arrests, admissions.

All within a twenty-four-hour window.

The chief said they would entertain questions now as Major Kovacsev stepped forward to take over.

The first question, focused on a potential serial nature, revolved around "the three"—Jennifer (Mee), Lamont, Laron—and if they had been doing this for a while, or was it their first time?

The major said all three had no criminal records to speak of, and the SPPD believed this was their first foray into setting someone up and robbing him.

"Was Mee aware that someone had been shot during this robbery?" one reporter asked.

"She was aware as it was progressing," the major explained. "The altercation occurred between the three subjects"—Laron, Lamont, Shannon—"as she was walking away, and she was in the vicinity when the gunshots were fired."

A vital question came up next: Did Jennifer know "they had a gun"?

"She did," Major Kovacsev said. "She knew who

brought the firearm there and knew the firearm was going to be utilized in the armed robbery."

The SPPD was "still looking" at the "angle" of how Jennifer might have seduced or lured Shannon to the location. They were conducting an investigation and needed further examination of the electronic evidence before commenting more on that end. Yet Kovacsev gave the impression that Jennifer Mee was the carrot in all of this, dangling there for a week on a long, sexy stick that Shannon Griffin found too appetizing to resist. Whatever Jennifer had said to Shannon—or promised him—in order to get him to that location on that night, the major clarified, it was enough to make Shannon believe he was in for a night of fun and romance with a girl he liked and who was attracted to him.

The topic of drugs came up next and the SPPD indicated there was no evidence whatsoever drugs played any role in the crime.

"The victim in this case had no criminal history whatsoever," the major said. He was on his way to meet a female for a romantic night out—that was the impression he gave to family members before leaving his house.

"Did Jennifer show any remorse?"

"Ah, she was . . . emotional," Kovacsev said. He seemed perplexed at how to answer this question. And it was legit. Jennifer Mee was hard to read for those who did not know her. The Tourette's tics she suffered from gave the impression that she was preoccupied or making faces or not really paying attention.

Shannon Griffin was a social introvert, Kovacsev explained. He had been on vacation from his Walmart job. Yet, interestingly enough, "*He* friended *her*," the major explained. (The emphasis is the author's.) Shannon had actually reached out to Jennifer after finding her in a chatroom online. It wasn't as though Jennifer went on the Internet and began preying on an unsuspecting, shy man, hoping to find the perfect victim to set up for a robbery.

Or had she?

The chief had something he wanted to add to this thread of meeting people online. He stepped forward, saying he wanted to give parents "out there" a warning, which by itself came across as reasonable and with good merit. Yet, when compiled with the context of Jennifer's case and the allegations (charges) against her at the time of the press conference, it truly spoke to whatever evidence they had against Jennifer, in that their case must be a strong one: "So, for those out there that are parents or friends or whatever, the message is—'Be careful who you are having a conversation with online, you just *never* know.'"

There was a moment of quick, penetrating silence after that comment, until a reporter spoke out and asked, "Who was holding the weapon?"

The chief nodded, smiled coyly, and said, "We're still working on that."

The notion was floated next that perhaps Jennifer was being overcharged or maybe she didn't really know what she was getting involved with, as far as the robbery and murder. Could Lamont and Laron have heard about her meeting/date and piggybacked on it, with the nefarious intention of rolling Shannon, without ever letting her know what they were planning?

It seemed unlikely, really, for the simple fact that Jennifer was dating and living with Lamont, and, according to many of her friends during this period, she loved him. Why would she go and make an online date with another guy?

The chief quickly explained how Jennifer was part of the case. "The two male participants were actually involved in the robbery, but like I said before, the felony murder rule *allows* for somebody to be charged if they *conspired* to do that, or were at the actual act when the thing occurs—like she was. She was *well aware* this was going on, and knew about it. Regardless of who was holding the gun, in the eyes of the law, they all get charged the same."

The press conference concluded shortly thereafter. There was still work to do, obviously, including the SPPD gaining access to the two computers involved. When the police were asked about this as a final question, the major could not answer with any authority. Thus, the SPPD had not yet concluded its investigation. Most of what they had left to do involved computer forensics, along with who spoke to whom, when, and where. Which led many to believe as the press conference dispersed that it was one thing to prove—and quite easy—that one computer or phone communicated with another on a particular night, what time, and where. Yet, it's quite another to prove who was actually sitting behind that computer or on the other end of the phone. With three other people in the apartment where Jennifer Mee lived, all of whom had access to the same computer and, arguably, the same phones, one had to assume the SPPD had some fairly strong evidence proving that it was, in fact, Jennifer Mee behind the keys and phone all week long, leading Shannon Griffin on a deadly path toward a date with murder.

CHAPTER 14

RACHEL ROBIDOUX HAD not heard much from her daughter since Jennifer was arrested and charged with felony murder and they had that short, two-minute telephone call. At home with Chris, both of whom were now frantically trying to figure out a way to accept what was happening to their family, Rachel was aghast to learn what had been reported at the press conference by the chief and another cop she believed to be Dave Wawrzynski, the lead detective in Jennifer's case. Watching that press conference, Rachel could not believe the entire focus of the announcement had pointed at Jennifer.

"Sure, go after Jennifer because she's the Hiccup Girl!" Rachel said.

To Rachel, the SPPD had put the case into sharp focus: they were aiming to make a strong, big case against Jennifer based on who she was, not what she had or had not done.

"I thought the whole thing was disgusting," Rachel said later. "Really? They had a press conference only because the case involved Jennifer, period. I listened and thought, 'They're going to find her guilty any way they can.' So many things didn't add for me as the so-called 'evidence' began to emerge. For one, Shannon Griffin's cousin [had come out and] said Shannon was going to meet a girl to go on a date. [He said] that he was 'dressed to the nines and had a grin, ear to ear.'"

This indicated to Rachel something far different from what the SPPD had just announced in their impromptu press conference—and, in Rachel's opinion, involved the SPPD's "secret" witness, whom they refused to name: Jennifer Charron.

When she heard that Detective Dave Wawrzynski was the lead in the murder of Shannon Griffin, Rachel recognized Wawrzynski's name as a cop she'd not only heard of, but had some personal interaction with in the past.

"When Jennifer went missing," Chris Robidoux said.

Detective Dave Wawrzynski had been involved in helping to find Jennifer in 2007 when Jennifer walked out of the house and, after a visit to the local park, disappeared. Apparently, scared of the future and what was happening to her, Jennifer left the house one night and never returned. She was fifteen then. She'd taken off without telling anyone. She wanted to be alone and try to figure out where her life was headed. Rachel and Chris knew she had probably gone down to the park to sit with friends and hang out. It was unlike Jennifer to take off on her own without telling anyone, and certainly unlike her, back then, not to come home. So when she left in a huff that early evening with Ashley, Rachel and Chris considered that she and Ashley would go to the park, Jennifer would blow off some steam, and then she'd return with Ashley some time later. Jennifer still might not be over her little fit, but she would begin to accept that Rachel and Chris were her parents and wanted what was best.

Ashley came home some hours later, but she was alone.

"Where's Jennifer?" Rachel and Chris asked.

"I saw her at the park," Ashley said, referring to the Roberts Recreation Center, not too far away from where they were living at the time. "That was the last time I heard from her."

Chris had called Ashley on her cell phone while she was at the park that evening and asked where Jennifer was.

"Did you see her?" Rachel wanted to know.

"Yeah. I told her dad wanted her home after he called me."

It was Sunday night, June 17, 2007. Instead of doing what she was told, however, Jennifer took off and started walking, eventually making it to Bartlett Park, a little over four miles away, a ninety-minute walk.

They figured Jennifer would come home late that night, as she always had in the past when she got angry and needed to be alone.

Nearly eleven hours had gone by and Rachel, worried sick that next morning after not hearing from Jennifer at all throughout the night, decided to call the SPPD.

It was now Monday, June 18.

"My daughter's run away. I don't know why," Rachel explained. She phoned the cops as the rest of the family quickly went into action, making flyers and calling as many of Jennifer's friends as they could to see if she was hiding out or if anyone had heard from her. Chris had Jennifer's phone turned back on—he'd taken it away recently and canceled it, which had started the entire tiff among Rachel, Chris, and Jennifer—just in case she wanted to call home. But when Chris called Jennifer's number after having the phone company turn it back on, the phone rang inside Jennifer's drawer.

Chris took the phone and scrolled through Jennifer's numbers, calling anyone he could, focusing on those numbers neither he nor Rachel recognized. Since Jennifer had become internationally known as the Hiccup Girl back in January of that year (2007), she had strangers coming up to her and asking for autographs and noticing her wherever she went. On top of that, people were somehow finding her phone number and calling Jennifer at random.

"Strangers!" Chris said later. "I didn't want her talking to strangers on her phone." When he found that out and thought about it, combined with some other things Jennifer was involved in, Chris decided she didn't need a cell phone anymore.

One thing Rachel noticed after chatting with police that morning was that Jennifer had left behind her purse, too. This was alarming in and of itself.

Why would she not take her purse? Rachel wondered, growing more concerned by the minute.

Then, picking up Jennifer's phone, staring at it, Rachel knew: *She's mad. She's pissed off at us.*

Jennifer had become angry with her mother and Chris over the decision to turn off her cell phone, the one salvation in Jennifer's life she could turn to and rely on for comfort at the time. Her phone was a direct connection to her friends and a social media life she had created and was becoming more deeply immersed in every day. More than those strangers calling and Jennifer talking to them, however, Chris had searched Jennifer's social media pages and found some rather disturbing conversations between her and several people, including much older males. All of it put together scared Rachel and Chris.

"There are a lot of parents that trust their kids," Chris said. "I wouldn't recommend it. I found so many accounts of highly explicit conversations on her social media pages."

Chris was worried Jennifer was getting involved with things that she didn't understand. Jennifer was someone that gave everyone the benefit of the doubt. She never judged people on race, class, social status, or

education. Jennifer treated everyone equally. In a lot
of ways, Chris knew, she was naïve and had a hard time
protecting herself from herself.

Deep inside, however, Jennifer was harboring deep-
seated resentment and anger toward Chris, she said
later.

"I've always felt out of place because I'm not Chris's
biological daughter. I feel as if he has always treated me
and my half sister [Ashley] different from the other
three girls."

One thing Jennifer said she noticed while growing
up was how Chris "spoiled the three girls, but when it
came to me and Ashley, it was always 'no.'"

"He was always very strict on me," Jennifer claimed.
There was a resentment Jennifer had against Chris she
could not shake.

Once Jennifer got a "taste of the real world," she
said, beyond the confines of a home where her mother
had gone through a lot of "B.S. . . . in her marriage,"
Jennifer never looked back. "I wanted more."

So she ran away.

CHAPTER 15

THE SPPD TOLD Rachel on the morning she reported
Jennifer missing that it would issue a BOLO (be on the
lookout) immediately and see what happened. Beyond
that, the officer explained to Rachel, they would assign
a detective to the case and begin a search.

Rachel didn't know what to do. She sat and thought

about Jennifer's life over the past six or seven months and realized the child had been on a whirligig of celebrity because of her hiccups, which had suddenly come to an end. It was enough to throw any child Jennifer's age into a plunge of confusion, depression, and hostility. Add to it Jennifer's learning disabilities and sheer lack of understanding regarding what had truly taken place as her celebrity rose and fell, and it was no wonder the kid had run away. She had been a celebrity one minute, known by name and face around the world. The next moment, she was the butt of jokes and online taunts, threats and absolute disparaging comments so vile and degrading that Chris and Rachel wondered if the sheer bullying and cruelty of some of the comments were enough to push an already depressed young girl over the edge.

"I saw a drastic change in Jennifer's personality and believed most of it was due to the medication [for the hiccups] she was taking and the international television exposure she had endured," Rachel commented later. "She was being called so many names and people hated on her so badly, saying she was making it all up for the attention. It was awful."

A lot of the name-calling and insult hurling brought Jennifer back to when she was a youngster in school, she later explained.

"I remember growing up and always being picked on because I had a mustache and because I am overweight," Jennifer recalled. "Plus, I think I lost all type of feelings when I was raped."

Rachel once referred to her daughter as having a "defiant nature."

Perhaps like many kids her age, Jennifer was ramming horns with the authority figures in her life, but she had been cut some slack because she had been through so much in such a short period. Jennifer was not momma's girl any longer, as she had been much of her life.

Rachel began to see the change transpire as the hiccup celebrity status, which Jennifer had gotten so used to, all of a sudden diminished. One of the telltale signs for Rachel was how Jennifer started to come and go as she pleased, without paying any mind to what Rachel and Chris asked of her. She stopped saying where she was headed when she left the house, and Rachel and Chris feared she was falling in with the wrong crowd. It was about this time, Chris later noted, when he discovered several racy letters between Jennifer and a boy.

"I'm hoping she's just acting out," Rachel told Chris as they waited at home that next morning for word that Jennifer was okay. They convinced themselves she just needed some time alone to work things out.

But it went much, much deeper for Jennifer. That "taste" of the outside world, which she had always talked about, felt so good.

"Chris never let me have my freedom," Jennifer claimed. What's more, they had always lived in small houses and the girls shared one bedroom—that's five girls in one room. Jennifer never felt she'd had any privacy growing up.

"I never had my own room. . . . I was always getting the shit end of the stick because I am the oldest. I always had to take the heat."

When a reporter reached Rachel after word got out that Jennifer had run away, Rachel said, "I am very close with Jennifer. That's why this is really bothering me. I have always tried to be her friend and her mother. I want her to feel like she can talk to me about whatever she wants to talk about."

Obviously, however, that intimacy between mother and daughter had been over for a while. Jennifer had become a renegade.

SPPD detective Dave Wawrzynski soon became involved in Jennifer's missing person case.

"Very briefly," Wawrzynski told me.

Wawrzynski went out searching for Jennifer as part of a law enforcement team put together by the department in order to locate the girl. There was some pressure from the media to find Jennifer because she had been a celebrity. All eyes were on the SPPD to find the girl.

"And as [Wawrzynski] was looking for her," Rachel later claimed, "he was driving his car slowly and Jennifer popped out from somewhere and he nearly ran her over. This really pissed him off. It got to him. He was upset to begin with that they were made to all go out looking for the Hiccup Girl, and here it was, he had almost struck her with his car. Ever since that day, I believe, in my opinion, Detective Wawrzynski had it in for Jennifer. He wanted to nail her on *something*."

"With regard to a 'vendetta' against this girl," Wawrzynski later explained to me, "that's really, uh, comical. My entire dealing with her was so minute. . . ."

The reason why Wawrzynski had come in contact with Jennifer in 2007 in the first place was because he was in patrol at the time, involved with Crimes Against

Children (CAC), which Jennifer's case—and that BOLO—fell under.

"Running away is not a crime," Wawrzynski clarified. "It's a civil problem the department takes very seriously. You call the police for help. If that kid runs from us, we cannot go chase them, tackle them. We have to say, 'Damn, there they go again.' And begin to look for them."

And as the search for Jennifer progressed, that's what happened. Jennifer Mee did not want to be found. Every time the SPPD got close, she took off.

Wawrzynski was told by department heads that because Jennifer had some "sort of semblance of notoriety," they needed to find her quickly.

"So I was asked to help them look for her," Wawrzynski told me.

Wawrzynski went out searching that day. As he was driving down an alley, he explained, "she ran out and I almost ran her over."

Jennifer knew cops were looking for her and she was purposely trying to avoid them. Was Wawrzynski a little perturbed that she'd dashed out in front of his car while she was trying to slip out of the grasp of the police department?

Absolutely.

But it was that one instant, maybe ten seconds, Wawrzynski said, that became his total involvement with Jennifer Mee in 2007. He said he might have also been inside the Robidoux residence as another officer discussed the search with the family, but that was the extent of his involvement.

"So, for that one instance to become a vendetta later, wow," Wawrzynski said with all due respect to Rachel and Jennifer's family. "If every person that ran in front of my car, if I had the ability to go back and get even with them, I would have burned out a *long* time ago."

By the time he became the lead in the Shannon Griffin murder investigation, three years after that runaway incident, Wawrzynski was an experienced detective. He realized and "totally understood" that the family—Jennifer's—needed someone to blame for everything that had happened.

"That's okay, if they want to cast me in there as well as a bad guy, that's fine," Wawrzynski concluded. "But unlike a TV show, that's not the way it happened."

What's more, until Jennifer Mee had told him her name when he met up with her in 2010 as part of the Shannon Griffin investigation, he "had no freakin' clue as to who she was."

CHAPTER 16

ON THE DAY Detective Wawrzynski almost ran Jennifer over, she was out there dodging the cops any which way she could. She had slept in Fossil Park on a park bench overnight, and had made a decision that she was done with being a child in the Robidoux household. She was now going to strike out on her own and live on the street among those friends who knew her best.

"For the most part," Jennifer recalled, "I had an okay family. Don't get me wrong—all families have problems. Like I said, the thing I wish could have been different was my mom being home more. My stepdad was not ready to raise a child, let alone a child that was not his."

No one could locate Jennifer Mee that day. But as evening came, a neighbor called Rachel and Chris and reported that Jennifer was at the park, sitting on a bench all alone. She looked tired and hungry and in need of some love.

Chris and Rachel rushed to the park.

As they walked up to Jennifer, she looked as though she wanted to run again and be done with everyone. However, Jennifer slumped into the park bench and cried, instead.

Rachel nestled up against her firstborn. What a ride they had been on since those days in Vermont, when it was just Jennifer and Rachel.

"What are you doing?" Chris asked. He was frantic and ecstatic all at the same time. Pissed at what she'd done, happy they'd found her. What a scare. Chris loved this girl, despite how Jennifer saw it. Rachel knew that. Why was Jennifer having such a hard time with it?

Rachel said, "Jennifer, we've been up all night, worried sick."

"You haven't slept?" Jennifer asked, looking at them.

"No, Jennifer," Rachel said through tears.

Jennifer looked up and saw that Chris was crying, too. "A grown man," she said later. "He was crying for *me*." And that, coupled with her parents being awake all night and worried sick about her, was when she realized she'd screwed up.

"I had done wrong," Jennifer said later. "I realized this in that one moment."

"Let's go home," Rachel said.

"I'll never do that again," Jennifer promised.

They decided that Jennifer would spend some time with her grandparents over the next few days, out of the house, on her own, so they could all have a moment to breathe, some quality time away from one another.

Rachel was considering counseling for her daughter. She wanted to learn how to handle what they had gone through with the international fame—not to mention the rise and fall of celebrity, Jennifer's Tourette condition, and an entire host of other problems now coming to light.

"I need to know how to cope with it all," Rachel said.

Jennifer had a different take. Sounding quite articulate and fairly knowledgeable about what was going on in her life as she worked her way back into the Robidoux fold, she told the *St. Petersburg Times* in the days after she went back home: "We need to do something about all the drama that's going on. We need some help so we can be a family and not a bunch of strangers living in one house."

CHAPTER 17

ACCORDING TO RACHEL, when the opportunity arose with the murder of Shannon Griffin and Jennifer's "potential involvement," Detective Dave Wawrzynski saw an opportunity and went after Jennifer with everything he had at his disposal. If that was the case, one might reckon any cop in Wawrzynski's position of being employed to solve a murder might do that same thing. Rachel was under the opinion that the SPPD wanted her daughter for this crime from the moment they realized Jennifer was part of the drama surrounding it.

"There are too many unanswered questions," Rachel remarked.

Wawrzynski was a smart detective with a variety of investigatory accolades, with hardly a blemish on his career. As a detective who has seen just about everything the street has to offer, Wawrzynski knew there was the Jennifer Mee her family had been familiar with and knew intimately, and then there was the Jennifer Mee whom they had *not* been familiar with—a young woman they knew nothing about. It did not take a team of investigators to figure out that Jennifer had led a life at the time of Shannon's murder away from her family, and she did not want anyone to know about it. Not to mention that one had to look at this case—and Rachel's accusation against the detective—through a clear, unbiased lens: would a decorated detective, like Wawrzynski, "go after" a young girl on murder charges solely because she had run in front of his patrol car, on top of a resentment rooted in the notoriety she had acquired while suffering from an uncontrollable condition brought on by Tourette's?

It hardly seemed plausible. In fact, once all the facts of the case were made clear, it would become obvious that it would also be nearly impossible.

Let's begin with Wawrzynski's life. He was an army brat, growing up not in one place, but rather moving all over the country, and sometimes the world, with his military family. Yet it was St. Pete, Wawrzynski later said, he'd choose if he had to call one of those places home.

That's where Wawrzynski graduated high school after moving with his family to the city in the mid-1970s. After a stint in the army himself, part of which included the military police, he decided to apply to the SPPD in 2003. It was the comradery and working with a unit, pooling ideas and collectively discussing and figuring things out, that attracted the law enforcement latecomer to the job. Wawrzynski was thirty-seven years old when he put on the blues for the first time, not quite your typical, wet-behind-the-ears criminal justice major.

Wawrzynski had offers to join the Customs Department and even the Secret Service, but it was the SPPD he chose. His goal, of course, was to become a detective— and within a short, two-year period he did just that.

The caseload Wawrzynski ran into as a detective in Crimes Against Children was enormous. Each detective in the unit dealt with between thirty and forty cases per month. And when you're talking crimes against children, you show up every day and your hours are generally not filled with happy stories of reuniting families and children. Your days, instead, are consumed with the vilest, most violent, disturbing, and chilling acts committed against the most innocent people on the planet.

Yet, Wawrzynski explained, a lot of what he faced every day included the unit "disproving crimes more than it did proving" them. There were so many false reports that came into the Crimes Against Children unit, at any given time, they outnumbered the actual real cases almost three to one.

"That's what made testifying so much easier in CAC cases, because when you built a case against someone that did not fall apart, one that you were able to back up with physical evidence and/or testimony, and it never fell apart, those were *so* rare."

Seventy percent of the time, Wawrzynski commented, "we are out there disproving allegations."

A lot of it revolved around "regret sex": a fifteen- or sixteen-year-old who'd had sex with her boyfriend, and the mom and the dad didn't like him, so a case was filed.

"Certainly, some of this is criminal," Wawrzynski said, "but it may not always rise to the level of prosecution."

Needless to say, Wawrzynski learned through his involvement there how to deal with families: to feel them out and develop a general consensus of what's going on behind the words they speak and the allegations they make, and, beyond all else, what's happening behind closed doors when no one is around.

Those years in the CAC laid the foundation for Wawrzynski to step into the Homicide Unit. Within a short period while in the Homicide Division, as Wawrzynski began to learn the ropes and get a feel for the types of cases St. Pete saw on a usual basis, there was one certainty he ran into in just about every murder: "Unlike any other crime, in a homicide, the victim cannot lie."

As far as murder cases, Wawrzynski explained, "you go where they take you. There is always something to do in a murder case until it is closed. They're permanent— always yours."

It wasn't the number of murders, or a particular case, that Wawrzynski recalled when he was asked about "that case" every cop has in his memory bank. It was something else.

"I have never been shocked or surprised by what I've

seen, but the level of depravity," he said sincerely, "or how cheap life is to some people is what gets me."

He once had a case where two guys got into an argument over a bicycle. One guy stabbed the other guy in the throat and the guy died in under a minute.

All because of a disagreement.

The value on human life today, without a doubt, is the lowest it's ever been.

There was another case in which the driver of a car in a mall parking lot "almost" ran over the foot of another man walking into the store. Never did, mind you, but came awfully close. The guy broke into a rage and followed the driver. As he got out of his vehicle, the pursuing man pulled a gun and started to fire into an open crowd of people, killing one—and it wasn't even the driver.

CHAPTER 18

JENNIFER MEE THOUGHT the world of her mother and called her life with Rachel "awesome—she was my best friend and she did everything she could for me."

The only complaint Jennifer had with her mother and the life they shared up until her arrest was that she wished her mother had "been home more while [I was] growing up."[4]

I asked Rachel about this. I had heard it from several sources close to Jennifer—how Jennifer had complained about having a mother who was never around much, someone she could confide in and talk to when needed. Was it an excuse? Was it a legitimate complaint from a girl who needed guidance and felt like she could only go to her mom? (Chris was home all the time, after all, so why not go to him?)

"I worked a lot of hours as a server while Jennifer was growing up," Rachel explained. "And when I wasn't working, I was helping my parents out." Rachel's father had ailments all his life and she needed and wanted to be there for him and her mother. "My mom was legally blind. She couldn't do much. . . . Chris was home."

It's quite clear when you speak with Jennifer Mee about her stepfather, Chris Robidoux, that there was a gulf there between them based on an event or series of events that had happened. Jennifer did not have many good things to say about Chris.

Rachel said that "they always butted heads." This was part of Jennifer's rebellious nature, Rachel suggested. It had to do with how much she wanted to spite Chris, especially when Jennifer started dating boys.

Her sisters, Jennifer explained to me, are "my little angels." They've had issues in the past, like any siblings, but Jennifer said she loves them dearly and always has.

It is her childhood (or lack thereof), Jennifer claimed, that she looks back on now and sees where things went terribly wrong.

"I feel like I had to grow up way too fast."

Part of it was being the oldest, she claimed. Many people didn't realize that being the oldest in a large family came with responsibility. The younger kids always got away with more, Jennifer said of her home life, while she took the brunt of the punishment and accountability.

"My guess would be some of the things that happened to her at a young age," Rachel said. "I just learned recently that [a family member was] buying her thong underwear and tried teaching her to drive . . . and let her smoke pot with her, at, like, ten or eleven years old. Maybe the fact that she was the oldest and needed to help with her sisters—be a 'little mom' in her mind while I was at work."

Allison Baldwin became the one and only true friend Jennifer said she ever had.

"She was my li'l rider," Jennifer recalled. "We did everything together. She took me in when I ran from my problems."

It was not until she moved out of the Robidoux house and on her own that Jennifer said, "I became ruthless."

That was the word she actually used: "ruthless."

It said a lot about her.

She was buying and selling drugs. She felt she needed to "rebel" against Chris and Rachel, maybe just to hide who she was becoming and stuff down the pain she claimed to be feeling at that time. Part of her emotional distress, Jennifer explained, had nothing to do with becoming the Hiccup Girl. It was centered, she said, around not feeling loved at home while growing up.

"Sometimes I felt as if I was just taking up space," she said.

CHAPTER 19

RACHEL MADE THE trip, as did Jennifer's lawyer, John Trevena. Although they did not travel together, they both arrived in New York to speak with Matt Lauer on NBC's *Today* during the weekend of November 9,

2010, for a scheduled appearance on November 10. Introducing the story, Matt Lauer was more serious than he had been when Jennifer had made other appearances as the Hiccup Girl back in 2007. This was Rachel's first full-length interview—an "exclusive," Lauer promoted—since Jennifer's arrest on murder charges.

"Mr. Trevena encouraged me to do it," Rachel later said.

Rachel bore a striking resemblance to her daughter. When the camera first panned on Rachel as she sat on the couch alone and Lauer teased the interview with a brief setup videotaped prologue, Rachel looked dazed, with an obvious sheen of despondency consuming her. But more than that, she appeared confused and affected, as if she still did not have a handle on what was actually happening.

Jennifer had been in jail for three weeks. Her latest attempt at bond had failed. Trevena argued during a recent hearing that Jennifer "posed absolutely no risk of flight." As Trevena spoke on Jennifer's behalf to the judge, she stood by his side, her hair pulled back and tied into a tight ponytail. She was dressed in prison blues and looked like a hospital orderly. Perhaps as a nervous condition, every once in a while she hiccupped, adding what was an eerie, sobering reality to the situation.

That cursed condition had never really left her entirely—and never would.

As Trevena spoke, Jennifer broke down and cried.

"She has absolutely no prior criminal history, juvenile or otherwise," Trevena explained. He was right. This girl was no flight risk. Where would she go?

Shannon's cousin Doug Bolden stood at the lectern next and told the judge, "It's just wrong, Your Honor.

Just wrong!" Bolden, still quite in shock by the murder of his little cousin, shook his head, speaking elegantly and softly, saying: "He just thought he was going on a date. Here was the kid just grinning, ear to ear, about to go on a date . . . as happy as could be."

Shannon left the house to meet a girl and wound up dead, Bolden proclaimed. Now the girl who had allegedly lured him to his death wanted to walk out of this courtroom. Doug Bolden didn't understand why they were even discussing this matter.

Rachel stood next to her daughter. She explained to the judge that Jennifer had several learning disabilities and did not comprehend the severity of all that had taken place. She needed to be home. She needed to begin to prepare for the fight of her life. After all, the charge Jennifer faced could land her in prison for life if she was found guilty.

Since the time of her arrest, police had come out and said that based on their investigation, they knew Jennifer was not likely at the scene when the murder took place. However, under Florida law, because she had purportedly lured Shannon to that location under a ruse of some kind and knew that he was going to be robbed, she was just as guilty as the shooter.

The judge seemed harsh in his ruling that "the family" had been unable to "control" Jennifer and her behavior up until this point, and so why should he allow them another opportunity? There was no good reason why he should release Jennifer now to those same people who could not contain or control her in the past.

Jennifer's bond was denied. She would stay in jail.

CHAPTER 20

ON THE *TODAY* couch, Rachel sat next to John Trevena. She had one leg crossed over the other, her foot bouncing nervously, both hands crossed over her knees. Her being there at this raw stage of the game seemed awkward, to say the least.

Matt Lauer asked if she had seen Jennifer lately and how she was doing.

"Holding up," Rachel said after indicating she had just visited Jennifer before flying to New York.

Lauer made a point to say Rachel had said Jennifer didn't comprehend what had been going on and had failed to understand things for what they were, based on Jennifer's low IQ and her grade level of an eleven-year-old. So he wanted to know if Jennifer had any indication that she was facing one of the most severe charges on the books.

"I honestly don't think so," Rachel said. "She mentioned to me the last time I saw her that she hoped to be home for Christmas. . . ."

Lauer made a good point, and perhaps spoke for much of America, when he said that he and the rest of the *Today* team had always remembered Jennifer as a shy, innocent little girl with hiccups she couldn't get rid of. As he spoke, a video montage from Jennifer's several appearances on the show played. She looked so young at fifteen and sixteen, so happy, despite fighting the hiccups, so focused on beating her condition. There was a subtle indication on Jennifer's face that she not only had the support of viewers, but it was that support that empowered her for maybe the first time in her life. Rachel, too, appeared relaxed and grateful that someone had cared enough about her daughter's odd condition to make it a pop culture phenomenon, which, in turn, could lead them to serious help. Jennifer's round and plump face was full of life, her smile radiant, and her attitude positive. Fast-forward to the video of her latest court appearance, juxtaposed with these past images, and America was looking at two different people. Now Jennifer appeared gaunt and passive, perplexed and confused, as Rachel had suggested, and also shaky and fragile. It appeared as though she'd break down if someone said the wrong thing.

When Lauer asked Rachel about her reaction to the charges when she first heard them, Rachel's voice cracked. "Absolute state of shock . . . I thought it was a nightmare."

Lauer seized on that moment to get into what Jennifer's life had been like since the hiccups had made her an international "reality"-type, disposable celebrity.

Rachel explained that Jennifer moved around a lot and stayed in "different places, but that she always had a roof over her head."

Matt Lauer termed Jennifer's existence then what it was: a "transient lifestyle."

Rachel agreed. Then she added, "Kind of running with the wrong crowd."

Matt Lauer asked if by running with the wrong people, Jennifer had maybe given the family an indication that she was headed down a slippery slope of what could be a criminal path. Maybe her life on the street, he suggested, had been a clear sign of what was to come.

"Not with me," Rachel said, speaking to a specific concern that Jennifer might have let on that she was heading for trouble. "She wouldn't want to let me down. . . ."

Clearly, Jennifer kept a lot of things from Rachel.

Then the point of Jennifer being diagnosed with Tourette's after her bout with the hiccups came up. Matt Lauer asked John Trevena if he was considering using her condition as a defense. There had been reports of Trevena perhaps dabbling in those murky waters of blaming whatever Jennifer did and the lifestyle she led on her Tourette condition.

"Well, it certainly adds to the extent that it is a mitigating factor," Trevena explained quite articulately. He said they were going to have Jennifer examined. "A whole battery of neuropsychiatric-type tests needed to be conducted. But yes . . ."

Rachel dabbed at her watery eyes as Trevena spoke to how Tourette's was a condition that was generally accompanied by additional psychiatric conditions.

Matt Lauer was ready for that statement because he had in his hand—which he then read aloud, word for word—a statement from the National Tourette Syndrome Association, in which the association blasted any claim that Tourette's could have been a motivating or mitigating factor in the criminal and murderous ways Jennifer might have acted. The association said in the statement that Tourette's, under those circumstances, was "no more the reason for, or an excuse for, such offense than other medical diagnoses—such as asthma or rheumatism." Moreover, the association went on to state, under the banner of science there was "no evidence of a causal relationship between having Tourette syndrome and criminal behavior."

The official statement was a major blow to any case of Trevena arguing that Tourette's had made Jennifer act a certain way in allegedly luring Shannon Griffin to that death location on the night he was blindsided and murdered.

"I think to pure causality that is an accurate statement," Trevena agreed. "But certainly, for example, if a young lady is pregnant at the time of sentencing in her case, that's a factor that the court's going to consider. That doesn't mean that pregnant women are killers. It just means that it's an issue that's taken into consideration." He went on to clarify that Tourette's, in Jennifer's case, "not only explains the hiccups, but could also explain some of her poor judgment."

Alcohol would also explain poor judgment, however. But was alcoholism a defense for getting behind the wheel intoxicated and then driving down the road the wrong way and taking out a family of four?

If this was his strategy, Trevena was fighting an uphill battle.

"And I knew it," he later told me.

Rachel had always called Jennifer's celebrity and her condition "the curse of the hiccups," not the "case of . . ."

Matt Lauer picked up on that explanation and asked Rachel to explain.

"I kind of felt like she was more and more trying to withdraw," Rachel said through her broken and emotional voice. This was so difficult, talking about Jennifer in that capacity. Also, the idea of sitting on the *Today* couch without Jennifer by her side had been devastating to Rachel, who had sat with Jennifer on the same couch several times under more manageable, seemingly constructive circumstances. Out of the corner of her eye, on the stage monitors, Rachel could see the video they were playing for viewers of Jennifer trying every old wives' tale imaginable to get rid of the hiccups back when she was more the butt of jokes and a sympathetic victim to a condition rather than an accused murderer.

Part of that "withdrawal," Rachel concluded, centered on Jennifer hopping onto many of the social media sites and wading in waters Rachel said she had "no business" being in "because she was so naïve—and it just escalated."

And that was it. The interview was over.

If there was one thing that came out of the interview, it was that the future did not look good for Jennifer Mee.

CHAPTER 21

AS A CASE against Jennifer Mee, Lamont Newton, and Laron Raiford was built by the SPPD in conjunction with the state's attorney's office (SAO), the public began to learn some of the facts surrounding what happened on the night of October 23, 2010. The entire narrative of the murder was still very much unknown and uncertain as the SPPD kept many of its cards close to the vest, but certain facts trickled out during those early days after the murder.

At home, Rachel and Chris were trying to piece together what happened, with bits of information from Jennifer, who could not say much on the prison phone, along with John Trevena, who himself was not sharing much of what Jennifer had been telling him during prison meetings. The one fact, however, which could not be denied as Shannon Griffin's family came out and spoke publicly, demanding justice for Shannon, was that this was not some sort of ghetto murder surrounding a drug deal gone bad, as some might have suspected and suggested in the media. According to his family, Shannon wasn't some sort of hoodlum or "gangsta" wannabe, out in the middle of the night, lurking on the streets of St. Pete. He was a grown man on vacation from his job, rebuilding a life that had been destroyed by a hurricane.

"He was a good kid," Shannon's brother told reporters. "He didn't hurt nobody. It just doesn't make any sense for a good kid like that to be murdered for no reason—just to be set up and murdered! He was only *twenty-two* years old."

Shannon Griffin's family struggled to deal with such a devastating, disrupting loss. Shannon was enjoying his first paid leave from his job at Walmart. He was a young man with a prosperous, bright future. He had dreams. He had set goals for himself. He was planning on making a life in Florida. He wanted a family of his own. He had left his house that night, thinking he was meeting a girl.

As far as a "playa" mentality, Jennifer Mee seemed to fit into that mold quite effortlessly, a fact that became clear as the press dismantled her life and dug into her social media sites, publishing what was Jennifer's online presence during those days leading up to Shannon's murder. On Facebook, back on September 4, 2010, six or so weeks before the murder, Jennifer wrote: *DIS WEEKEND IS FINA BE A GREAT WEEKEND. BAE GOT A SHOW THEN A AFTA PARTY. THEN ME N MY BAE GETEN A RENTAL N GOING 2 DA STRIP CLUB.*

Jennifer's boyfriend, Lamont Newton, fashioned himself a rapper—that "show" was a gig Lamont had.

Reading this later, Jennifer's family wondered if they ever knew her at all. It surely didn't sound like the Jennifer in the years before she left the house and went off on her own.

That strip club Jennifer referred to was, of course, Bottom to the Top, where Lamont had purportedly hung out while Jennifer sold drugs on the streets around the club.

A few former friends of Jennifer's spoke to reporters in those days following her arrest. While many could not believe what she was being accused of, others had seen it coming for a long time. One boy said Jennifer was texting him recently and all she ever talked about was "getting drunk and high."

Jennifer's Myspace pages told a similar story. The photos she had posted and the things she wrote would lead one to believe Jennifer was getting in over her head, but she was also embracing and even enjoying a life she had created for herself away from the family.

The wallpaper on her Myspace page depicted stacks of pink money. Her status of where she lived was "St. Pistol, Florida." She referred to herself as "Diva," bragging in a bodacious manner about her new lifestyle, sharing one of her most common sayings during those days: *[I am the] female version of a hustla, maken so much money idk what 2 do wit it.*

"Some of those things," Rachel explained, "were posted on her sites by [others]. But Jennifer allowed them to stay on the sites, I know that."

In jail, all Jennifer could do at this point was wait it out. There was no chance of her getting out on bond. A trial date would soon be set as John Trevena declared he needed time to figure out what type of defense to lodge in Jennifer's case. Yet, as the New Year holiday came and went, and Shannon Griffin's family members were left to celebrate what would be his twenty-third birthday on January 23, 2011, tragedy struck the Robidoux household.

CHAPTER 22

ONCE AGAIN IT was a phone call in the middle of the night. Rachel was at her own home this time around, sleeping. It was February 4, 2011. She awoke near 3 A.M. to the sound of her phone ringing.

"Yeah . . . hello?"

The person on the other end explained what was going on.

Rachel dropped the phone, woke up Chris, and got dressed. Soon, both were out the door and on their way.

As they drove from Spring Hill down to St. Pete, Rachel thought about how ill her mother had been. She'd spent some time in rehab lately, but Rachel had been under the impression that she was getting stronger and working toward going back home.

Now, this.

It took about an hour for them to make it into town, but they were too late. When Rachel and Chris arrived, they were told immediately that Rachel's mother, a woman Rachel called "the best friend I ever had," had passed away from congenital heart failure. She was relatively young, just sixty-eight years old.

Rachel was devastated.

Three weeks later, it wasn't a call this time, but Rachel had stopped by to see how her dad was doing since the death of his wife, and she found him on the floor, unresponsive, and had to call 911.

It felt to Rachel as if her family was taking a pounding, one blow after another. And all she could do to defend it was to sit back and accept that these were the cards and she had to make a hand of some kind out of them.

Rachel had been going over to the house every day to look after her dad since he'd lost his wife. She was even staying there during the week again, because her work was so close and her dad was alone.

As it turned out, Rachel's father lived, despite having had a heart attack and a stroke. But life for Jennifer Mee's grandfather would never be the same.

"This was the craziest time of my entire life," Rachel said later. "My mom and I were . . . It was to the point where she would be thinking something and I would know what she was thinking." That loss alone, on top of what was going on with Jennifer and then her father's stroke, wore Rachel down. "It just tore me up."

When she heard, Jennifer blamed herself for all of it.

"Jennifer felt because of her arrest and all that was happening," Rachel explained, "she had killed my mother."

For a lifeline, some sort of saving grace out of the black hole Rachel found herself falling in, she kept going back in her mind to that one thing Jennifer had said to her long ago on the telephone, on the night of her arrest: "Mom, it really was a date. . . ."

Rachel seized upon this. She felt there was something to it.

The theory Rachel put together in her mind, and began to believe, was that the "date" Jennifer referred to had been set up between Jennifer Charron (Laron Raiford's girlfriend) and Shannon Griffin. Not Rachel's Jennifer. After all, if it really was a date, how could Jennifer Mee justify it when she was supposedly in love with Lamont Newton? Why would Jennifer Mee be setting up a date with a man she met online, to begin with?

It was a part of the murder narrative that didn't make sense to Rachel. But, as Rachel later explained, if you place Jennifer Charron into the same scenario, it made all the sense in the world.

In April 2011, Jennifer Mee gave a jailhouse interview to *Today* under the guidance and direction of her attorney, John Trevena, who had explained to Rachel and Chris that the right television appearance could help Jennifer's case in the end.

"Mr. Trevena actually pushed it," Rachel said. "Mr. Trevena is very close with [someone who works for the *Today* show], to the point where they go out together and so forth, so he set it up."

Jennifer was being held at the Pinellas County Jail in Clearwater, Florida, where NBC News correspondent Amy Robach sat down with her for a formal, "exclusive" interview, as NBC billed it. The first Jennifer had given any media outlet since her arrest.

Jennifer was dressed in blue prison johnnies. Her

greasy, unkempt hair was set in a tight ponytail, with
two distinctive, thick bangs outlining her pudgy baby
face. She was emotional and cried through much of
the interview, often wiping away tears that dripped out
of her eyes without warning, lending credence to the
notion that they were genuine.

As Jennifer explained to Amy Robach, it wasn't until
she had been placed inside the back of a police car and
on her way to jail that the weight of it all "hit" her and
she was not living a dream—that her life had taken a
complete 180-degree turn for the worst.

There were moments when Jennifer smiled during
the interview and did not cry, mostly while describing
her life, as Amy Robach put it, being the "it girl" after
returning from *Today* as the Hiccup Girl. Everyone in
school, Jennifer said, had now noticed her for the first
time. It was clear that Jennifer enjoyed the limelight,
the attention, and whatever she was able to glean from
her brush with stardom. Yet, when it faded, Jennifer
was left to deal with life afterward, all on her own.

"What did you do with that fame?" Robach wondered.

"I basically let it all go to my head and started doing
what I *wanted* to do."

With her eyes red and swollen, and those tears
streaming down both cheeks, Jennifer talked about
how her life went from fame to emotional and moral
famine. She said, "I took the path of the Devil, I really
did. Instead of keeping my faith with the Lord, I let the
Devil overcome me."

Without tears, Jennifer said she did think about
Shannon Griffin, the victim, "every day . . . every day I
do." But her thoughts about him were centered on
Jennifer herself possibly being the victim and how close

she had been herself to death. "Because I think, what if that was *me* behind that barrel—that could have been *my* life taken. He didn't deserve to . . . ," she tried to say next, stopping for a brief moment, unable to get the next word out, instead adding, "He was very young. He was just only a couple of years older than I was. I think about it every day and it eats me alive."

Jennifer cried after Amy Robach asked her if she felt responsible for Shannon's death. Then, answering, Jennifer hesitated, looked off to the side and clearly thought about what to say before uttering, "Ah, I cannot tell you the truth . . . because I"—and she smiled here a bit, perhaps out of nerves—"I didn't do nothing wrong. I'm not guilty of anything."

NBC reported during the interview that it had spoken to the SPPD and gotten "two versions" of statements Jennifer had given on that night she had been arrested. And for the first time the public got a small taste of the state's case and what happened during those hours after Jennifer and the others had been arrested. At first, during an initial statement, Jennifer told detectives that Shannon Griffin was murdered as part of a love triangle between Laron and Shannon and another woman, presumably Laron's girlfriend, Jennifer Charron.

"When Laron found out, I guess, that [Shannon] had some type of relationship with his girlfriend, he snapped. . . ."

That excerpt from an SPPD interview that NBC played was only half of the story, however. During a second interview later that same night, after admitting that she had lied during the first statement, Jennifer Mee broke down and told SPPD detectives that she had actually lured Shannon to that location so Lamont and Laron could rob him. And that the first statement was a story they had all concocted to try and get away with it.

"He was calling Laron's phone, asking me where I could meet him," Jennifer said in a tape of that interview, referring to Shannon.

With Amy Robach, Jennifer switched gears again and told the reporter that she had been "coerced into taking the blame."

So Robach asked the obvious next question: "Why would you implicate yourself in a murder?"

"Um," Jennifer responded, again with a nervous smile, "from . . . uh, I don't know. It's hard. It's hard to explain. I made a mistake. I thought because I was quote/end quote"—and she used both her hands here to make air quotes with her peace sign fingers—"famous, so young, nothing would happen to me. So I went with a story I thought I wouldn't get into trouble with. But in all reality, it put me behind bars . . . and I could be facing life."

Jennifer talked about how "rough" daily life was for her behind bars. For three days leading up to the interview, she explained, she was on "lockdown twenty-three hours a day. . . ."

What broke her heart, Jennifer said as the tears came on once again, was that she had missed her grandmother's funeral, again mentioning how she believed she played a "big part" in her passing because of all the turmoil and strife she'd caused the family with her behavior.

Robach wanted to know what Jennifer thought about the outcome of her trial down the road. Could she make a prediction?

Jennifer said she didn't even want to think that far in advance, but she was "scared."

As the interview wound down, Robach explained that Shannon Griffin's family would likely be watching the interview when it aired and she wanted to extend to Jennifer the invitation to speak directly to them.

Jennifer became more emotional than she had been during the entire interview; it came across as sincere and honest as she began by saying she was sorry for their loss. She added, "I wish that everything would have been different from what it all proceeded out to be." She paused. Sniffled. "He didn't deserve it. He didn't. He did not deserve to go and be shot." She had a hard time getting those final few words out because her emotions took over.

What was clear postinterview was that Jennifer Mee had just changed her entire defense, maybe without realizing or even knowing what she was doing. John Trevena had been saying that his defense for Jennifer was going to be grounded in her diagnosis of Tourette's and the idea that she did not have control over what she had done. Some were claiming that the Tourette defense was the basis for an insanity plea. Yet, Jennifer, all by herself, was now saying that the second statement she gave to police amounted to a false confession. Because based alone on what Jennifer had admitted to the SPPD, she herself claimed she lured Shannon Griffin to that location so Lamont and Laron could rob him. And under Florida law, if Jennifer Mee knew that Shannon Griffin was going to be robbed and she took part in the planning and carrying out of that robbery, and Shannon was murdered during the course of that crime, even if Jennifer ran away as Shannon was taken behind a building to be mugged, she was just as guilty of first-degree felony murder as Lamont and Laron were.

Not once during the interview with NBC that aired did Jennifer Mee hiccup.

CHAPTER 23

THE SPPD'S RESPONSE to Jennifer Mee going on national television and proclaiming she had nothing to do with luring and/or killing Shannon Griffin was immediate. New evidence in the case was released to the media and with it came some rather shocking allegations by law enforcement, explaining at least part of the state's case against Jennifer.

The evidence was in the form of text messages between Shannon Griffin and the person on the other end of Laron Raiford's cell phone, which the SPPD suspected to be Jennifer Mee (because she had told them it was, in fact, her). There was some indication that the meeting between Jennifer and Shannon was not a "date," after all, which had been previously reported, but was a setup by Jennifer Mee to sell Shannon a "half ounce" of marijuana. Initial contact between the two had been made on MocoSpace (a social media website for networking, chatting, and game playing); but on the night Shannon was murdered, according to the SPPD, Jennifer communicated with Shannon via Laron's cell phone, texting him as he made his way toward a location Jennifer had given him.

Just across the street and around the corner from where Jennifer, Lamont, Laron, and Laron's girl, Jennifer Charron, lived was a vacant, renovated home. Jennifer Mee had told Shannon to meet her in front of that building. The first text message the SPPD released had taken place at seven twenty-two that night, October 23, fewer than three hours before Shannon Griffin was murdered.

I WIL DO 55, Jennifer allegedly texted Shannon, leading law enforcement to believe that $55 was the price they agreed on for that small amount of weed.

ALRIGHT, Shannon texted back.

There was a break for a few minutes.

Then Shannon indicated he wanted to confirm the address: IT WAS 5TH AVE, 6TH ST?

NAW CUM TO GROOVE N 7TH ST NRTH, Jennifer supposedly texted back.

Six minutes passed and Jennifer did not see Shannon where they had agreed to meet. So she texted him: DAMN BRO WEA U AT?

Shannon answered right away: OK IM ON 7TH AN GROVE.

AM CUMIN, Jennifer said. Then: CALL ME.

The SPPD made it clear that Shannon received a final call on his phone—allegedly from Jennifer Mee, who was using Laron's cell phone—at 9:44 P.M. And when Shannon arrived at the scene where they had agreed to meet, just in front of that vacant house at 511 Seventh Street North, Jennifer greeted Shannon and led him "behind the vacant house . . . knowing Raiford and Newton were waiting" in the shadows to rob Shannon at gunpoint.

There was more evidence, plenty more, but the SPPD did not want to release it at this time, seeing that the SAO was building a case against Jennifer Mee, Laron Raiford and Lamont Newton. The feeling was that Laron and Lamont were going to plead out their cases separately and had given the SAO what it needed to prosecute Jennifer on murder charges.

CHAPTER 24

"BEFORE SHE STARTED dating one particular boy, you have to understand something," Rachel Robidoux later said, "Jennifer was very clean-cut, pretty much a normal teenager."

Rachel didn't know it, but that statement was not entirely true. It was an idyllic image that a mother, Rachel, and a stepfather, Chris, had of Jennifer. As Jennifer herself later explained to me, she was a different person from that "clean-cut" girl inside the home once she stepped outside and entered her own world beyond the family.

Whether they didn't realize it, or chose not to accept who Jennifer was becoming, there were glimpses of this other Jennifer obvious to both Chris and Rachel. For one, they had intercepted several letters a boy named Tyrone O'Donnell (pseudonym) had sent Jennifer while he was incarcerated in a juvenile detention center.

Tyrone was Jennifer's first serious relationship. Or, as she later explained to me, "My first love and crush."

Jennifer was a mere twelve-year-old child, just about to turn thirteen, when she and Tyrone started "dating." Later, it was clear that Rachel did not even know Jennifer was dating Tyrone until she and Chris seized those letters.

What became obvious in the letters between them, Rachel explained, "was that he had taken her down a clear path to hell."

By the time Jennifer moved in with Tyrone in the months before her eighteenth birthday, they had been dating for many years already, which could have made it all right in her fragile, young mind.

"He was very abusive to her," Rachel said. "He had even knocked her out one time. She showed up with a black eye. I questioned her. She told me [Tyrone's] nephew threw a toy car at her."

Jennifer later said Tyrone "beat me and introduced me to drugs."

According to Rachel, Jennifer had gotten pregnant while living with Tyrone; and when he found out, "he punched her in the stomach and caused her to have a miscarriage."

Tyrone had been in and out of youth detention centers (and, after turning eighteen, jails) since the age of eleven. His record is enormous. One of his most vicious crimes was that during the time he was with Jennifer, Tyrone had beaten and robbed an elderly woman. He had a foot and fifty pounds on Jennifer; he was five feet ten inches tall, 175 pounds, most of it muscle—an explosive, intense, uncaring, cold soul, who could walk into the apartment while living with Jennifer and erupt into a hurricane of violence for no reason other than Jennifer saying the wrong thing or looking at him the wrong way.

Jennifer first told me she met Tyrone at a nearby park one day while she was hanging out with friends, watching the boys play basketball. Taking all of what

Rachel and Jennifer said about Tyrone, the obvious questions become: Why would Jennifer choose such a person for a lover? Why hadn't she seen the signs? Why hadn't she taken the warnings of his explosive temper, not to mention the beatings she received, and run from the boy? Why would she stay in this abusive, toxic relationship for years?

Jennifer had grown up in a Christian household with reportedly no violence, according to Rachel and Chris Robidoux. She had never been abused, Rachel said, by Rachel or Chris. She had been given the proper amount of discipline and moral guidance. Thus, how does a girl grow up in that seemingly stable environment and then go out into the world and choose the polar opposite for a companion? Was it as simple as Jennifer made it out to be later on: "My mother was never around."

In Rachel's view, it started for Jennifer in early childhood, when she was allegedly raped.

"And I didn't know it," Rachel said, "and we . . . weren't told about the abuse until later."

It was several months after Jennifer had been (allegedly) raped, when she was outside in front of the Robidoux house playing with her sister one afternoon. Jennifer had on these shorts that were too big and they kept falling down. After it happened several times, and wasn't so much of a joke anymore, Jennifer's sister ran into the house and found their mother.

"Jennifer doesn't like her shorts falling down, Mommy—she's scared that what happened to her . . . will happen again, Mommy."

This piqued Rachel's interest.

"What are you talking about?" Rachel asked.

The sister explained best she could.

Rachel and Chris questioned Jennifer. She told them what her attackers had been doing to her.

They called the police.[5]

"There was never a time when she came to me and Chris with this and we did not believe her," Rachel later clarified, answering a later allegation by someone that she and Chris told Jennifer it was all in her head after Jennifer mentioned being abused and, at first, did not believe her.

If true, this violent and altogether self-esteem-draining sexual assault experience, which was Jennifer's introduction to sex at an age when a kid should not even hear the word, Rachel later said, set Jennifer up for many personal problems that had arisen from the abuse.

". . . We would have rather wanted her to date within her own race," Rachel explained at the risk of sounding racist, "but it was her choice and Jennifer chose to start dating only black men."

CHAPTER 25

THE SECOND STORY of meeting Tyrone O'Donnell, which Jennifer shared with me (perhaps forgetting the first), went like this. She was standing outside a friend's house waiting for the "church bus" to pick her up and take her home. It was the spring of 2003. Jennifer was twelve, almost thirteen. They had recently moved to Florida. Tyrone O'Donnell just happened to be there, waiting for that same bus, according to what Jennifer later explained in a letter. So they started talking. It was the beginning of a multiyear relationship that, after she turned fourteen, led to her losing her virginity, Jennifer said. And for those first few years, she explained, Tyrone was a "nice" guy—though it's hard to rely on a then-fourteen-year-old girl's judgment of what constitutes "nice." One could argue that Jennifer's entire perception of good and bad had been skewed. She had no idea how to make healthy decisions for herself within the context of a relationship. She was too damn young to be dating, anyway, and had no idea what was unhealthy for her emotional well-being.

Still, if you ask Jennifer, she and Tyrone hit it off. "He thought I was beautiful . . . ," Jennifer said. "Little did I know he was nothing but trouble."

Losing her virginity to the guy, she explained, "was the worst mistake ever."

It was this relationship, Jennifer claimed, that introduced her to the world of drugs and sex and everything that her parents had taught her not to get mixed up in. She referred to it as a "life I never thought I would have experienced."

What's clear here is that Rachel never understood—or maybe comprehended—the depth of this relationship as it was going on, because Jennifer kept it hidden, for the most part, from her parents.

"First, I'll say moving to Florida and a big city was a shell shock," Rachel later commented. "I saw good in all people unroll about a year after that, [but] then got a reality check dealing with city life—thugs, the hood, and streetwalkers were all new to me. Until then, I didn't see people of color as different. That being said, I didn't judge one way or another until [Tyrone O'Donnell] gave me a reason."

Rachel went on to say she knew when the two met that Tyrone "was already in and out of the system." For the three years Jen and Tyrone dated, because he was in and out of juvenile detention centers so often, they wouldn't speak or see each other for six months or more, but then would start to talk again as soon as he got out. Obviously, it wasn't until Rachel and Chris found those letters that Rachel realized the relationship never really slowed down when he was locked up.

"I didn't like him because of his lack of respect," Rachel remembered. "They started living together. . . . I hated the idea, but, of course, I didn't know the real [Tyrone] until later on—the drug dealing, women beating, stealing. . . . I truly believe that's where her life took a turn for the worst—being exposed to the ghetto thug life."

As far as an overall change in her daughter, Rachel said she didn't notice anything different about Jennifer until "about six months or maybe a year before she got locked up" due to the felony murder charges. Thus, despite that road in which Jennifer traveled with Tyrone, it wasn't until early 2010 that Rachel said she realized Jennifer was in over her head.

With Tyrone, Jennifer fell hard. She was just a teenager, Jennifer said, contradicting an earlier statement that she had been well versed in "weed" and "sex" *before* meeting Tyrone. But Tyrone brought an entire new level of understanding of that drug life into Jennifer's world.

Cocaine.

Tyrone led Jennifer into a life of smoking crack and snorting coke, she later alleged in a letter to me.

I remember I sold my first piece of crack at thirteen years old, Jennifer wrote, referring to a time just after meeting

Tyrone. *He showed me the fast life and from there, that's all I knew.*

After admitting this to me, Jennifer wrote (for about the third time): *The only thing I wish that could have been different would have been that my mom could have been home more.*

As she explained that her life after meeting Tyrone took on a criminal, dark path, in the same breath, Jennifer wrote: *I'm not trying to be funny, but people put me in a category of goin' "hood." In reality, I was a follower, when I should have been a leader.*

Jennifer said she has done bad things in her life, but she'd "never been a violent" person. Indeed, there is no record of Jennifer becoming violent with anyone. Before her arrest on felony murder charges, there is no record of Jennifer ever being arrested. Yet being charged with felony murder didn't require a history of violence. To be clear, Jennifer was charged as someone who knew there was a robbery about to take place, knew there was a weapon involved in that robbery, and took part in planning and carrying it out. The fact that a murder took place within the framework of that initial crime made the charge against her felony murder. It didn't mean she planned to murder Shannon Griffin. It meant a murder took place under the commission of another crime, and Jennifer Mee had knowledge of it and took part in it.

I'm very calm and laidback, Jennifer continued, *unless you piss me off, and even that takes a lot.*

She went on to write how she didn't understand how she got caught up in a mess like this: *Now [I'm] goin' to prison I am afraid I'll let this place get the best of me. . . . I'm really trying to show everyone I'm not the type of person* they [emphasis mine] *made me out to be. . . .*

The types of people Jennifer meant by "they"—the "media, police, and prosecutors"—were trying to portray her as just a "ghetto thug" after her arrest. Her mom, Rachel, agreed: "I know what type of person she is. [Jennifer] would give a person in need her last dollar even if she didn't know them, if she knew that they needed it. She always wanted to make people happy and to be a friend."

There's evidence to support that statement about Jennifer Mee by her mother. On the other hand, there is plenty of additional evidence, including what Jennifer herself told me, to indicate that when she was away and beyond the confines of parental boundaries, Jennifer Mee was a completely different person—very close, in fact, to that person "they" had made her out to be. You add to that what Jennifer wrote on her Myspace and Facebook pages, the way she talked, the people she hung around with, the lifestyle she led at the time of her arrest and in the years before, and the person Jennifer Mee claimed she *wasn't* had been the exact person she *had become.*

"With Jennifer," Rachel said, "she and I [were] very close. She had another life I didn't know about, maybe out of shame and disappointment of not wanting to hurt me. It seems she was able to be what people wanted her to be, depending on who she was with at that time."

Her boyfriend at the time of her arrest, Lamont Newton, was a guy Jennifer described in her letter in glowing terms: *Wow, we dated for about [five months and] he was amazing. He treated me like a queen. He was perfect.*

In the next statement, which sums up that *perfection* within a relationship Jennifer accepted in the place of love, she wrote: *He never put his hands on me. The only thing that I can say would have been better would be him [not] selling drugs.* . . .

Jennifer Mee's life was a contradiction: she was a known drug dealer.

Jennifer was already selling crack before I met her, Lamont wrote to me. *She was selling when she was with [Tyrone].*

CHAPTER 26

RACHEL'S FATHER DEVELOPED dementia after suffering that terrible, life-altering stroke, a condition that made all of their lives even harder to deal with as the spring of 2011 brought in balmy Florida temperatures and Jennifer sat behind bars. The only silver lining out of it all had been that Jennifer was being housed at Pinellas County Jail and had not been transferred or moved far away. So the family could see her when time and the prison permitted. Yet all they could do was wait and hope, wondering what the future was going to bring: a deal with the prosecution or a murder trial? Rachel and Jennifer did not know.

As Rachel went about her days, trying to deal with what life was throwing at her nearly on a daily basis, she couldn't help but think that Jennifer had gotten mixed up in being at the wrong place at the wrong time. Or maybe that was her hope, anyway. Rachel had no idea, of course, that Jennifer had admitted to police by this time that she knew they were going to rob Shannon Griffin. For Rachel, the evidence she had heard explained a scenario that did not involve her daughter at all.

"I kept hearing her saying, 'It really was a date . . . ,'"

Rachel said later, referring to that first phone call she and Jennifer had after Jennifer's arrest. To Rachel, this meant Jennifer Charron had set up a date with Shannon. And when Laron found out, he followed her there and snapped, killing Shannon in the heat of a jealous rage.

"Mr. Trevena had told us by then about [my daughter's] first statement," Rachel recalled.

That first statement Jennifer gave police, beginning at 5:45 P.M. on Sunday, October 24, 2010, not yet twenty-four-hours after the murder, was rather telling. Jennifer sat with Detective Gary Gibson. It's important to note that the SPPD had been investigating the case around the clock since Shannon's death and the evidence investigators collected led them to bringing Jennifer in on that day for questioning. She hadn't been targeted in any way, and, truthfully, Laron and Lamont had been arrested hours before the SPPD even realized Jennifer Mee was part of it all.

Jennifer had been inside the SPPD for "several hours" by the time Detective Gibson sat down with her to talk. Right away, Jennifer agreed with the detective that she had been treated "fairly" and was now ready to give her version of the events that led to Shannon's murder.

"We're talking about a homicide," Gibson said into the recording device.

Jennifer said she was speaking with police under her own free will and there were "no problems" with the SPPD and her talking. In other words, she waived her right to an attorney.

Her first mistake was to sit and talk without an attorney. Whether she was guilty of anything or not, it didn't matter. The fact that Jennifer was talking (and purportedly lying) became a hole Jennifer Mee would have a hard time digging herself out from during the coming years.

Rachel and Jennifer later said that in Jennifer's delicate mind-set at the time, she did not think she had done anything wrong.

Before they started to chat, Gibson showed Jennifer a photograph of a revolver and then asked if she had ever seen the weapon before and if she knew who might own the gun.

"Laron," Jennifer answered without hesitating.

Gibson wanted a last name.

"No, sir," she said, indicating that she had no idea what Laron's last name was.

But she had recognized the gun in the photograph.

Gibson encouraged Jennifer to explain what happened.

Jennifer told Gibson she was at the park up the street from the apartment the previous night when everything went bad. As Jennifer talked through what would be her first explanation of the events (there would be a second version later), she referred to Shannon as "the suspect" several times.

Until, that is, Detective Gibson corrected her, calling Shannon "the victim."

"I mean 'victim,'" she said. "That's what I meant . . . I apologize."

At first, Jennifer told her story in one long breath, saying Shannon was "supposed to meet us or whatever the case may be. Let me rephrase it—was trying to meet *Jen,* the other Jennifer."

Jennifer Mee was talking about her roommate, Jennifer Charron. Mee said she had no idea that Shannon Griffin and Jennifer Charron "had any type of relation going on, and then when Laron had, I guess, found out that [Shannon] had some type of relation going on with his girlfriend, Laron snapped, grabbed the man up, choked him, and pulled the gun out of the book-bag and put it to the man's head and told the man not to say anything and brought the man to the back of the house and shot and killed him."

She also admitted knowing the gun was inside a bookbag.

As seemingly straightforward and simple as it sounded, that entire explanation felt much too cut-and-dry to the detective, although he did not let on that he felt this way. Now was not the time to badger Jennifer Mee and throw evidence of the contrary in her face. Gibson wanted to let Jennifer talk. See what type of role she placed herself in regarding this crime. If he could then go out and back up Jennifer's state-ment with evidence, well, they were onto something.

Within Jennifer's explanation, there was motive and opportunity present for Laron. Love, money, and re-venge are the three major motivations for murder. In a jealous rage, apparently, Laron carried out an execution-style murder.

It seemed to fit.

Jennifer said she heard "two" gunshots, but she did not see the "actual shooting" take place.

After the murder, she recalled, "I didn't stay around. I left. I fled from everything. I didn't know what to do."

After being asked, Jennifer said it was "me, Jennifer [Charron], Lamont, and Laron" at the park—a flagrant lie, which would be proven false.

She referred to Lamont as a "friend."

Jennifer Mee and Detective Gibson then began to talk about possible evidence at the scene. Gibson wanted to know if Jennifer could explain to him anything she might have seen that had been left at the crime scene.

"A pair of Jordan Slides," she said. They were Laron's. And she knew this because Laron was "the only one that came back with no shoes on."

Right after the shooting, Jennifer told Gibson, Laron was frantic.

"Make phone calls," Laron said to no one in particular. They were all standing in the park, perhaps thinking: *What in the hell just happened*? "We need to leave," Laron continued. "I think I killed the man. I think I killed the man."

So they ran from the park at that moment and wound up back at the apartment they shared.

Jennifer explained how she "thought they were just going to try and rob the man and leave him alone. Then when the man tried to grab for the barrel, Laron thought . . . the man was trying to take Laron's life. Well . . ."

Although he did not come out and explain it to Jennifer, Gibson had a major problem with this. Jennifer had started off saying it was a quarrel between two men and a girl, a sort of love triangle that went bad. Now she was saying it was a planned robbery gone bad. Which was it?

In any event, despite whatever the motive might have been, Gibson had important pieces of a case against Jennifer Mee in place: an admission from her that she "knew" there was a weapon involved and "knew" beforehand there was going to be a robbery.

Gibson asked Jennifer where she was getting this information from—had someone told her, or had she witnessed it for herself?

Jennifer said she was there; she saw the entire incident unfold: "I seen it. . . ."

Then she explained that sometime after Shannon arrived, Laron took out his weapon and put it to Shannon's head. According to Jennifer, Laron said: "Don't. Say. Nothing."

Shannon reacted instinctively and grabbed the gun by the barrel.

Laron moved quickly and "snatched it back," Jennifer recalled for Gibson. And once he had the barrel pointed at Shannon's head, Shannon was a hostage, willing to do whatever Laron asked. "And then [he] brought him all the way to the back and that's when I heard the gunshots and I left."

Some other facts supported by Jennifer, which came out during this first interview, included how Shannon, according to Jennifer, became aggressive when he showed up at the park and realized Laron and the others were there. He didn't expect anyone but Jennifer Charron to be there, Jennifer Mee explained. "He was coming over there to chill with [Jenni], I guess."

Gibson wanted to know which of the two men became hostile first.

"Laron did," Jennifer said, "because he seen—he asked for Jennifer [Charron] and he also was asking me because I was sitting next to [Lamont]."

Detective Gibson asked Jennifer if she could give him some insight into Laron's demeanor and if it changed when Shannon showed up looking for Jennifer Charron.

Jennifer said it definitely did. She used the word "snapped" for a second time.

And that was it. They concluded the interview around 5:50 P.M.

Jennifer had given the detective a narrative of what happened, placing herself in the role of supporting the robbery by taking part in it, and potentially knowing Laron was bringing a weapon with him.

This would not be the last time the SPPD spoke to Jennifer Mee about the murder of Shannon Griffin. When they once again shined that interrogation light in her face, for a second time, boy, would her story change!

And so one had to wonder: What happened that night and in those days leading up to the murder of twenty-two-year-old Shannon Griffin? Who was truly involved? And was it a robbery, or was it a jealous man in a rage murdering a man he thought was hooking up with his lady?

The answers to those questions began years before Shannon Griffin rode a scooter down to a vacant house in South St. Pete on the night of October 23, 2010, parked the two-wheeled motor vehicle on its kickstand, and walked across the street toward a death trap.

PART TWO

CHAPTER 27

UNSUCCESSFULLY TRYING TO manage a life that Jennifer Mee later described as nothing short of disappointments amid depression and other emotional conflicts, Jennifer fell into a routine of school, going to the movies on Friday nights, hanging over friends' houses, and walking down to the nearby park to see who was around. It was late 2006 and the early part of January 2007. On the surface, her life seemed to fall in line with what many fifteen-year-old kids consider the daily grind. Unlike many of her peers, however, Jennifer and her friends would smoke weed, laugh, cry, maybe take some pills, have sex with specific boys, and complain about being teens in such a judgmental world, especially when you're considered among the unpopular. Jennifer indicated that she despised school and everything about it then.

"I thought it was for punks."

On a typical day during this period of her life, unbeknownst to Rachel or Chris Robidoux, Jennifer would arrive home around one-thirty in the afternoon from school. Instead of studying or maybe watching some television, having an afternoon snack, Jennifer would sneak boys into the house to party and have sex. It was as if she lived in a bubble where anything she wanted to do was okay: no parental supervision, no rules, and no one to answer to.

This routine was disrupted, however, when Jennifer's life dramatically changed one morning. And from that moment on, things would never be the same for her. It was a time during her high-school days that Jennifer recalled as if it had happened the day before.

January 23, 2007, was a Tuesday. President George W. Bush was slated to give his State of the Union speech that night. Earlier in the month, Apple CEO Steve Jobs gave the world the iPhone. Robert Pickton, thought to be Canada's worst serial killer on record, sat in court as his jury trial got under way. It was cool in Florida that January, much cooler than normal. Light-jacket weather, as they say.

Jennifer was sitting in science class, her mind wandering off to whatever she was planning for that day after school. It was early morning. Sitting at her desk, Jennifer felt a tremendous pain in her chest come on unexpectedly and suddenly: a tightening, throbbing, penetrating niggle of some sort. She had no idea what was happening. It was as if some boy had walked over and thrust his fist directly between her breasts. The excruciating pain grew and lingered with each moment.

Damn, what's happening? Jennifer asked herself.

Then it started.

Hic.

A pause.

Hic. Hic.

Water, Jennifer thought. *I need some water and these hiccups will be gone, same as the last time.*

She'd had the hiccups before. Not quite in the same manner as most kids (a bit more powerful and extended), but they always went away. And they had never been accompanied by so much pain. Where had that staggering pain in her chest come from—the damn hiccups were causing it?

No way, she thought.

Jennifer asked to be excused from the classroom.

"Sure, go ahead," her teacher said.

Her classmates looked on as Jennifer, seemingly panicked, hiccupping repeatedly, fast and furious, walked out of the room.

All the way down the hallway: *Hic. Hic. Hic.* The hiccups came in quick repetition, in groups of three or four or even five.

Hic. Hic. Hic.

Pause.

Hic. Hic. Hic. Hic.

She took a drink of water from the student fountain. Held her breath. It had worked once before.

Not this time.

Thirty minutes passed. Jennifer was back in class; that pain still there, and the hiccups continuing. Fellow students were looking at her strangely, wondering what in the world was going on. Was she drumming up the hiccups for attention? Did she want to get out of class?

Hic. Hic. Hic.

Students to her left and right were already becoming impatient. It was disruptive and irritating.

What the hell, Mee?

That chest pain grew more intense.

Jennifer raised her hand: "Can I go down to the nurse's office?"

"Certainly," said the teacher.

An hour passed and Jennifer was still hiccupping. The pain, still generalized in the center of her chest, was now unbearable, as if someone had been punching her, over and over, not letting up. A brain freeze from eating ice cream too fast times ten.

The nurse had Jennifer hold her breath.

Didn't work.

Breathe into a paper bag.

Nope.

Drink a glass of water while holding her nose.

That was a damn old wives' tale.

Of course, it didn't work.

"Try this peanut butter," the nurse told her.

Tasted great, but had no effect whatsoever. If anything, Jennifer was hiccupping more now, faster, so it felt harder. The pain was deeper and so overwhelming she couldn't lie down. Her diaphragm hurt. Her stomach ached.

Jennifer called her mother.

"You're kidding? I don't believe you," Rachel told her daughter. "You must want to leave school early." According to Jennifer, Rachel even laughed. She had never heard of such a thing: the hiccups coming on and not going away.

"No, I'm not—*hic, hic, hic*—kidding, Mom. I'm serious. . . ."

Hic, hic, hic.

The nurse got on the phone with Rachel. "It's true."

"Okay, if they persist for another thirty minutes, call me and I'll come and get her," Rachel said.

Jennifer had started to cry moments after arriving at the nurse's office because she had no idea what was going on. This bout with the hiccups, she could tell right away, was different from anything she'd ever experienced. It was painful, and it scared Jennifer.

Thirty additional minutes passed. Now, ninety minutes or more into it, Jennifer called her mother and told her to hurry up. She needed to get out of this school.

Now.

"I want to go home," Jennifer said through tears.

"I'm on my way, honey."

Rachel knew it was no ruse to get out of school; her Jennifer was in pain.

After arriving home and trying various tried-and-true remedies, none of which worked, Jennifer tried to go to sleep, thinking that a good night's rest might shake the hiccups. If not, at least she could take a break from what was now a condition beyond irritating and alarming and painful.

CHAPTER 28

HE WAS INSIDE the barn preparing a 350-pound hog for slaughter. While picking up the beast and trying to hang the thing so he could butcher it humanely with a rather large, serrated knife, which lay on the table by his side, he bent down and something popped inside his head.

Charles Osborne, a father of eight, slipped, fell, and was knocked out cold.

"I felt nothing," Osborne later said.

As he came to, Osborne noticed something different right away.

Hic. Hic. Hic.

He had the hiccups. One nearly every second and a half.

Hic, hic, hic, hic . . .

It was involuntary. He couldn't control it. As if lifting that pig and falling down had broken something inside him. Had he blown a brain gasket or something?

Weird.

In fact, it wasn't so strange. Without knowing it, Charles Osborne had ruptured a small part of his brain that controlled the hiccup response in his body. His body had no choice *but* to hiccup.

If, when she awoke on the morning of January 24, 2007, Jennifer Mee thought eighteen hours with the hiccups had been a long spell, Charles Osborne had her beat by sixty-seven years, 364 days and six hours. Osborne had developed the hiccups on that 1922 morning when he lifted an oversized hog and a blood vessel popped in his head. They lasted until 1990, the year before he died at ninety-seven years old, when the hiccups mysteriously stopped on their own without warning or reason. It has been said that Mr. Osborne, a farmer and former military man, had started out hiccupping at least forty times per minute, but cut it down to twenty during those latter years just before the irritating condition stopped. In order to eat, he had developed a way of breathing taught to him by Mayo Clinic doctors, who had tried for years to cure him.

Still, any bout with the hiccups longer than the norm of ten or so minutes was torture—anyone could agree with that. For Jennifer Mee, as she opened her eyes after a night of not sleeping much, lots of tossing and turning and chest pains, not to mention thoughts of what was happening to her, they were still there.

Hic. Hic. Hic.

Jennifer Mee rolled over and started to cry.

What was she going to do?

Mom got on the telephone to Jennifer's doctor first thing that morning after realizing that this was more than a routine bout with the hiccups that all children (and even adults) experienced from time to time. Something was terribly wrong with Jennifer.

"Make it stop, Mom. Please."

The hiccups involve a "sudden, involuntary contraction (spasm) of the diaphragm muscle" near the base of the lungs. Hiccupping is considered a digestive disorder. When that contraction takes place, in the same instant, the vocal cords close and what we refer to as the hiccup sound is produced. Most, if not all, medical texts report the causes as eating too quickly, drinking or eating too much at once, surgery in the adnominal region, strokes, brain tumors, even noxious fumes, and some medications, which can bring on a bout with the hiccups. As most people have experienced, hiccups that come on unexpectedly generally go away after a glass of water or swallowing air or after a few hours/minutes on their own. The rule of thumb in the medical community is that hiccups lasting more than twenty-four hours should not be a cause to become frenzied and think the world is coming to an end. Rather, they're perhaps a minor concern and a call to your doctor to see what to do next is warranted. After all, the doctor might think there is an underlying problem. According to the most recent research: *Some illnesses for which continuing hiccups may be a symptom include: pleurisy of the diaphragm, pneumonia, uremia, alcoholism, disorders of the stomach or esophagus, and bowel diseases. Hiccups may also be associated with pancreatitis, pregnancy, bladder irritation, liver cancer or hepatitis. Surgery, tumors, and lesions may also cause persistent hiccups.*[6]

Jennifer was suffering from a serious condition—much more severe than perhaps she or Rachel knew then. Her hiccups were not the type that lasted a few minutes or, at the most, a few hours and then went away. Here it was twenty-four hours later and she was still hiccupping. Her stomach now hurt a lot because of the constant, uncontrollable contractions. She had a headache. The chest pain had subsided some, but was still present. Her throat was sore. She had back pain from the constant jerking. Her hips began to bother her.

All she could do was cry.

"Why?" she asked her mother.

They went into the doctor's office after Rachel called and spoke to a nurse.

"Intractable hiccups," the doctor told them during that first visit.

Generally, an intractable hiccups diagnosis is not made until one has the hiccups for two weeks or more. This was a good indication, though Rachel had no idea at the time that her doctor was not at all familiar with how to deal with Jennifer's condition. Perhaps like most other physicians, Jennifer's doctor figured the hiccups would go away on their own after some time.

Rachel and Jennifer looked at each other.

"Chronic" was what the doctor meant when he said "intractable."

"What can we do?" Rachel wanted to know. Frustrated already.

The doctor explained that they needed to find out why Jennifer was hiccupping so often. What was the root cause? Was there some sort of underlying issue that started the hiccups and kept them going, like in the Charles Osborne case? Jennifer was not new to having the hiccups; she'd had them before for periods of an hour, two, maybe three. There was something going on here that Jennifer felt was different—that she was now involved with a condition that was going to take over her life more than it had already.

Treatment involved a wide variety of remedies (some old, some new, some urban legends, some not) and even medication.

What hurt Rachel most was seeing Jennifer cry and break down, experience that pain brought on by the side effects of having the hiccups for an extended period of time.

"We tried to keep her spirits up," Rachel said later. "We wanted to keep her smiling. But when she starts hurting, it breaks my heart."

For Rachel and Chris, it was the helplessness. The fact that there was nothing Rachel and Chris could do for their child.

They left the doctor's office with a fraying sense of hope—and, of course, medication. It was the only remedy the doctor could think of.

The first round, Chlorpromazine, a med that is commonly given by doctors for intractable hiccups, came with a host of side effects. Among them were drowsiness and faintness, palpitations and tachycardia (a dangerously fast heart rate). Yet, Jennifer experienced none of those. Instead, after taking just one dose, she broke out in hives all over her body and had trouble breathing.

The doctor suggested Valium: ten milligrams, four times a day.

This calmed Jennifer down and allowed her to deal

with the hiccups—or at least *feel* as if she could deal with the hiccups.

"But she walked around the house like a zombie," Rachel recalled.

It was a Band-Aid. It masked the symptoms and made her feel doped up. It did nothing to correct the problem.

Two days turned into a week

Hic, hic, hic . . .

Jennifer went to several pediatricians and a neurologist. She had an MRI, CAT scan, X-rays, bloodwork. She saw a cardiologist.

"Nothing," Jennifer said. "They could not tell us anything."

One week turned into two and then three.

"We tried peanut butter again, tablespoons of sugar, mustard, gallons and gallons of water. . . ."

She even drank vinegar.

None of it worked.

Quite interesting, when Jennifer was interviewed by a local news crew during those weeks after the hiccups began, she said, "Someone told me to take a hit of marijuana—yeah, right!"

Then the reporter asked, "You're definitely not going to go that route, right?"

Jennifer responded, laughing, "Definitely not."

But the sad fact was that she had been smoking weed and taking other drugs leading up to this time. And none of that had worked, either.

Rachel had no idea what to do. Doctors in Florida were saying they couldn't do anything more than they were: doping her up on meds she had allergic reactions to.

Jennifer cried and complained about the pain. The irritation and the sheer frustration of this dreaded condition that had taken over every second of her life was almost too much to bear. Her depression deepened. She felt as if nothing was going to work.

"I'll never get married . . . ," she told Rachel. "Never get to have kids."

More than that, wherever she went after word spread around town of her condition, Jennifer was being recognized and, at times, ridiculed.

Kids would mimic her and yell things at Jennifer.

"Stop faking!"

"Are you drunk, bitch?"

"You pregnant?"

Jennifer's self-esteem, which before this was considered seriously low, anyway, sank to even lower levels and compounded what was a growing self-consciousness and self-hatred. She began to feel that everyone was looking at her and talking about her wherever she went. One of Jennifer's favorite things to do on Friday nights was go to the movies with friends. She couldn't do that anymore because kids from school would chastise her, get in her face, call her vicious names, and bully her. Just the hiccups alone would irritate other people watching the movie.

And then the accusations began: a majority of the people in town believed she was making it all up for the attention.

Rachel sat by and watched her daughter suffer. It was horrendous.

At one point, Jennifer said something that Rachel could not ignore. Rachel now had to do something drastic. She would have to act.

"She was getting picked on in school and public," Rachel recalled. "She was not sleeping much. Always in pain and she didn't see an end to it."

Jennifer came to Rachel one night.

"No one is going to want to date me. . . ."

"We'll figure it out, honey. Don't worry."

Jennifer had heard this now for weeks.

"We will figure out how to stop it, I promise," Rachel said.

"I want to jump off the Sunshine Skyway," Jennifer said.

"What?"

Jennifer indicated that suicide was now an option.

Hearing this crushed Rachel.

"It might have been idle talk," Rachel said later, "but I knew then I had to do whatever I could to try to stop the hiccups."

Sitting at home, wondering what to do next, where to go, how to deal with this problem that had taken over their lives, realizing her options had all run out, Rachel decided to take control of the situation and do something she would later be ridiculed for, but she felt she had no other alternative but to at least try. It was, Rachel felt, their only option for getting rid of the hiccups for good.

CHAPTER 29

RACHEL THOUGHT ABOUT what she could do to help her ailing daughter. Sitting idly on the sidelines, watching Jennifer agonize and manage tremendous pain, was slowly destroying the mother of five. The hiccups were their life now. There was no other focus in the Robidoux household. All of the doctors they had gone to could do nothing more than shrug their shoulders and whip out a prescription pad. Rachel needed to speak with a bona fide expert—someone with experience in battling long-term, acute hiccups. Pickle juice and drinking water upside down was stupid. All those so-called remedies did nothing more than cause Jennifer to become more frustrated. She was hiccupping now about fifty times per minute, almost once per second.

"Stressful," Jennifer recalled. "I couldn't go anywhere. I just stayed inside my home."

She felt like a sideshow . . . a prisoner.

When Jennifer did dredge up the courage to go out, some offered prayers, while others tried to sneak up behind Jennifer and scare the hiccups out of her. The prayers and good wishes were thoughtful, sure, but the negative and mean people of the world overshadowed any good that anybody was trying to send Jennifer's way.

One astute doctor they visited during this period suggested Jennifer's hiccups were signs of a "tic disorder" often associated with Tourette's. But Rachel wrote it off, saying Jennifer never showed any signs of twitching or having erratic, inappropriate, often vulgar, and obscene outbursts, all of which are symptoms of Tourette's.

By now, Jennifer's hips were hurting so badly from the constant jerking of her body every time she hiccupped, it was hard to walk. Her diet consisted of applesauce, Jell-O, and ice cream, all foods she could swallow in an instant, between each hiccup. She was actually scared of eating anything solid, for she feared she might choke to death.

As Rachel and Jennifer started to research the lasting effects of long-term hiccups, they did not like what they found. Decreased physical strength, depression, and possibly even death, reported an article from the University of Colorado, Denver. Death had occurred in patients suffering the hiccups and a secondary, underlying condition. Were the hiccups a sign of some other ailment Jennifer had that could potentially kill her?

Just one more thing to worry about.

The concern everyone had more than most anything else was the fact that Jennifer had been prone to depression already. Would her condition now send her into an abyss of sadness she couldn't come back from? Was that momentary mention of suicide by Jennifer an actual cry for help? Was Jennifer thinking that suicide was the only way to put an end to the pain and ridicule?

The bottom line here was that it was no laughing matter: This was not some child getting the hiccups and everyone sitting around a BBQ thinking it was cute because they sounded silly and lasted a little longer than usual. This was chronic, extreme, and had taken over every waking moment of Jennifer's life. She was no longer going to school because it was too much for her and too much of a distraction for everyone else.

Rachel was desperate. She needed to make something happen. She was at the house one afternoon, lying down, trying to get a handle on what to do next.

"It came to me that I should maybe call the local newspaper, see if I can get a Letter to the Editor printed and maybe a doctor or someone who had dealt with this condition would see it and I might be able to get her some help," Rachel explained later. "I didn't know where else to turn."

It was a decision that would change the course of everything.

"I was only looking for answers," Rachel added. "By that point, we were willing to do and try *anything*."

From the moment she called the newspaper, Rachel

explained, Jennifer's story took off. They could never have considered or predicted how fast it would spread or how big it would become. Jennifer's condition went from a small story in the local newspapers and local television news station to international media calling her and wanting to put her in front of a worldwide audience.

According to Rachel, the *Tampa Bay Times* sent a reporter to her house to interview the family. At the same time, some of the interview was recorded on a small handheld video camera for the newspaper's website. Before the print story was published, the video went up online.

"Before the print story published the next day, we got thirty to fifty calls from media wanting Jennifer to do a story with them," Rachel explained.

That was it: Jennifer's story was now part of the endless transom that is the Internet pipeline, traveling all around the world, being shared and shared and shared with comments attached.

"After they got hold of it, the blogs made it seem as if I was trying to sell Jennifer's story," Rachel explained, defending her decision to take Jennifer's hiccups public. "Like I wanted to make money off her. But, in fact, I wanted a *cure*. . . . She was depressed and had talked about jumping off a bridge. My mission was to find a cure for my daughter and not to show her off like a freak show."

Rachel believed any parent would have done the same thing.

"I just wish," Rachel said later, reflecting on her decision to call the newspaper on that day, "I had been more informed when I did it. I never wanted to put

Jennifer out there like that. I was *just* trying to get her some help."

When Jennifer's story printed in the *Tampa Bay Times* the following morning, Valentine's Day, February 14, 2007, it took on an entire new level of pathological (viral) vitality. The big networks latched on. Rachel's phone, still ringing from the Internet video story the previous night, was now on fire. ABC, NBC, CBS, FOX, CNN, HLN, and MSNBC were calling; some of them offered to fly Jennifer to New York on the first flight out so they could put her on their morning shows.

This story of the "Hiccup Girl"—a nickname that, in and of itself, had a funny, pop culture ring—was perfect fodder for that early-morning audience, many of whom liked their news served with a sidedish of fluff and a dash of celebrity crash-and-burn seasoning. A fifteen-year-old girl like Jennifer, cute and seemingly innocent and naïve and altogether the classic American child, was the ideal ratings grabber as a winter ratings sweeps period was under way for the big networks. Jennifer would appeal to everyone. People would feel sorry for her. They'd offer help.

Rachel's hope was that an expert would see Jennifer's story and offer his or her help—and cure the damn hiccups.

That was the goal.

Nothing more.

That one story on February 14 by *Tampa Bay Times* reporter Mary Jane Park sparked a storm of criticism, too. But as Rachel fielded calls from producers all over the world, the one she took most interest in, mainly because of what they were offering, was NBC's *Today* morning show. Producers promised Rachel that if she and Jennifer appeared that Friday, February 16, they would have a medical expert appear with them and the doctor would try to help Jennifer get rid of the hiccups. It seemed to be exactly the reason why Rachel had called the newspaper in the first place.

What a major coup—ratings-wise—it would be if a network morning show could make the claim that its in-house doctor had cured the Hiccup Girl.

"That's the reason we're doing this, to try to get her some help," Rachel told the *Tampa Bay Times* in a follow-up story a day before she and Jennifer packed their bags and flew off to New York. "We don't want to give the wrong impression that Jennifer's just going for fun."

Good Morning America, more than the CBS *Morning Show,* wanted Jennifer to sit on its couch, too. But Jennifer and Rachel felt that appearing on *Today* was enough.

Fly in, do the show, fly back home.

Chris Robidoux told the *Tampa Bay Times* they did not want Jennifer's condition or her life "to turn into a circus."

But, of course, it was far too late for that already.

CHAPTER 30

MEREDITH VIEIRA INTRODUCED Jennifer as the camera focused on her face—and she hiccupped repeatedly. Both Jennifer and Rachel looked good, all dolled up by the *Today* crack team of makeup and hair personnel. Both wore black blouses, Jennifer black pants, Rachel brown, and Jennifer had a red ribbon of some sort wrapped around her right wrist. They did not appear to be nervous. Both seemed interested in getting to the bottom of what was happening to Jennifer and hopefully finding the child some relief. The only respite Jennifer had experienced over the past three weeks was when she slept. According to her and Rachel, Jennifer's hiccups ceased during the hours she was sound asleep; but the moment she opened her eyes, they started once again.

On the *Today* couch, Vieira sat next to Matt Lauer, Jennifer next to Lauer, and flanking them on each side, in single chairs, Rachel and a doctor. The segment was billed as a *"Today* Show Exclusive: 3 Weeks with the Hiccups."[7]

NBC brought in Dr. Roshini Rajapaksa ("Dr. Raj"), a gastroenterologist from nearby New York Medical Center. Dr. Raj sported solid credentials. She graduated from New York University School of Medicine in 1997. A beautiful woman with long, dark black hair, blemish-free bronze skin, and a million-dollar smile, the doctor was there to help Jennifer and give her advice as to which steps the family could take next.

As Vieira had suggested at the top of the story, everyone and their mother seemed to have a suggestion to get rid of the hiccups, but nothing had worked for Jennifer.

After saying good morning, directing her attention to Jennifer, Vieira said, "I feel so bad for you. . . ."

It was a sentiment felt by everyone simply by watching the segment, listening to Jennifer hiccup relentlessly, her entire body jerking, and her facial expression lifeless. No one would want to be in Jennifer's position, and it was easy to sympathize with this poor young girl who just wanted the hiccups to go away so she could move on with her life.

What would later provoke scores of haters (most "Internet trolls") to come out from underneath their bridges and publicly demean and hate on Jennifer, calling her a liar, was that when she started to answer questions posed by the *Today* team, the hiccups stopped. As she sat waiting to talk, before the first question of how they were coping, Jennifer hiccupped repeatedly, second after second. However, as soon as she opened her mouth to speak— "I can't do what a normal teenager would do. I can't go to a movie like I would like to do every Friday. I can't go somewhere out in public without people staring and saying something. I've had people ask me if I was drinking or if I was pregnant"—she did not hiccup once.

Yet, as soon as she stopped talking, there they were again.

Hic. Hic. Hic. Hic. Hic. Hic . . .

Quick pause.

Hic. Hic. Hic. Hic. Hic. Hic . . .

Matt Lauer picked up on it and mentioned how Jennifer had stopped hiccupping while she answered Vieira's first question. "So there's the solution right there," Lauer said humorously, everyone smiling, "don't stop talking."

They discussed the pain. Jennifer said it hurt so bad all she wanted to do was cry. That she was actually putting on her best face for the show, because inside all she wanted to do was break down.

She seemed a little manic as the segment progressed. She talked about how a combination of Benadryl and Valium was helping her cope and sleep.

Matt Lauer asked Rachel about all the doctors they had seen and if there was any sort of indication as to what was going on, medically speaking.

"Nothing yet," Rachel said. "That's why we're here. . . ."

Rachel's goal was clear. It didn't matter what anyone

had said or posted online, what those knuckleheads at the mall screamed at the family as they shopped, or what idiots called and said on the telephone when they accused Rachel and Chris of trying to pimp their daughter into an overnight celebrity. Rachel was determined to help her daughter beat this condition. If that meant hopping on a jet and flying to New York, well, damn it, so be it. Rachel wanted her daughter to find relief.

Lauer encouraged viewers to go to the show's website and write in "any solution" they might have, no matter how crazy it may sound.

Vieira asked Dr. Raj, who had sat listening, what caused the hiccups.

The doctor explained how common they were and also warned how the medical establishment really didn't know a lot about the causes. Dr. Raj explained how the hiccups were associated with the diaphragm and the muscles in the chest. Meanwhile, the *Today* producers put a graphic on the screen to explain what was happening in the body as a person hiccupped.

In the background, while everyone talked, viewers could hear Jennifer hiccupping incessantly.

After a very brief explanation by the doctor, Lauer patted Jennifer on the knee and said good luck.

The entire segment clocked in at two minutes, fifty-three seconds—most of which Jennifer hiccupped throughout.

Rachel and Jennifer were given no new remedies or any advice from Dr. Raj. The segment, basically, introduced Hiccup Girl to the world, showed how aggravating and frustrating the hiccups were for Jennifer and Rachel, and that was it. NBC had scored the first national interview with Hiccup Girl.

Jennifer and Rachel hung around the studio after the segment. Keith Urban was slated to play on the outside stage—the Plaza—later that morning, and Jennifer, especially, wanted to see the performance.

When it came time for Keith Urban's performance, the outside temperature was 15 degrees. Absolutely freezing. The wind blew. Crowds shivered. Quite the culture shock for Jennifer and Rachel, who pined for the warmth of Florida they were used to. But there they were, dressed in winter clothes, outside at the Plaza, waiting for Keith Urban to do his thing.

When cameras panned to the stage as Keith Urban stood in front of the microphone, that signature Fender Stratocaster hanging around his neck, Jennifer was off to the side of the stage, trying to stay warm, wearing black gloves, an ankle-length, cowboy-like leather jacket, smiling best she could manage under such extreme conditions.

Keith Urban felt so bad for Jennifer he brought her up on the stage and gave her a big hug as the crowd went wild.

Jennifer smiled. She had met her first A-list celebrity.

Since Matt Lauer had made that announcement earlier in the morning to e-mail the *Today* website any solutions viewers might have, the website had received about ten thousand e-mails from people commenting on the Jennifer Mee story, many of whom offered advice and remedies of all types: lemon juice, apple juice, massage therapy, hypnotist therapy, and acupuncture.

It all seemed so glib. Jennifer and Rachel had heard it all before. There was nothing new, other than maybe the acupuncture, which Jennifer was opposed to, "because of the needles," she claimed.

Back at the hotel, preparing to catch a flight back

home, Jennifer and Rachel took a call from one of the *Today* producers. The show wanted them to stay in town for another appearance on Monday morning. The segment had gone over so big, with so much national and international interest, they wanted to revisit the story again next week, maybe get a new doctor and talk some more about what they could do to help Jennifer.

Back in Florida, Chris reported the phone ringing as relentlessly as Jennifer's hiccups. Calls were coming from everywhere. It was overwhelming and difficult. They had no idea what they'd gotten themselves into with all of this. The story was taking off at a rate that seemed unbearable and unpredictable. Already there were ten pages of links to stories about Jennifer on Google, more showing up with every page refresh.

Jennifer and her hiccups were now an international wild fire burning out of control. Jennifer felt special all of a sudden. Everyone now recognized her wherever she went. She felt like a bona fide celebrity. Some of it was already going to her head after *Today* promised the royal treatment for Jennifer and Rachel if they agreed to stay in town for an appearance on Monday: spa, restaurants, spending money, maybe a Broadway show.

That weekend, as they waited inside the hotel for Monday to come, *Good Morning America* producers called Jennifer's house in Florida a reported fifty-seven times in one day. While all of this craziness happened, Jennifer and Rachel watched as notes from *GMA* producers were slipped underneath their hotel room door. *GMA* had found out where they were staying and were desperate, according to Rachel, to steal Jennifer away from *Today*.

Rachel was loyal, she said. She was not going to

jump over to the other, competing network and have Jennifer appear there. This wasn't about turning Jennifer into a commodity.

Meanwhile, Jennifer was soaking up all this attention— and loving it.

"We're going to move you two," said a producer from *Today* after Rachel explained what was going on with *GMA*. "We're going to put you up in a new hotel under fake names."

Thus, Jennifer and Rachel were shuffled under the cloak of secrecy to a second hotel, checked in under aliases, and told to stay in the room until they appeared on Monday morning.

In what would become a sore issue for some later on, *Today* paid for everything that weekend Rachel and Jennifer stayed in town. They had their clothes washed, and Rachel couldn't believe the laundry bill was close to $300. They gave Rachel money for missing work, because she told them she had to go back to Florida so she could earn money. Every day in New York was a missed day of work. Rachel and her family needed the money.

Jennifer got herself a French manicure. They needed to eat, so *Today* bought them meals. The show even picked up the tab for two packs of cigarettes. In total, Rachel later said, she was given $2,200 for expenses, which included some pleasurable things to do while they waited and that work money she lost while in New York with Jennifer. Those who would later criticize Rachel and claim she was making money off her daughter, selling her out, were quite ignorant to the situation because there was no money to be made. No one was paying Jennifer for her story. And $2,200 was not a payday that would change the family's lives in any way. Even Jennifer would later tell a friend she was "upset" because Rachel and Chris spent all the money she made from the hiccups. But in reality there was no money. It was just one more way for Jennifer to, as her celebrity rose, allow it all to go to her head—and also one more in a long line of contradictions posed by Jennifer.

On that Monday morning, Jennifer did a second interview with *Today,* which amounted to much of the same fluff from the previous Friday. The main focus of this second interview was the response *Today* had to Friday's segment. Jennifer and Rachel spoke with Natalie Morales, and once again Dr. Raj was there. This time, Dr. Raj suggested treatments such as acupuncture, chiropractic manipulation, massage therapy, and even certain types of injections, intravenous medication, and endoscopy.

That afternoon, before flying back to Florida, Jennifer taped an interview for *Inside Edition.* She'd made the rounds. She was an overnight media sensation and now a recognizable, albeit disposable, celebrity.

When they arrived home, people stared, pointed, and whispered at the airport. Some came up and asked for an autograph. Others hurled insults. Some wished her well.

Jennifer took it all in as if she were walking the red carpet. The elation on her face was derived from all the attention she was getting. Here was the other side of all that pain: being noticed, being wanted, being popular.

Walking out of the airport, Jennifer said all she wanted to do was go see her friend. "I haven't seen her in a million years." She wanted to reconnect with this friend and bring her into the fold. She wanted to allow the friend to hang with her and enjoy the ride.

Rachel needed to get back to work. She was the breadwinner of the household. With Chris on disability, Rachel needed the income. Many doctors were donating treatment, but bills would start to pile up. All this traveling cost money, even though NBC Universal had paid for most of it.

The local media was waiting at the airport, of course. Jennifer did several local interviews while exiting the airport. She was told the *Ellen DeGeneres Show* had called and was hoping to book her. Additional calls had come in from Britain and Canada and Australia and other countries. For some reason, Japan was crazy for the story. Everyone wanted a piece of Jennifer Mee. There was also word that a husband and wife team in Pennsylvania that had apparently invented a cure for the hiccups wanted to speak with Jennifer, allow her to use their product, and talk about a possible endorsement deal.

As the whirlwind continued, *Tampa Bay Times* reporter Mary Jane Park spoke to Chris Robidoux, who was rather tired of all the calls, e-mails, and knocks on the door. Chris wanted their lives back. He needed peace. He wanted life to go on quietly again.

But all of this had just begun, essentially. There was no turning it off now.

"We went to the media for one reason only, but now I just feel like she is being used," Chris told Park. "She's not for sale. She's a human being."

CHAPTER 31

JENNIFER MEE WAS back in St. Pete after what turned
out to be two appearances on *Today* and a taped segment for *Inside Edition*. Now every media outlet in
the Tampa region wanted her, as well as media from
all around the country and world. Jennifer was smiling from ear to ear, enjoying every moment in the
limelight.

By February 26, 2007, the *Tampa Bay Times* had received more than two hundred thousand hits on its
website, most of those interested in the stories about
Jennifer's hiccupping ordeal. Two thousand e-mails
had come into the newspaper inquiring about Jennifer, many of those offering advice, remedies, and well
wishes. Mary Jane Park had received upward of over
one thousand voice mails regarding the stories she'd
published. What was interesting, Park pointed out in
an article published in late February, now just over
one month after Jennifer began hiccupping, was that
Britney Spears and Anna Nicole Smith had been the
subject of tabloid banner headlines and consistent and
constant rumors—salacious and scandalous and likely
false as they were. Both women were continuously in
the news. Yet, Jennifer's story had trumped even those
two headline-grabbing celebrities, usurping them as
the latest pop culture phenomenon.

Most of the attention was built around public sym-
pathy for Jennifer. Americans in general felt sorry for
her. Sure, there was a group of Internet haters, alongside some people out in public, who liked to ridicule

and make fun of Jennifer. But for the most part, people felt horrible for the predicament she found herself in by not being able to stop hiccupping. As all of the attention grew, incredibly, Jennifer's hiccups grew louder and more animated. Whenever she went into a building for an interview or a doctor's appointment, the focus would be all on her and her hiccups as she could be heard from one end of the building to the other. Often, Jennifer would be placed in a room by herself because the hiccups were so loud and disruptive.

One expert whom Park interviewed nailed it when he said the public likely viewed Jennifer as a "damsel in distress."

Today was not leaving the story alone. The show had a crew following Jennifer whenever she went to a doctor's appointment. A local radio station, which had had Jennifer on as a guest, spoke to a local theater owner at the Channelside Cinemas in Tampa. Going to the movies had been one thing Jennifer said she loved and now missed since the hiccups had started. The movies had been a Friday-night habit for her and a few friends. Thus, after hearing her disappointment about missing out on the movies, the theater owner closed the theater on that Friday night after she returned from New York and allowed Jennifer and a few chosen friends the run of the place. Jennifer chose to see the Eddie Murphy movie *Norbit*. She and her friends were given the red-carpet treatment with free popcorn, candy, and soda.

As Jennifer went to see a new round of doctors, there was some indication that a recent bout Jennifer had had with strep throat and a vertebra compression picked up on a new MRI scan might have contributed to her having developed acute, intractable hiccups. Yet, the cause, Rachel felt at this point of their ordeal, was insignificant to the fact that Jennifer was still hiccupping relentlessly.

Some professionals had a different theory: "I believe the cause of her hiccups," said one professional who saw Jennifer near this time, "was much, much deeper and more personal. Jennifer *wanted* to have the hiccups, effectively."

Still, those diagnoses, along with the suggestions of many people writing in and e-mailing, were enough to push Jennifer, who had been against it from the start because of her fear of needles, to seek treatment from an acupuncturist.

"The treatment wasn't bad," Jennifer said afterward. "It was actually very relaxing."

Yet, it did nothing to stop the hiccups.

CHAPTER 32

AFTER SEEING JENNIFER'S story in the media, Pennsylvania entrepreneur Michele Ehlinger decided to give Rachel a call to find out if Jennifer would be interested in testing a product Michele's husband had invented especially for Michele in 1990. The company they created had become a side business for the two of them.

Their company, Hic-Cup Ltd., manufactured and sold a cup (or "cure") for the hiccups. The product is an actual stainless-steel cup with a brass anode, or strawlike apparatus attached to the side with a non-electricity-conducting clip.

Michele explained how the cup works, telling me: "Our product was developed by my husband when I was pregnant with our first son. . . . [My husband's] background is in architecture, and he does a lot of invention and creative fabrication in metal, wood, and other materials."

It came about like a lot of inventions: out of the necessity to try and fix a problem. Due to the fact that most of the traditional "home hiccup remedies were inappropriate for a pregnant woman," Michele said, her husband started looking into any type of relief he could find for a terrible, pregnancy-induced bout of the hiccups, which Michele was experiencing then.

Thus, the Hic-Cup cup was born.

"Medical literature seemed to suggest that hiccups are influenced by the vagus nerve," Michele added. (*Vagus* is Latin for "wanderer.") "The longest nerve in the body, it is involved in many body systems. Although we have no medical education, it seemed like something that influenced the vagus nerve may help interrupt the hiccup reflex arc."

Michele's husband experimented by creating a low-level electrical current inside the cup, manufacturing a "metal cup with two different metals immersed in a potable liquid. . . . Ultimately, the first prototype was a stainless-steel Coleman camping cup with a copper rod sticking up on one side. When filled with regular tap water, an electrical test meter records about one hundred and fifty milliamps of current produced by the cup and its metal parts. Too low a current to feel, but apparently enough to stop hiccups," Michele explained.

"[Jennifer] might be the perfect person to try the Hic-Cup on, and if it cures her, we could maybe get her to promote the cup," Michele told her husband while discussing Jennifer Mee's condition.

Picking up the phone, Michele was skeptical. She had seen Jennifer and Rachel on television and had reservations about the veracity of Jennifer's hiccup claims. Why? She never said. Still, Michele questioned her own judgment because she knew that from dealing with people affected by the hiccups all over the world (with the exception of only four countries), every person suffering from intractable hiccups experienced different symptoms. Moreover, Michele understood that every hiccup sufferer hiccupped differently—the sound, the rhythm, and the amount of hiccups per minute.

"What the heck, why not call and talk to them?"

Michele made the call and Rachel said she and Jennifer were interested. They made plans to meet as soon as Michele could secure a flight from Pennsylvania to Florida.

Within a few days, Michele called Rachel back and gave her a day and time she would be in St. Pete. ("And Rachel said she and Jennifer would be there waiting. . . .")

Michele hopped on the short flight.

She had decided to stay the night. There was no sense in meeting with Rachel and Jennifer and flying back the same night.

Fresh off the plane, Michele called the house. The line rang and rang, but nobody answered.

Strange, Michele thought. *They're expecting my visit.*

She had explained she'd call the moment she got off the plane.

"We'd made a setup time to meet, and it wasn't that

far away from that exact time when I called," Michele explained later.

She had some time to spare, so Michele did a few things. Got her bags and a cup of coffee. Sat down and caught her breath.

Fifteen to thirty minutes passed.

She tried the number again.

Chris Robidoux answered this time, according to Michele. "Yeah?"

She explained who she was.

"Um, they're not here," Chris said to the utter shock of Michele. "Rachel, Jennifer, and a few of her friends went to the local amusement park with a camera crew."

Michele was aghast. She'd made plans with Rachel. She'd flown all the way down to Florida. Her flight was leaving at six o'clock the next morning.

Amusement park?

Michele found out that a local television station had agreed to pay for Jennifer and her friends to go to the park, as long as they could film it.

"Not sure when they'll be back," Chris said.

"Ah . . . *really?*" Michele didn't know what to say, better yet what to do.

"Call back," Chris said. "That's all I can tell you."

Michele checked into her hotel. Then she went and found the neighborhood where Rachel and Chris lived, pulled into a nearby restaurant, and called the house again.

"Nope, not home yet."

Michele was astounded. She had plans to meet Jennifer and Rachel at a specific time, a specific date. What was going on? Did they not take this seriously?

She ordered some food. She called the house again after dinner—it was now well into the evening—and they were finally home. Rachel gave Michele directions to the house.

It was six o'clock at night when Michele arrived.

"They seemed almost uninterested in my presence," Michele recalled, referring to her first impression of Rachel and Jennifer. "I thought that if they were truly interested in curing the hiccups Jennifer had, they knew I was going to be there and that we were supposed to meet at noon, and yet she's at an amusement park with friends?" If it had been one of Michele's children with the hiccups, she later noted, and a possible cure was flying in, "I would have met them at the airport!"

The Robidoux house was cluttered and "busy," lots of things placed everywhere. You could tell a lot of people had been packed inside a small area.

"Hi," Michele said, shaking hands with Rachel and Chris after they let her in.

Rachel asked Michele to get comfortable in the dining room.

In the company founders' opinions, the Hic-Cup cup had worked for the many people whom Michele and her husband had sold it to. The company had received a patent for the apparatus in 2006. The patent described "curing" the hiccups with the Hic-Cup cup in a way that involved pouring tap water into the stainless-steel cup and creating an electrical current between the stainless steel and the brass rod. Thus, when one drank the electrically charged water, a microcurrent and "flow of ions" traveled from the lips to the vagus nerve, stimulating the nerve with an electrical charge that was enough to stop the hiccups. The charge allegedly went down the throat and gave the vagus nerve a little jolt, and that "slight shock is enough in many cases to stop the hiccups," Michele asserted. "If you use orange juice, the charge is slightly stronger because of the acidity in the juice."

In published reports, Joel Richter, a gastroenterologist and chairman of medicine at Temple University School of Medicine, called the cup "hocus-pocus," while many in various medical fields agreed. Furthermore, there was no scientific research the company presented in 2006 to establish that there had been a study done indicating that the Hic-Cup cup actually worked in clinical trials.

"When my husband was developing the product in the 1990s," Michele said, "we immediately discovered that it seemed to work every time I got hiccups. . . . We had no scientific proof, just anecdotal observations."

Throughout the years, Michele went on to say, her husband produced many prototypes of the Hic-Cup cup. They handed them out to family and friends.

"All reported that it worked every time and was especially popular with children, who seem to get hiccups more frequently than adults. Indeed, we used the cup with our own children, and their friends would often come over when they had bad hiccups, just to use the cup. . . ."

It was then that they decided to form a small company, locating suppliers for the cup and its parts. They launched the business with a website.

"It was always just a little side business, and we never quit our day jobs. We explored getting FDA 510K approval of the Hic-Cup cup as a medical device because we learned from customers it was very effective in treating postsurgery anesthesia-induced hiccups. Ultimately we decided that people don't take hiccups seriously enough to justify the expense of FDA approval to get the device into hospitals."

The point that Michele made to Rachel as they chatted inside Rachel's dining room was that the cup generally did not work the first time a patient used it. The cup took repeated effort to cure the hiccups.

Jennifer was in another room. She came in and shook Michele's hand.

"We can give it a shot," Michele said. "You're just going to have to be patient, however. It's going to take more than one time."

Jennifer and Rachel seemed mildly interested, Michele said.

Maybe skeptical was a better way to put it. By this time, it's important to note, Jennifer had been promised cures from all around the world. She had tried just about every imaginable remedy, and nothing had come close to working. So, yes, to Rachel and Jennifer, there was a bit of sarcasm and disbelief that a cup was the answer.

"You mind if I videotape this?" Michele asked.

Rachel didn't have a problem. Neither did Jennifer.

Michele took out a tripod and video camera and set it up.

She had her finger on the RECORD button. "Okay, sit over here," Michele said, directing Jennifer, hitting the button to begin recording. "You ready?"

She placed Jennifer in a chair so the camera was focused directly on her. She took out the cup, filled it with water, and gave it to Jennifer.

She took a sip.

Nothing.

"Let's wait a little while, try it again."

They waited.

Once again, nothing happened.

"Do you have any orange juice?" Michele asked. She explained how when the user put orange juice in the cup and drank out of it, the acidity in the juice was akin to giving the cup a "turbocharge." This had worked especially well for chemotherapy patients that developed chemo-related hiccups, Michele later explained.

"We don't," Rachel said.

As she watched Rachel, Michele said later, Rachel seemed "very nonchalant about it all," as if this was the next thing to do. "And so did Jennifer."

But for Jennifer and Rachel, here was one more broken promise and failed remedy.

The entire time Michele was there, Jennifer hiccupped repeatedly, except when she spoke.

"Orange juice might help," Michele suggested.

"Well, then, let's get some orange juice. Chris, go get some orange juice at the store."

Michele, Rachel, and Jennifer sat and waited for Chris.

When he returned, they tried the orange juice and it did not work, either.

After a few more tries, Michele later said, "None of it worked." So she packed up her things, said her good-byes, and left the cup with Jennifer, telling both Jennifer and Rachel: "You know, if it ever does work, please call me. Maybe we could enter into a business relationship—that would be great."

The implication Michele left them with was that if the cup worked, Hic-Cup Ltd. would be interested in perhaps hiring Jennifer in some capacity to help promote the product. For Michele and her husband, of course, it all depended on whether the cup did indeed work for the Hiccup Girl. Jennifer was getting a lot of attention. If their cup worked to stop her from hiccupping, it might be just the boost the business needed to take off. But without the cup working—which it clearly hadn't, a fact Michele got on tape, no less—how could they claim that it had cured the Hiccup Girl?

Disappointed, but not at all upset, Michele was content that at least Jennifer came down and gave it a try. After all, part of the trip was business and another part was her wanting to help the girl stop hiccupping.

Michele went back to her hotel room, slept the night, and flew home the next morning—"And thought, 'I'd never hear from Rachel again.'"

CHAPTER 33

DEBBIE LANE WAS sitting at the local coffee shop near her office on March 2, 2007, enjoying a cup of coffee, when her cell phone rang. Lane had been following Jennifer's story in the newspapers. She was profoundly affected by Jennifer's personal struggle and the torment that Lane perceived the affliction had caused Jennifer and the Robidoux family. A certified, practicing hypnotist, Lane wanted to help from the first moment she heard about Jennifer's case. She truly believed that with properly administered hypnotherapy, she could help Jennifer eliminate or overcome whatever underlying, troubling issues from Jennifer's past (or present) that were the foundation of what was causing her hiccups.

It was Rachel Robidoux on the other end of Lane's phone line. Someone whom Lane did not know personally and had never spoken to before, but had certainly heard about in those news reports of Jennifer. As Lane saw things, she felt bad that Jennifer was being whisked around town, flown off to New York, and put up on a public stage for everyone to gawk at. The hypnotist worried about Jennifer's delicate, young psyche being exploited by the media.

"I am Jennifer Mee's mother. A reporter gave me your name and number. Are you willing to work with Jennifer?" Rachel asked during that first phone call.

"Absolutely," Lane said. She explained that she would even waive her fee. She wanted to help Jennifer any way she could.

They made plans to meet that evening after Lane rearranged her schedule to make room for Jennifer.

Rachel and Jennifer arrived at Lane's Palm Harbor office in the early evening hours of that same day. Jennifer's friend Allison Baldwin was with them. Jennifer and Rachel were somewhat skeptical about the procedure, but they claimed they were willing to try anything at this point. It had been thirty-seven days and counting, and Jennifer was still hiccupping.

A typical session Lane conducted lasted one hour to ninety minutes. The hypnotist would spend some time with the client alone and learn as much as she could about the person before beginning the actual hypnotherapy. Hypnosis is designed to reach the inner awareness of a person, his or her primary sense of consciousness, and pick up on what the principal issues are surrounding a particular problem—i.e., lack of sleep, smoking, alcoholism, excessive eating, belching, farting, hiccupping, whatever. At its fundamental core, hypnosis aims to focus on the client's goals: what does he or she want out of the session?

Lane warned: not everyone will benefit from hypnotherapy.

Right away, she realized, "Jennifer was a malleable young lady." In Lane's opinion, she felt, just by speaking to Jennifer briefly that Jennifer was being manipulated, maybe even used in some way. Or perhaps Jennifer was herself using the hiccups as a means to an end of some kind?

Debbie Lane was the 2007 "Hypnotist of the Year" internationally (with hypnotists from as many as twenty other countries in the running); she is a certified member of the National Guild of Hypnotists, along with several other certifications. Hypnosis isn't some Houdini-like, spiritual, *Long Island Medium*-type of psychic, junk science. To the contrary, Lane said: "Hypnosis is a method of achieving a relaxed state of heightened focus and concentration—intensified attention and receptiveness to an idea or set of ideas. Hypnosis produces the ability to experience thoughts and images as real, bypassing the 'critical factor' to establish selective thinking. When the conscious mind is bypassed, the subconscious mind is open to suggestion. This hypnotic trance state makes it possible to increase motivation or change behavior patterns."

Hypnotherapy also allows the hypnotist to understand why the condition, problem, or personal issue in the client's life is occurring in the first place, which can, in turn, lead to that change that the person is seeking to take place.

The type of treatment Lane began with Jennifer, "hypnotherapy," is what she referred to as a "complementary treatment of a health problem, using hypnosis following a diagnosis. Hypnotherapy is performed by a hypnotherapist. By law, hypnotherapy must be performed by a trained professional who is a medical practitioner, or under the supervision or direction of a licensed practitioner. Some issues require a script from a medical doctor for a referral."

Lane sat Rachel down in her office and explained how the session was going to work, once she and Jennifer were alone. "You cannot be here. You'll have to wait outside the room. I'm going to tape-record the session. . . ."

Rachel said she was okay with all of that. She then signed the waiver forms the hypnotist required because Jennifer was a minor.

"Rachel came across antsy after I explained things," Lane recalled. "She agreed to it all . . . but I saw distance."

Even though she sensed something going on with Rachel, Lane said, her main concern was Jennifer.

Debbie Lane is an articulate, well-dressed professional woman from head to toe. She was there, as a practicing hypnotist, to help a child overcome what she viewed as a horrible condition that had saddled Jennifer's life and put her teenage years on hold. She had explained to Jennifer and Rachel before the session began that hypnosis required the client to have the desire and commitment to achieve the goals of the therapy. More than that, the client must have an unencumbered belief in one's self that it can work, alongside a positive expectation for an outcome they all seek to achieve.

Lane wondered: *Is this the "next thing" in a long list of remedies Rachel and Jennifer have lined up? Are they going about the business of checking things off a so-called list only to turn around and say, "We tried everything! She still has the hiccups."*

After speaking with Rachel, Lane got the feeling it was all of the above.

Meeting and speaking to Jennifer alone, Lane felt the properties a hypnotist needed for a positive and rewarding outcome were there, even if she had to pull them out of the girl.

"What are your goals?" she asked Jennifer. By this point, they were alone in a relaxed setting inside an office Lane had maintained exclusively for therapy sessions. Lane had asked that Rachel and Allison Baldwin wait down the hall. She told Rachel not to expect her and Jennifer anytime soon and not to interrupt the session at any time, under any circumstance.

Rachel took off outside and had a cigarette as the hypnotist and Jennifer got started.

"Intense," Lane said of Jennifer. "Right from the start."

Immediately after Jennifer was "under"—a term that probably doesn't best describe the state of consciousness the client is placed in by the hypnotist—Jennifer went back to those days before she had the hiccups. This was an important space Lane needed to explore without prodding. Getting Jennifer to realize and feel what life had been like without the hiccups was important to Jen's stopping.

"She talked about the secondary gain and fear before she even came down with the hiccups," Lane recalled later, speaking about the session.

Within every action a human being takes part in,

there is a secondary gain—a positive outcome he or she is chasing, so to speak.

"Or he/she wouldn't have it to begin with," Lane explained.

"For her to continue those hiccups," the hypnotist said, "at a subconscious level, there *had* to be a gain—something in it for Jennifer's benefit."

A payoff, in other words.

In Lane's opinion, Jennifer had been hiccupping all this time for a reason. Jennifer was herself continuing to allow the hiccups to control their lives because she was receiving gratification of some sort for doing it. Through the hiccups, she was getting something she had wanted and craved for a long time, Lane claimed.

"Attention," the hypnotist said (a few others agreed with this overall observation). "When you're living in a house with that many people and you're not being heard, your body's responding to it. Jennifer Mee wanted attention."

The hiccups were certainly getting her plenty of it.

At one point, Lane asked Jennifer: "Your mom said you were her oldest?"

"Yes."

"How many siblings do you have?"

"Four."

"How old [are they] and what are their names?"

"Um, the youngest one is five and her name is McKenzie. Destiny is seven. Kayla is twelve, and Ashley is fourteen."

Jennifer was in a comfortable space for Lane right now.

"Okay, okay," she asked Jennifer, "do you get along with all of them?"

"There have been times when I have, and times

when I don't," Jennifer answered. "It's like every normal family, but yeah, I get along with them, for the most part."

"Do you share a room with any of them?"

"Yes. We live in a two-bedroom house and, unfortunately, we are all crammed into one room."

Compelling in and of itself, especially to Lane as she got to know Jennifer more personally during the session and learned what she perceived as the root cause of her hiccupping, was a moment while Jennifer had filled out the paperwork for the hypnotist before the session started. Jennifer had to be told to go into a room down at the end of a long hallway and close the door because she was hiccupping so loudly and disruptively. It was so bad that some of the other tenants in the building stuck their heads out of their doors to see and ask what in the world was going on. For Lane, it was as if Jennifer had arrived wanting to make sure everyone in that building knew she was the Hiccup Girl.

As the session continued, Lane noticed that Jennifer's hiccupping, which at the start of the hypnosis therapy was loud and rapid and obnoxious, had slowed down as she talked her way through what was bothering her at a fundamental, emotional core level. Jennifer's deep feelings were spilling out of her and the hiccups were beginning to subside.

"What I discovered during the session was that the more I asked questions and just listened to her, the quieter the hiccups became," Lane recalled. "And it was in that silence, if you will, that I heard an answer."

CHAPTER 34

AS JENNIFER BECAME more relaxed, slipping deeper under hypnosis, Debbie Lane heard what she believed was the answer to the hiccups, which then pointed toward a direction to take Jennifer with the session.

"We're going to work together as a team until we can get the solution that we want," Lane told Jennifer. She paused.

"Okay . . . ," Jennifer responded.

"And what is it you want?" Lane asked.

"I want them to go away and to be a normal fifteen-year-old again," Jennifer said.

This hardly sounded like a child faking the hiccups for attention.

"And what is a normal fifteen-year-old?" Lane asked, trying to get a clear indication from Jennifer how she saw herself in the world.

"Um, being able to go out to the movies every Friday. Hanging out with your girlfriends and doing stuff that I would like to do, like talking on the phone and stuff like that."

Sounded pretty average.

"Okay. And what else?"

Jennifer took a breath. Without hiccupping, she said: "Um, just, I would like to be able to go to the movies every Friday, which I can't do anymore because I would be a distraction. Going back to school. That may sound a little silly for saying that 'cause most teenagers don't like school, but I'd like to go back to school and see all my friends and be able to be with all my classmates again."

As Jennifer continued, she talked about wanting privacy and more attention from her parents. She then listed her goals in life, one of which included having her own bedroom. Jennifer talked about how tired she was of living in a two-bedroom house with four sisters, her uncle (who had been living with them since 2005), and her mother and father. There was nowhere for her to go and be alone.

Another part of this for Jennifer, which Debbie Lane said Jennifer never mentioned (but Rachel had mentioned a few times), was that Jennifer had been kept on such a short leash by Rachel all her life. Rachel had been scared to allow Jennifer or any of her children the freedom to go out on their own, she claimed, especially due to living in downtown St. Pete. Jennifer certainly wanted to break free from that and be her own person.

The situation in the house had been like this for as long as Jennifer could recall, she told Lane, and she just wanted to be noticed and heard in what was a chaotic existence inside a home that was far too small for eight people.

The hiccups, Lane thought while listening, were Jennifer's way of getting that attention she had sought all her life.

"To be noticed," the hypnotist said. "Jennifer told me she just wanted to be *heard*."

One of the reasons she held on to the hiccups, Lane considered while listening to Jennifer talk about what bothered her, was because "she was afraid of letting go and what might happen to her if she stopped hiccupping."

"Death," Jennifer said.

Death? Lane asked herself. This was shocking. What was Jennifer talking about?

"She said she was afraid of dying," Lane explained.

The hypnotist was interested in this thread of Jennifer's life. She tried to get Jennifer to explain herself more fully, but Jennifer backed off the subject. The one thing about hypnosis that Lane was quick to point out was how careful the hypnotist had to be not to lead the client into any answers by carefully chosen (and leading) questions. Lane had to allow Jennifer to talk her way through whatever she wanted and needed to say, without coaching or holding her hand and pointing her down a particular path. In doing that, Jennifer could effectively cure herself, or at least get to the heart of what was troubling her most.

Jennifer explained that she would stop hiccupping if and when she felt "safe."

"Is it now safe to stop?" Lane asked Jennifer softly, almost in a whisper.

Debbie Lane's perspective after sitting and counseling Jennifer with hypnotherapy, hearing Jennifer speak under hypnosis about her life both before the hiccups and after, changed as she realized what she felt were Jennifer's biggest fears.

"When I first heard about Jennifer, it was this tiny, little paragraph in the newspaper," Lane explained. "But the story leapt out at me as if the entire paper was a blur except that little paragraph."

Hypnosis has come a long way since the days of a magician waving a pocket watch in front of a preselected audience member, uttering those abracadabra words of "you're getting very sleepy." Debbie Lane, a board-certified hypnotherapist, had helped many people "make those changes they've been promising themselves for a long time."

Part of Jennifer's therapy included her looking into the future and seeing herself not hiccupping. She needed to feel the calm she was experiencing under hypnosis and believe that all of the fear she felt being lifted as the safety she desired was put in its place so she could live her life without hiccupping. This was important to the long-term outcome of the session.

One of the main issues Jennifer returned to was that while she felt cramped inside her small home, Rachel and Chris had gone and allowed Chris's brother to move in with them. It bothered Jennifer that as she stated her opinion to her parents about there not being enough room inside the house, they wouldn't listen.

"She felt as though she was the one everyone in that house was picking on," Lane said. "Now, that is typical teenager stuff, and they may have *all* felt that way in the house."

As Jennifer talked for hours about her life before and after having the hiccups, not once, Lane confirmed, did she mention being raped. One might expect that such a traumatizing moment of Jennifer's life would be front and center within a session such as hypnotherapy, a barrier she needed to overcome in order to heal. But it never came up. Neither did the later revelation by Jennifer of dealing crack cocaine at thirteen and having been beaten by Tyrone O'Donnell.

Perhaps Jennifer had blocked all of it out for some reason?

When later pressed for details about being raped, Jennifer explained to me that she was "very young." She "felt as if what they were doing" to her "was okay." She talked about being by some water one time where the two males liked to hang out. "We played house and it started with [one of them] playing with my hair and led to other things." She recalled being "raped in [a building by water]." She didn't remember how long it lasted, but she was certain the males "did it every chance they got." Moreover, Jennifer's sister Ashley was a witness to it all. "You will never talk about this," the males allegedly said to Ashley and Jennifer on more than one occasion, "or you will die." There was once, Jennifer said, when she tried to scream as she was being raped and one of them shoved an "object in my mouth."

Was this that fear of dying Jennifer referred to in her hypnosis testimony? Experts who study rape and how the mind deals with the trauma afterward feel this type of trauma, left untreated, could manifest in various ways throughout a lifetime, including post-traumatic stress disorder (PTSD) and rape trauma syndrome (RTS). One of the most persistent symptoms of both includes "avoidance of stimuli that remind of the trauma. . . ." Within this, the victim "avoids thoughts and feelings associated with the trauma. . . ."

Jennifer's not recalling many details about the rape, nor sharing it under hypnosis, falls in line with the mind's normal way of dealing with such a painful, disturbing event.

When Lane later heard about that "thug life" Jennifer spoke of being involved in from the age of thirteen, she couldn't help but think that as Jennifer looked back on her life years later, she "fantasized" about aspects of it to draw even more attention to herself, especially after all of her hiccup fame diminished.

"Look, if, in fact, that is true," Lane said later in her quiet, soothing voice, clearly thinking through her answers before speaking (referring here specifically to Jennifer's crack dealing at thirteen, not the rape), "I'm stunned, because Jennifer was fifteen when she saw me and there was no evidence of any of that type of behavior. She came across as a tough little girl, but at the same time, a *little* girl. She won my heart. . . ."

After a long period of silence during their session, Lane said, "You may slowly begin to bring your awareness back to the room."

"Oh, you don't know how much I love you [right] now," Jennifer said. "They're gone! I can't believe it."

CHAPTER 35

JENNIFER WAS COMING out from under hypnosis as she and Lane realized the hiccups were completely gone. Not partially, or for a few moments—but Jennifer Mee was not hiccupping anymore.

"I love you, too, sweetheart," Lane said.

"They're gone. I'm in tears."

"May I hug you?" Lane asked, being certain not to invade Jennifer's space.

Crying, Jennifer said, "Yes! I love you. Oh, my God."

"You now know they are gone," Lane stated, wanting to be clear.

"Yeah, I do."

"And you're safe?"

"Yes, I am. Oh, my God!"

Again, this did not sound like a young woman who had been faking the hiccups and was suddenly now "cured." Jennifer came across as a young girl suffering from social isolation, which was now going to be lifted because the ball had finally been cut from the chain.

As Jennifer acclimated herself to the room and opened her eyes, she was weeping profound tears of joy and adulation. It was as if she had dumped all of her emotional baggage and was starting from a fresh outlook—one that did not include her hiccupping anymore.

"I love you. . . . I love you. . . . I love you," she said to Debbie Lane, jumping up and hugging her. "I cannot believe this. . . ."

The hiccups were completely gone.

"Mom? Mom?" Jennifer called out. Jennifer was still "heavy from the trance . . . and remained relaxed in a recliner," still coming out of it.

Rachel was outside smoking, according to Lane, who went to fetch her while Jennifer waited.

"What's going on?" Rachel asked, walking into the lobby area and sitting down.

"I have a surprise for you," Lane said.

But as Lane later explained, the next part of the night made her "stomach hurt."

"Rachel could not have been more distant," she opined. "Almost disappointed."

Disappointed?

Yes!

As she stood there, divulging the good news, judging Rachel's reaction, Lane believed that the hiccups were finished. Jennifer's claim to fame was gone. Therefore, the Hiccup Girl saga was over.

Rachel, however, didn't see it that way. Rachel told me later: "She was in there maybe forty-five minutes to an hour, and when she came out, the hiccups were gone." She said she asked Lane, "How the heck did you do that? I was absolutely elated. I was in tears, and Jennifer was in tears. I gave [Lane] a hug. I hugged Jennifer."

Jennifer later confirmed much of this, as did Allison Baldwin.

According to Lane's notes, the session went well over three hours. "And I never saw Rachel shed a tear," she added.

Rachel described Lane as a "typical" professional who asked "medical questions about the patient. She told me she hoped the therapy would work to stop the hiccups. She asked me if I thought Jennifer could be hypnotized and told me the only people who couldn't be hypnotized were people who were insane or had mental illness."

After the session, when Jennifer appeared not to be hiccupping any longer, what Lane surmised was that Rachel was upset because Jennifer would no longer be a media sensation, thus deflating the air out of any future earnings.

"Ignorant," Rachel said of that accusation. "Nobody knew us and lived in that house with us, and understood what we went through. It's totally ignorant to make claims like that when the truth was the total opposite."

"I love you," Jennifer said to Lane again in the waiting room as Rachel and Allison Baldwin, Jennifer's friend, looked on. Then she looked at her mother. "They're gone!" She walked over and hugged Rachel.

According to Lane, Rachel was not happy.

"People are going to say what they feel—I've gotten used to it," Rachel commented later after I explained that some were saying she wanted Jennifer to have the hiccups. "I would tell them to look at her medical files and see that she has a medical condition. At no time did I ever seek to exploit her. I looked for answers as to why this was happening. Instead of being haters, they should have spoken to me directly or even gone to a few doctors' appointments!"

Rachel was disturbed by the notion that several people, she explained, having no idea how taxing this entire ordeal was on the family and especially on Jennifer, had judged them without knowing any of the facts.

"The way I see it is, if people are uninformed enough to think that she/we staged and faked and manipulated her medical condition, rather than coming to me and talking to me and getting correctly informed, well, 'ignorant' is the nicest word that comes to mind. I could say much worse, but I won't sink to their level."[8]

After she thought about it later and learned all of the facts, Debbie Lane said, "If she *was* faking it, she missed her calling in theater."

As the session ended, Lane explained to Rachel

that Jennifer needed to return for several follow-up appointments, that this first session was, essentially, only the beginning. Jennifer had stopped hiccupping; but in order to keep Jennifer in this "new" state of not hiccupping, she would need to continue to see the hypnotist and finish the therapy.

They agreed, Lane said later, to return. So the hypnotist booked a few appointments.

"I don't believe she mentioned a follow-up and I don't believe she gave Jennifer anything," Rachel said regarding the end of the session and what she and Lane had spoken about. "I think it was kind of a onetime thing. There may have been a follow-up appointment, but I don't know that we ever went back."

There was no reason for them to go, Rachel went on to say. Jennifer's hiccups were gone. After the hypnotist, Jennifer went to see a neurologist, Rachel explained, and she was then diagnosed with Tourette's.

"Another point that needs to be made," Chris Robidoux added, "is that if we were coaching Jennifer, making her fake the hiccups, wouldn't we have 'made her' stop them the first few times she had used that Hic-Cup cup?"

It's a fair assessment of the situation. If making money and exploiting Jennifer and her ordeal by controlling it had been the intention, wouldn't Rachel have told Jennifer to stop once she began using the Hic-Cup cup so they could collect on an endorsement deal?

Lane watched Jennifer, Rachel, and Allison Baldwin leave. She had reservations about what had just transpired and how Rachel and Jennifer were going to deal with it. By Lane's personal and professional estimation, she had just cured Jennifer of the hiccups. They were completely gone as Jennifer exited her office. Jennifer appeared relaxed and totally able to breathe now. Lane had given her a fresh start.

Those reservations of Lane's came to fruition, she said, the following day. As Jennifer made her rounds, talking to local media and a few syndicated radio shows, she started off by saying that the hiccups had stopped the previous night inside the hypnotist's office. However, as the day progressed, Lane's work would be totally wiped out of the picture as Jennifer was saying she wasn't really sure how they had stopped.

"I couldn't believe how she was saying that they weren't sure," Lane said later. "It had gone from Jennifer telling the world it was in my office to 'we're not sure.' I was shocked."

Even though Jennifer and Rachel had effectively "dissed" her and the hypnotherapy, Lane vowed to honor the appointments she had made with Jennifer, wanting nothing more than to help the girl.

So she called and called, but Jennifer or Rachel never returned her calls or showed up for another appointment.

The hypnotist had given Jennifer a CD of some relaxation techniques and things to do, which they had created together during the session, and told Jennifer to use it regularly.

"We did the equivalent of 'three sessions in one' that night."

Lane wanted to make sure that within all of the information Jennifer had gotten, she knew what to do and how to focus on relaxing within that hiccup-free zone Lane had created for her. But Debbie Lane was now seriously concerned that without Jennifer returning for those follow-up hypnotherapy treatments, she would start hiccupping again.

CHAPTER 36

IN THE DAYS following her experience with Debbie Lane, Jennifer Mee remained hiccup-free. She had a new lease on what she had described for the hypnotist as a chaotic life inside a small home—all of the above partly responsible for her hiccupping in the first place. She could finally think about school again or going out with friends to the movies and to the park. She could just be normal—whatever Jennifer's new normal was at this point in her life. Of course, there would be a wave of publicity surrounding the hiccups being gone, which Jennifer could ride; but after that, Jennifer could go back to her life. Something she claimed to want more than anything else.

Jennifer asked her mother about going shopping for clothes. Jennifer talked about desperately getting back to high school and how some new duds would set her on the right track.

"Of course," Rachel said.

That feeling of being a bug in a glass jar that everyone was gawking and squawking at began to diminish for Jennifer as the middle of March came and she finished a small round of publicity surrounding her being "cured." She had enjoyed the celebrity life. She had taken in all of the attention, and she had loved it. But she and Rachel knew from day one that it would all end someday, and Jennifer would have to cope with the result. The question was (and perhaps Rachel and Chris Robidoux had been unprepared for this part of the entire experience): Was there a plan to bring Jennifer back down to earth?

With the hiccups gone, Jennifer felt she could perhaps even turn her life around, using the experience and notoriety as a starting point toward a better way of life. Arguably, according to her, Jennifer was not the innocent little girl her mother—and America—thought her to be. If what Jennifer later told me is true, she had been dabbling in some very hard-core drugs, smoking weed, having sex, hanging out with "thug"-type people, and carving out a life on the streets for herself—all while staying with a boy who was beating her anytime he felt like it. The hiccups had slowed that lifestyle down some, along with Tyrone O'Donnell going into juvenile detention, but her previous life was still percolating there in the recesses of Jennifer's soul—that is, if she chose to step back into it. Jennifer could not escape from who she had become. The only difference now was that everyone knew her name, and many her face. Her ego was already getting the best of her, her head a bit bigger than it had ever been (just about everyone around her later agreed with this), and she realized that doing things in a big way could get her the attention she told Debbie Lane she had craved so much.

Still, Jennifer Mee had the opportunity to cut that cord and begin anew. She was at a fork in the road of her life right now. It was her choice. And what was the big attraction to that life on the street, anyway?

"I don't know what made me want to live the hustla

life," Jennifer told me. "I guess 'cause maybe it was fast and easy money and that's what all my mind knew? I cannot really tell you."

Rachel had purchased an iPhone for Jennifer, something Jennifer never had. Jennifer had been in the dark about most things until she heard it from a friend or saw it on the news. Not now, though. She had a direct link to the world outside the door via her own phone.

"I did not want a computer, ever," Rachel later said. "Moving into the 'big city' of St. Pete," Rachel added, "I was overwhelmed by what the kids could be exposed to just down the block. For that reason, I kept them all close to me and never allowed them any room beyond the household. I wanted to know where they were and what they were doing at every moment. I figured a computer would invite elements into their lives I didn't want them to know about."

"I blame myself for everything that happened to Jennifer," Chris Robidoux said. "We should have never moved into the city. It exposed Jennifer and the kids to all kinds of things they should have never seen or heard. I'm responsible."

"With me working as much as I did and taking care of my parents, I realize now that there was a lot going on I did not see," Rachel said, "or chose to look the other way and *not* see."

The one thing Jennifer could now do was text, which became a habit she took to effortlessly. As her hiccups subsided—now back at home with a hic here and a hic there, but nothing like what she had suffered from—Jennifer texted back and forth with friends and met new people. She wanted to get back into the social campfire of school and what was happening down at the park. Tyrone was still in juvenile detention, but he would be getting out soon enough and Jennifer had decided to give the relationship another chance.

When she and Rachel returned from shopping, Jennifer met with Karen Ardis, a teacher who had come to give Jennifer the Florida Comprehensive Assessment Test (FCAT) inside her home. Jennifer had gone into school weeks before to take the test but was "kicked out of the classroom," according to Rachel, because she was disrupting the test with her hiccups. Taking the test at home at least made Jennifer feel as if she was getting back into a way of life she had known before the hiccups had taken over. After taking the test, she could go back to the classroom, especially now that she was not hiccupping (and disrupting class) anymore.

"The one thing I want, Mom," Jennifer had said on the evening she approached her first twenty-four hours totally hiccup-free, "is that we never use that *H* word again."

Rachel agreed.

What Rachel looked forward to most was returning the household to its normal daily routines of kids and school and meals and problems to solve that did not involve going to doctors three and four times a day, several days a week, on top of meeting with an infectious-disease-control person (which they were scheduled to do) and being under the microscope of the world. It was no way to live. No way to raise a family of five girls.

"Jennifer had even spoken to a faith healer over the telephone at one point," Rachel remembered.

Was it actually all over? And did Rachel and Jennifer *want* it to be over?

"There was nothing I wanted more," Rachel said.

"It was incredible," Jennifer added, explaining the relief she felt from not being a slave to the hiccups any longer.

CHAPTER 37

SOMETIME LATER, ACCORDING to Jennifer, it started all again. Without any warning this time: *hic, hic, hic.*

They were back.

Just like that.

As quick as they had left her, the hiccups were again controlling Jennifer Mee's life.

The satellite trucks had not yet pulled away, and the calls had not stopped coming into the house from media across the globe, when Jennifer looked at her mother with a grimace, her shoulders drooped, indicating they were now back to square one.

Hic-hic-hic . . .

There seemed to be something different this time around, however. "I need to go to the hospital," Jennifer told her mother. Her hips and chest hurt worse than she could ever recall. It was an intense pain and she was unable to deal with it.

So Rachel and Jennifer were off to the All Children's Hospital emergency room once more—a familiar task they had gotten used to by this point. But again, like the past few times they had seen a doctor, there wasn't much the hospital could do but prescribe medication and tell Jennifer to go see a specialist.

Thorazine, a very strong and powerful antipsychotic medication, was a common prescription Jennifer was given. The medication turned Jennifer into a zombie every time she took it, Rachel knew. Thorazine was generally used to treat psychotic disorders, such as schizophrenia or manic-depression, on top of severe behavioral problems. It was the go-to for doctors after diagnosing children between the ages of one through twelve who were exhibiting those symptoms. The generic term is chlorpromazine, and it is a common drug handed out to children showing signs of tics, twitches, nausea and vomiting, anxiety, and chronic hiccups.

"She had seen a chiropractor who got in contact with me through e-mails to the *Tampa Bay Times*," Rachel explained later. "He saw her five times. She saw an acupuncturist and Debbie Lane, the hypnotist. The chiropractor she saw multiple times found some compressed vertebra. The first visit to the hypnotist and her hiccups stopped . . . but then . . . well, it was so disappointing, they came back."

As far as the hiccups coming back, Lane said, "The hiccups were always a go-to for Jennifer, a fallback for attention. It's where she learned people would care."

Not that she was faking, Lane was quick to point out, but the hiccups got Jennifer noticed. The thought was, Jennifer needed to be loved and the hiccups gave her that attention and love she so much desired. So her body, when she didn't feel those emotions, went into action.

"That's absolutely untrue," Rachel said. "The hiccups came back, were real, and we had to deal with it.

No one else. Just us. I wish people could understand what our lives were like. They don't. Instead, they judge us. Jennifer never faked the hiccups."

If Rachel and Jennifer did not realize how big Jennifer's story had become, all they had to do was turn on NPR on a Saturday morning near this time when everything seemed to crash. National Public Radio's popular show *Wait Wait . . . Don't Tell Me* led its broadcast with a report on Jennifer.

"All of you follow the news, so I know that you're concerned . . . about the fate of Jennifer Mee . . . who became the subject of an intense booking war between *Today* and *Good Morning America* because she's been hiccupping nonstop for four weeks."

The comment brought several laughs out of the live audience.

"She is still hiccupping, and apparently even Diane Sawyer banging on her door at four in the morning with flowers could not scare the hiccups away" was the next comment, which produced a big round of laughter for Peter Sagal, the voice behind this sarcastic game show built around news and popular culture stories.

It was quite insulting, actually, that a reputable, somewhat highbrow, and definitely ultraliberal public radio organization as big and powerful as the mighty NPR was poking fun at Jennifer (a child) and her plight. While Jennifer and her family were at home, pulling at their hair trying to figure out how to stop the hiccups and get Jennifer back on track and in school, Jennifer was a punch line. She was a person to laugh at and mock. That opening few lines recited by Peter Sagal truly proved how big a phenomenon the Jennifer "Hiccup Girl" Mee story had become.

Heading toward week seven, Rachel wondered what they were going to do. They'd tried just about everything. Nothing had totally worked.

Then, on March 14, 2007, out of seemingly nowhere, Jennifer opened her eyes on a new day with a different feeling.

She wasn't hiccupping anymore.

Jennifer had gone to four different doctors leading up to the hiccups once again stopping.

"That's all they did," Chris added. "Go to doctors."

The idea that they were gone brought Jennifer to tears, with a certain amount of trepidation, because she and Rachel had gone through this before and thought it was over, but the celebration had been fleeting. The hiccups had always come back.

Yet something told Jennifer this was it—they were gone for good.

Finally.

Recently, since getting her own phone, Jennifer had reconnected with her "real" father and they were calling each other every day.

"That was a big mistake," Chris Robidoux said of Jennifer hooking back up with the sperm donor known as her father.

Jennifer called her biological father to share the great news.

"Dad, they're gone. . . ."

"Holy shit," he said.

"Yeah, they're gone."

"Wow, that's great. Can you believe it?"

One day went by and they had not returned. Then it was two days.

Then three.

She'd experienced one or two hiccups, same as before, but the constant pounding of her diaphragm and that jerking of her chest and hips and stomach were gone.

Looking quite beaten, tired, and unkempt, Jennifer was interviewed by local 10 News reporter Beau Zimmer for the CBS affiliate out of Tampa Bay. It's a telling interview for many reasons, as it truly depicts the "little girl" and genuine person at the center of all this—that same young person whom NPR, like many others, had made fun of during this same time. Jennifer could come across as mercurial during the big media interviews, having been catered to by makeup artists and hairstylists, coached by producers about what to say and how to iterate her thoughts. But here, within the simplicity of this local news building, there were no red carpets and no limos. There were no elaborately produced setup pieces of television by the big network morning shows. This interview took place in the hallway of the 10 News newsroom, and felt as though it had been recorded on a handheld camera. Jennifer wore a 93.3 FM ("MJ in the Morning") T-shirt, her hair appeared to be unwashed and rather oily and tangled. She wore nearly no makeup. She came across as the person she actually was: an innocent teenager with a young mind behind her brown eyes, who was thrust into a media cesspool of pop culture celebrity she'd had no training for and had been totally unprepared to manage.

Beau Zimmer made a great point during the interview that no other reporter had focused on or talked about at any length. He pointed out to Jennifer that many people looked at her and her condition as silly and laughed about it, but it had been a very serious condition, hadn't it? Indeed, no laughing matter. She had suffered greatly (and would continue to do so). The public saw it all as some quirky news story. However, behind the sad eyes of Jennifer Mee, she and her family were at the end of their rope with all of this. Chris and Jennifer were especially having a hard time getting along. Their relationship was breaking down a little more every day, which, in turn, was causing big problems for the marriage. This was a family that had never wanted the publicity, or worldwide attention, all of them later claimed. Jennifer had been insulted so much, made fun of, ridiculed and called so many names, she said she couldn't even go out anymore without someone saying something stupid or personally attacking her. Maybe now that the hiccups were finally gone, she could get back to the life she'd had before it all went awry—and maybe take the experience and learn a lesson from it. After all, there had been far more positive comments and calls and cards and letters from the public, many people giving her well wishes, prayers, and advice. Jennifer had not been totally jaded by it all.

The relief alone for Jennifer was overwhelming, she told News 10 reporter Zimmer. There was a time when she had been so concerned about her condition she wondered if she'd ever have a relationship, go on to work, and have a home. But now, with the hiccups gone, she could relax and get back to her everyday life. She smiled so much during her time with Zimmer it was as if she had once again become that nervous little girl doing her first interview.

"I'm so relieved," Jennifer told Zimmer, "that the first thing that popped into my mind the other day was that I'm going to go back to school." She mentioned how a lot of her peers might think she sounded "crazy" for saying she "wanted" to go back to school, but she reiterated, "I'm going back to school!" She nodded her head in agreement, smiling.

The question came up whether there was any positive side effect to having had the hiccups for so long, her story garnering all that attention, and Jennifer quickly ruled that out.

"No!"

Her "hope [was] that they [would] stay away for a long time."

The tone she used, the feeling she displayed during the piece (something Rachel later agreed with), was that the hiccups ("they") were the enemy, a condition Jennifer and her family feared could return at any hour, any day.

Beau Zimmer wanted a timeline, a plan Jennifer had for going back to school and what she was going to do now that she could go anywhere and do anything she wanted to again.

Jennifer wasn't going back to school until the following Monday, so she could "start fresh" with a new week. After leaving News 10, she was going to see her neurologist and then to a meeting with her homebound tutor and then to the chiropractor.

"But they want to fly me back to New York as soon as possible," she added with a great big smile, indicating that the red-carpet treatment wasn't, in fact, over. *Today* wasn't finished. The show wanted a follow-up story—the traditionally packaged ribbon-and-bow ending to this American pop culture phenomenon.

Jennifer, a smile from ear to ear, said she was really looking forward to traveling back to New York, adding, "And actually when I get older . . . I want to move [there]."

CHAPTER 38

MICHELE EHLINGER WAS at her Pennsylvania home on Thursday, March 1, 2007, when her phone rang. On the other end of the line, according to Michele's recollection, was a very happy, excited Rachel Robidoux, who wanted to share the best news she'd had in quite a while.

"Gone!" Rachel said.

"What?" Michele asked, confused.

"The hiccups are finally gone. You cured her with the cup."

"Oh, my," Michele said, startled. "That's wonderful."

Michele and her husband had not paid much attention to Jennifer's story after Michele flew to Florida and the Hic-Cup cup failed to work. Michele and her husband had moved on to other ways of trying to build their company. But here was Rachel on the phone telling Michele that it had been the cup, after all, that finally cured her daughter.

Michele was thrilled.

"We would love for Jennifer to be your spokesperson and talk about how the cup cured her," Michele later recalled Rachel telling her.

Michele was ecstatic. She'd had a feeling that with

some effort and patience the cup would ultimately help Jennifer. And here it was, not two weeks after that trip south, and she was hiccup-free.

Rachel wanted to talk business so Michele handed the phone to her husband, who dealt in those matters.

Jennifer had been given a free Hic-Cup cup on that day Michele met the family in Florida. Yet, Michele said, since it did not work at the time, she left Florida thinking she would never hear from Rachel again. After all, there was no reason to expect further discussions: The cup didn't appear to work for Jennifer's hiccups. Thus, there was no reason to continue a relationship of any sort.

According to published reports that claimed Jennifer was offered a "generous and lucrative contract," along with an "immediate cash signing bonus" by Hic-Cup Ltd., the company had apparently agreed to pay Jennifer $2,500 as long as she mentioned the product on *Today*. Some later claimed Jennifer was paid a lot more money for signing the deal.

"That's outrageous," Rachel later said, laughing. "I wish!"

Jennifer confirmed published reports that it was $2,500. Michele's canceled check indicated the same. Documents provided by Rachel later said it was a "onetime fee" of $2,500.

Michele had a problem with the "generous and lucrative" comment, along with the "immediate cash signing bonus" information, which had been put out by the media after Jennifer signed with Hic-Cup. According to Michele's husband, who had spoken to Rachel on the phone that day she called to say the cup had cured Jennifer, "[Rachel] wanted more money, but finally agreed upon the [$2,500] amount offered. The agreement up front was if it helped Jennifer, she would be offered compensation for her television, video, and written testimonials. This was all that was promised. Since the cup did not even work for her at our initial meeting [in Florida], why would we offer her a 'signing bonus'? Her credibility was already in question and a payment up front would make it look like a fake endorsement for cash. She was only offered any compensation if it worked to cure her hiccups."

Michele said Rachel, Chris, and Jennifer knew this when she left Florida: the only way Jennifer could be compensated was if the cup "cured" her.

During this call from Rachel to Michele and her husband on March 1, reportedly after the *Today* show appearance had been booked, was to say that the cup had finally come through and "cured" Jennifer. According to Michele and her husband's recollections of the call, Rachel never mentioned anything about acupuncture or hypnotherapy. At the time of the call, Hic-Cup Ltd. knew nothing about either. As far as they were concerned, the cup had cured Jennifer and they were now prepared to enter into a business relationship with Jennifer's legal guardians, Rachel and Chris.

The $2,500 was a "flat fee," Michele said. "That was all she was getting."

Rachel told Michele's husband that she and Jennifer were scheduled to go on *Today* the following morning.

"She's going on *Today* . . . and she is *not* going to talk about [the cup] until we've been paid," Rachel explained to Michele's husband over the phone.[9]

"We will FedEx the check to you overnight—will that work?"[10]

"Yes."

They hung up. Michele FedEx-ed the check for

$2,500 as Rachel and Jennifer headed to the airport for a flight to New York.

Chris Robidoux received the check the following morning, according to Michele's records.

All was set for Jennifer to go on *Today* and proclaim to the world that the Hic-Cup stainless-steel cup with the brass anode, invented by Michele Ehlinger's husband, had cured her of the devastating, torturous condition of having the hiccups since January 23, 2007. It was set to be, as they say, a win-win situation for all involved.

CHAPTER 39

JENNIFER SAT ON the *Today* set and told America she was hiccup-free. Matt Lauer started the segment by high-fiving a smiling, cheerful Jennifer Mee. Rachel, barely unable to contain her excitement, sat next to her daughter with obvious joy illuminating her face.

Tell the world *how* they stopped, Matt Lauer suggested, quickly stepping out of the way so his interviewee could share the great news.

"Multiple things," Jennifer explained. Not one or the other, but several "things" contributed to the hiccups going away for what they believed was good this time.

"I had acupuncture, chiropractor, hypnotism, and a *Hic*-Cup," Jennifer said, highlighting that first word of the brand.

"A Hic-*Cup*," Lauer echoed. "In other words, something you drank *out* of?"

Jennifer shrugged, saying she believed it was a combination of all those things that made her stop. She did give Debbie Lane a nod—although she never mentioned Lane by name—by adding, "Trust me, while I was in hypnotism, something told me that I would have trouble with my heart if I didn't stop. . . ."

They discussed what life had been like for Jennifer over the duration of having the hiccups. Jennifer explained how it was "very hectic, a lot of stress in the family."

An understatement.

This interview was especially revealing. Jennifer and Rachel were beaming. There was a gentle, sincere radiance about them that cannot be denied. It was as if a burden had been lifted and they could now begin life with a fresh start. No doubt, Jennifer and Rachel were happier than they had been in quite some time. They couldn't contain it. Rachel had her legs crossed and one leg was moving rapidly, bouncing nervously along as she and Jennifer spoke. Jennifer was antsy and it appeared as though she was going to jump out of her seat and shout to viewers how delighted she was that the hiccups were gone for good.

Matt Lauer asked if Jennifer's life from this point on would be full of anxiety and fear, never knowing if the hiccups might return at any time.

She said no, not especially.

Rachel spoke over her daughter at one point, adding, "She's going to have her cup, because each time she's had one"—meaning a stray hiccup—"she's used that cup and it's only been one single hiccup."

"Yup," Jennifer agreed.

There was the Hic-Cup plug!

One thing Jennifer Mee was adamant about at this point in her life: The damn hiccups weren't coming back.

Yes, she had a stray hiccup here and there, but the way she felt—the resources she now had because of all the support she'd received—she believed they were gone forever.

And all that "attention" she had received along the way, some of which Jennifer had taken to like a snake to a field of corn, was soon going to vanish as Jennifer integrated herself back into the life of a teenager.

The question would soon become: how would Jennifer respond?

CHAPTER 40

WATCHING THIS INTERVIEW on *Today* from her home had made Debbie Lane cringe. She knew the hiccups had left Jennifer on the evening she provided her with pro bono hypnotherapy in her office. Jennifer had been totally "cured"—a strong word to use in this situation—by the hypnotherapy, Lane believed. Sure, they might have come back, but Lane's treatment started the ball rolling. And yet, here was Jennifer and Rachel—at least halfheartedly—backing away from that and giving credit to the cup, the hypnotism, a chiropractor, and acupuncture.

"I believe we said that these were the things she had tried very recently and it may have been a *combination* of them," Rachel commented after being asked if she felt as though she had dissed Lane's treatment on *Today.* "We felt pressured into talking about all [of the remedies]—they were all free of charge. . . . We never tried to dismiss anybody's kindness and effort in her recovery."

To the contrary, regarding dismissing one particular effort to help Jennifer, one could argue that Rachel had even asked and taken a moment out of the *Today* segment to give a broad thank-you to everyone that helped Jennifer throughout her ordeal. She and Jennifer were very grateful for all the well-wishers and their suggestions.

Michele Ehlinger and her husband were upset and felt duped after seeing the *Today* show segment, Michele saying later, "[Jennifer] offered only a vague partial credit to our Hic-Cup cup for helping end her hiccups. She instead said on [*Today*] and in follow-up interviews that it was a 'combination' of things that cured her hiccups. This was not what her mother told us over the phone when she was negotiating payment for the testimonial. We were let down and felt duped as she was paid [several] thousand . . . dollars by us based on her claim that it *cured* her hiccups. Yet she gave much less than a full-throated endorsement while speaking with the media."

Michele and her husband decided they "had been played by the family, and [Rachel and Jennifer] were only saying just enough to keep the cash, yet not actually stating that it cured her hiccups."

They were upset. They'd spent a lot of money the company did not have.

"We felt like we got ripped off by a fraud. We never spoke with them again, and in our last conversation, we made it clear we felt like they lied to us. We considered taking action, but it would be nothing but grief and bad publicity, which is the last thing we wanted, or a new company needs."

Nonetheless, Michele and her husband took a screenshot from the *Today* segment and put it up on their company website. It only seemed fair that they promote the notion that Jennifer mentioned the cup on *Today*.

"It was one still picture of the morning television show she appeared on and was used briefly on our website. . . . [It was] in the compensation agreement," Michele said.

It wasn't as if they'd gone and printed sales brochures, advertisements, or run commercials or radio ads using Jennifer Mee as their spokesperson—Hic-Cup Ltd. did none of that.

"As for the agreement we did have, it included the TV appearance for which she was paid, and we had the right to use a simple still frame of her at that public appearance. That is what we paid her for when she claimed it cured her hiccups—a claim she failed to repeat, after Rachel used it for her demand for money."

Michele and her husband shrugged it all off as a business loss, lesson learned, and considered they'd never hear from Rachel again.

CHAPTER 41

WHILE THE PRESSURE of being Hiccup Girl had been in its prime, Rachel and Chris had caved and decided to put a computer in the house, a laptop they bought with money borrowed from Rachel's parents not long after Jennifer first got the hiccups. They had done this mainly so they could log on to the Internet, Rachel said, and search for remedies, research other people who'd been through intractable hiccups, find support groups, and communicate with professionals via e-mail and instant message in the same way the rest of the modern world had been doing for nearly a decade. Documents provided by Rachel show a long history of communication between the Robidoux family and doctors, well-wishers, children, men, women, haters, and so on.

Although the computer helped them, Jennifer sat at it during the day when Rachel wasn't home and read what some people were saying about her. Even though she had stopped hiccupping, some of the comments posted by Internet trolls had taken her down into a burrow of darkness and self-hatred. What was most hurtful were the comments about her dating boys out of her race, how she was nothing but a "media whore," who was looking for attention, the allegation that she had been faking it all along, and how it had all been a show Jennifer had put on to see how much money the family could make off her celebrity.

"Don't read any of it," Chris told Jennifer. "Stay off the computer."

Now satisfied she was totally hiccup-free (save for a stray here and there), on March 14, 2007, Jennifer returned to school. Walking into Northeast High School in St. Pete was a strange experience for Jennifer. She felt as though she'd been gone a year or more. She was a different person—much more grown-up and experienced in the way that the world worked. She'd been to Manhattan (an alien place for this girl who had

never been on a plane before that first ride to *Today*).
She'd become comfortable with sitting and speaking to
millions of people.

"And it all went to her head," Rachel said later.

Everyone wanted to know Jennifer. Kids stared.
They whispered behind her back. She was popular
now.

Jennifer sucked it up. She loved being noticed,
being the center of attention.

"It felt good," Jennifer admitted.

All of a sudden, Jennifer Mee was somebody. Getting up every day and going to school mattered.

Northeast is one of the largest high schools in the
Pinellas County region. The school motto is: "Once a
Viking, always a Viking." On that first day Jennifer returned, she had embraced her stigma of Hiccup Girl
so innately, so pleasantly, so affably, that the same
nickname she had once rebuked—and said she wanted
nothing to do with—was now the only name she
wanted to be known by. As Jennifer walked down the
hallway, her shiny, Barbie-pink-colored fingernails
could be seen from down the hallway. And if a student
didn't happen to notice, Jennifer was quick to flip over
her hands and show anyone who asked what that was
written on each fingernail.

"What's that say?"

Jennifer smiled. She happily displayed them: *H-I-C-
C-U-P G-I-R-L* was spelled out, one letter on each fingernail, in black nail polish against that flashy pink
background. This was her new identity. Jennifer had
embraced her condition. She was now who the media
had said she was.

Hiccup Girl.

* * *

Throughout it all, Jennifer said later, "What bothered me was that people thought my parents and I were profiting financially from my hiccups." (In reality, all of Jennifer's medical bills that had not been donated were paid through public assistance.)

Yet, that was only one small after-effect of becoming a major pop culture celebrity. The Robidoux household, as a whole, was having a difficult time dealing with the fallout after Jennifer's star began to fade and she became just another high-school teen trying to wade her way through life. For one, the two-bedroom, ranch-style, small home they lived in was not the size home you'd expect five girls, Rachel, Chris, and Chris's brother (who slept on a couch they placed in the dining room for him) to live in. But it was what their budget could afford, Rachel explained, and they did the best they could with what they had. Jennifer and her four sisters slept in one bedroom. No one in that small bedroom went to bed until Jennifer fell asleep, one sister later said, because Jennifer was the oldest and did what she wanted and they looked up to her.

Still, if sleeping together in such tight quarters was hard enough, the younger girls were having difficulty understanding all the attention placed on Jennifer. Being seven and five years old at the time, Destiny and McKenzie didn't comprehend what was happening and why Jennifer was on television and in the newspapers, and why did so many people want her time and to pay attention to her?

"There was jealousy," Rachel explained. "They kept

asking me why Jennifer was getting to do things the others weren't."

And throughout it all, of course, Rachel was getting up at her usual 5 A.M. hour and heading off to her waitressing job, leaving the parenting to Chris, whose disability—a thyroid disease and several other "conditions," which Chris did not want to share publicly— kept his mobility and parenting to a minimum. It had been only on her days off during the week that Rachel was able to deal with Jennifer's hiccups and take her to appointments. Chris and Rachel, who'd experienced marital problems in the past, had not spent any time together as a couple in what seemed like months.

But when the hiccups went away, it was such a relief and burden lifted, Rachel felt as though, as a family, they could take on anything from this point forward and move in the right direction.

"I was relieved to say the least," Rachel remembered, referring to that period when they realized the hiccups were gone for good. "It felt like the tornado we got sucked up into put us back down on the ground and we had escaped its wrath, for the most part. I envisioned Jennifer going back to school and her little sisters not feeling neglected anymore. For all that time, it seemed all about Jennifer and doctors and the media. I just wanted it all behind us, and I know Jennifer did, too. It became very overwhelming. All of it."

During her first day of class, fellow students hugged Jennifer, one after the other. Some even clapped as she entered the building.

"I'm doing it," Jennifer said. "I'm back in school!"

CHAPTER 42

ON THURSDAY, MARCH 15, back for just her second day of class, Jennifer looked up at her science classroom clock, where it had all started back on January 23, almost two months ago, and felt a tickle of warmth on her upper lip.

It was 8:15 A.M.

Feeling an itch, along with that warmth, Jennifer put her hand up to her nose.

"Jennifer?" a classmate said. "Are you okay?"

Blood ran down Jennifer's nose and upper lip.

Then, all at once: *Hic, hic, hic.*

The hiccups had become a recurring nightmare for Jennifer, a hibernating beast waiting to lash out again. Now here she was in science class and her nose was bleeding and she was hiccupping.

What the hell? Jennifer asked herself.

The sound was quite a bit louder than it had been in the past. The hiccups, too, were much more intense, Jennifer could tell right away. They were also constant, same as when they began long ago.

Hic, hic, hic, hic . . . about fifty times per minute.

When Jennifer got home, Chris and Rachel looked at her and did not know what to say. It was horrible. This curse. This all-consuming nightmare was *not* over. Why them? Why again? Would the hiccups ever go away for good?

Jennifer was sitting down. A nosebleed, which she had contained shortly after it first started back in class, was now back.

Doctors recommended more medication. Rachel was tired of it all. Jennifer had not been herself since taking those medications—that is, those she wasn't even allergic to.

"I'm not sure the hiccups and her bloody nose were connected," Rachel explained. "I think it was just a coincidence."

Regardless, the hiccups were enough to contend with. Not only did they take over Jennifer's life every time they came back, but they kept her from going to school.

The only choice they could make now, if Jennifer didn't want to fall so far behind in school that she'd have to make up an entire year, would be to start the homebound program again and stick to it for the rest of the school year. There was no use in Jennifer returning to the classroom, and possibly having to leave again and again and again. The hiccups were coming and going. Likely, Jennifer would have them for the rest of her life in some capacity.

As summer came and Jennifer celebrated her sixteenth birthday on July 28, 2007, she was able to get her hiccups under control. She had started taking Prilosec, an acid reducer used in treating patients with acid reflux, and it seemed to help. The hiccups subsided.

"Sometimes I'd get them for half a day," Jennifer said later.

"But they always go away," Rachel added.

The one important diagnosis, Rachel commented later, that doctors began to focus on around this time was that Jennifer suffered from Tourette's, a claim that was supported by documentation Rachel provided.

That diagnosis, Rachel said, answered a lot of questions and set them on the right path, medically speaking. There was a connection, Rachel was told, between the Tourette condition and the hiccups.[11]

Jennifer had changed so much from that fifteen-year-old girl with the hiccups being paraded all over the media. She'd not so much matured—at least socially—as talked and acted differently. No more was Jennifer the innocent, naïve teen who spoke so fast that sometimes it was hard to understand what she was saying. She now smiled at odd times and twitched and seemed perpetually nervous (most of which were currently considered Tourette-based tics). But on the proper meds, she was much calmer and, in some respects, easier to understand and even seemingly somewhat subdued.

Still, from where Chris Robidoux sat on the sidelines and watched Jennifer's life unfold, he saw there was something about Jennifer that he was having a hard time dealing with: her attitude. Jennifer was cocky and belligerent. Plain and simple, she was a smart-ass. She felt as though she could parent herself, especially when Rachel was not home and Jennifer was just alone with Chris.

When her mom did come home, however, there was Jennifer, the pleasant teenager her mother thought her to be.

"I don't understand what you're talking about, Chris," Rachel would say when Chris explained how fed up he was with Jennifer and her insolence. "Ghetto" was how Chris described Jennifer's general demeanor.

"She had that street mentality—I *hated* it. She had grown up around it in St. Pete, and it's my fault."

Not only were Chris and Jennifer arguing all the time, but Chris and Rachel were tossing it around almost on a daily basis during those days, too.

"And didn't stop," Chris remembered.

For Jennifer, she told me she resented Chris deeply for something the family had gone through back in Vermont—a dark family scandal in which Chris had hurt Rachel emotionally and Rachel was able to forgive him eventually, but Jennifer, unfortunately, never could.[12]

As Jennifer sat and read about herself online, the Internet became more "vulgar" and "obscene" with postings about her. It was hard for Jennifer to read anything online any longer without recoiling and taking personally what people had to say. What didn't help matters was that after Jennifer had run away in June of that year, as the whirlwind of media subsided and she became just another girl with the hiccups, people questioned the authenticity of her hiccups by spreading venomous rumors online. Yet, as her birthday approached, Jennifer was already talking about going back to school when classes started again that fall. She was determined to do whatever she had to in order to make it back into class with all of her peers. If she let go of school, where would she go? What would she do? This was probably one of the most important decisions Jennifer was going to make.

Today contacted Jennifer again in August for a show titled "Where Are They Now?" Producers flew Rachel, Jennifer, and Chris to New York for a weekend entirely paid for by NBC Universal.

When Jennifer returned to Florida, having been speaking with her biological father since her first appearance on *Today,* she had an announcement to make for Chris and Rachel.

"I want to go spend some time with Dad in Vermont."

"I don't see why not," Rachel said. In fact, maybe some time away from each other would do Jennifer and Chris some good.

Jennifer took off for two weeks to stay with her biological father in Vermont.

When she returned, Chris noticed another round of immediate changes in the girl. When Rachel was not around, Jennifer was even cockier and wiser, telling Chris, "You're not my real father. *He* understands me."

Jennifer was more aggressive verbally, and entirely her own person. There was a clear indication from her that she was not going to be told what to do any longer, on any level. She was going to make her own choices and nobody was going to tell her otherwise.

As Rachel worked and Chris dealt with his disabilities, while also having to take care of three small children, they were not totally available for Jennifer. Jennifer was meeting people online and communicating once again with Tyrone O'Donnell, who was in juvenile detention. Writing to her, O'Donnell promised that when he got out, they were going to pick up the relationship where they left off.

"[Tyrone] was my first love ever," Jennifer told me. "He was one of those types of boys you wouldn't want your daughter around. But there was something about him that my mind and body wanted to feel."

Jennifer said she dated Tyrone because he was "very sweet at first." As she got to know the "bad-boy side" of Tyrone, however, as most other girls would have run far away from it, Jennifer was "attracted to that."

Tyrone told Jennifer what she wanted to hear. She later admitted that as she grew up, she suffered from low self-esteem and thought very little of herself. Tyrone fed off that and plied Jennifer with that "love" Jennifer felt she was not getting elsewhere.

It wasn't long after they started dating that Tyrone hauled off and smacked Jennifer in the face one day.

She cried and curled up into a fetal ball. Whimpering, she asked Tyrone, why? Why did he have to hit her?

Tyrone told Jennifer she had gotten out of line and he wouldn't stand for it. Not ever.

So Jennifer apologized for whatever it was she had done to "make him" hit her. In her mind, it was all her fault, which made it okay for Jennifer to live with it. That's a consequence and a lie that domestic violence convinces some of its victims to believe.

"'Cause I loved him," Jennifer explained. "So I stayed with him."

"I'm sorry, baby," Tyrone would say in one breath. In the next, maybe a day later, he'd smack her again, "You're a ho," he'd snap while bruising Jennifer up real good. "A real piece of shit."

"Why?" Jennifer would ask him.

"He would say," Jennifer recalled, "'I'm-a make you so ugly that no other motherfucker will want you.'"

The way she talked about this particular comment sounded as though, to Jennifer, Tyrone was giving her a compliment.

Jennifer went on to say she couldn't recall how many times Tyrone hit her because it was "so often."

"He used to always think I was cheating on him, when really, he was the one doing it to me."

CHAPTER 43

JENNIFER DECIDED SHE was finished with high school. She wasn't going back. What would it matter, anyway? By now, Jennifer was consistently meeting people online and going down to the park near their St. Pete home to meet up in person. The exact scenario that Rachel had feared by bringing a computer into the home had, in fact, come to fruition.

Most were kids Jennifer's age. Many just wanted to be friends with her because of her hiccup celebrity status.

Rachel explained that Jennifer wasn't at all disappointed the hiccups were gone for good—it was never about that. But she was, however, upset that the limelight was gone and she was no longer a household name. Jennifer, for many reasons, wanted to hold on to her fifteen minutes of fame for as long as she could, but it was over. She'd have to face it sooner or later.

"She got a big head on her," Rachel said, "and I used to tell her that she thought she was 'all that and a bag of chips.'"

Nobody was going to tell Jennifer what to do,

Rachel realized as she watched Jennifer go through dramatic changes that fall of 2007.

Maybe Chris is right?

People from all over still wanted to talk to Jennifer about her brush with fame. Jennifer had no trouble meeting new people online because all she had to do was mention who she was—there was hardly any person in the country who paid even the slightest bit of attention to pop culture who was not familiar with Jennifer's story.

Trying desperately to get their daughter back on track, Rachel and Chris had a tutor come to the house. Public assistance paid for it. "The paperwork alone," Rachel explained, "was a nightmare, but we got it done." Jennifer had left school a freshman and did not have enough credits to return as a sophomore, like the rest of her class would that fall. The more she fell behind, the deeper she sank. Jennifer wanted nothing to do with school any longer. She was going through the motions with the tutor, perhaps simply pleasing her parents. On top of that, there was talk of them moving north to Spring Hill, Florida, and Jennifer would have to transfer schools.

"I'm not doing this anymore," Jennifer told Rachel one day.

"What do you mean?"

"I'm done."

They talked about Jennifer getting her GED and maybe attending cosmetology school, a dream Jennifer had from childhood.

While Rachel worked, Jennifer was at home: no schoolwork to do, no obligations to speak of. Within that new family dynamic, Chris and Jennifer couldn't stand to be in the same room together—albeit, with a mere four rooms in the entire house to contend with. Chris was worried how much the hiccup fame had changed his stepdaughter. He'd never seen her act so arrogantly. Just the way she spoke, the language she used—it was a clear indication to Chris that the street had gotten hold of Jennifer.

"She's definitely trying to spread her wings," Rachel remembered, going back to those days when Jennifer was wandering through her teenage years, wondering what to do, waiting on that next thing.

"And the problem was that Jennifer was a follower," Jennifer's sister Ashley McCauley later explained. Jennifer's closest sister, who had sat by and witnessed all of what was happening, felt helpless. She looked on as Jennifer started smoking cigarettes at the age of thirteen, and Ashley warned her about the problems that would eventually cause. Ashley had watched as Jennifer moved on to weed and "took pills" and began having sex with various boys. Now, with the crowd Jennifer had started to run with, Ashley was telling Jennifer almost every day to watch herself. The game she was getting into on the street was for real. The streets played for keeps. Jennifer was not conditioned to survive that lifestyle.

"Let's send her to my mom's," Rachel suggested to Chris one night.

Jennifer had complained about privacy. She needed her space. The deal was if she went to Rachel's parents, she would meet with a tutor regularly.

Jennifer agreed. She was actually excited. Giving schoolwork another try seemed like the right thing to do. She'd have her own room. She could, at least, take the time to try and figure out what she was going to do with her life. Chris decided that Jennifer wasn't going to just sit around and wait for her life to begin. They were going to make those choices for her as long as she lived in the house.

That seemingly good idea failed. Rachel's parents didn't like people coming into their home during the early-morning hours, disrupting their lives, tutoring Jennifer. These were elderly people set in their ways. Jennifer was a lot to handle. Rachel's parents lived near downtown, too, so Jennifer could take off and meet her people. And it wasn't as if they could leave Jennifer by herself. If keeping her out of trouble was a goal, well, Jennifer needed constant supervision.

So Jennifer moved in with a friend. Rachel insisted the tutors go there and meet with her.

But that didn't work out, either.

So she moved back home—which was when things between Chris and Jennifer took on an entire new level of dysfunction.

CHAPTER 44

CHRIS SAT AT the family computer. Outside the window was another beautiful, picture-perfect Florida winter day with temps averaging around 72 degrees. The sun, of course, was perpetually shining its golden rays into the house through the blinds. As Chris scrolled through screens, he wondered what Jennifer had been up to. He didn't trust her, obviously. Ever since she'd returned to the house, their relationship had gone from bad to worse. He could sense something was up with Jennifer and she was getting involved with people who were easily influencing her. The arguments between them were more blistering and hostile every time they had it out. Insults and cusswords were hurled at each other as if casual conversation. Both Chris and Jennifer were guilty of screaming and swearing and saying things they would both one day woefully regret.

Staring at the screen, Chris logged on to Jennifer's Facebook page and scrolled through to see if he could gain some insight into what she was doing and what was going on in her life outside the house. Snooping? Spying? Sure! But this was where they were in their relationship. And social media was a great tool for a parent to learn about the "real world"—a way to uncover what a problem teenager was actually involved in outside the confines of the household.

"And that's when I saw it," Chris said later. It was one of the most startling, disturbing, spiteful things he could ever recall finding out about Jennifer at the time, clearly directed exclusively at him. It was altogether hurtful, dangerous, and unhealthy, not to mention the pain it would cause Rachel when Chris sat her down and explained.

Incredible! Chris said to himself, reading a few posts Jennifer had just made. *What in the hell does she think she is doing?*

At that moment, had someone suggested to Chris that Jennifer had been faking the hiccups, he might have leaned toward believing it. He wondered if he ever truly knew Jennifer and what she was doing on her own time. But later, after it was all done, Chris said the idea he and Rachel had been manipulating Jennifer to keep the hiccups going—a common accusation online—was absolutely preposterous. Their lives during the hiccup period and shortly thereafter were a testament to how much chaos the hiccups and the media attention had caused the family. Chris had sat and witnessed Jennifer's entire suffering play out before him, feeling the implications personally as his relationship with Jennifer dissolved into them hating each other.

"She was offered [a lot of money, by his perception] by Hic-Cup in the beginning to use the cup and see if it stopped the hiccups completely," Chris said, making what was an excellent point. "If we were manipulating her, um, that would have been the time to tell her to stop."

It's a solid argument: If she was faking, Jennifer could have stopped after the offer was made and said, *"Wow! This cup totally cured me."* She could have taken a payday and walked away.

According to Rachel and Chris, the family "lost money" during the time Jennifer had the hiccups. As Chris recalled, "We never capitalized on *any* of this. There was never *any* money. People said we used Jennifer like an ATM. I won't even try to explain or defend that, because we never made a dime."

As he sat and stared at the computer, Chris's jaw would have hit the floor if it could have reached that far. Reading what Jennifer had posted on her Facebook page, Chris was startled and hurt by what he read. He couldn't help but think back to that little girl he met when he first started dating Rachel. Jennifer was a mere eighteen months old. She was so fragile, Chris recalled, so delicate and cheerful.

"Just a joy," Chris said, speaking of that time in Vermont when it was just Chris, Rachel, Jennifer, and Ashley. Things seemed so simple back then. "I coached her basketball team and it was just wonderful."

Chris had not had the most picture-perfect life leading up to meeting Rachel. In 1988, Chris was arrested for attempted murder, which he was able to plea bargain down to a second-degree aggravated-assault charge. In total, Chris wound up spending five years in prison for the crime.

According to Chris's version, he was living with his brother and his brother's girlfriend at the time and something happened between them. Chris said the girlfriend made a "pass" at him, and, as one might suspect, that had caused a great friction between the two siblings. Chris was eventually kicked out of the residence. A few days after he left, Chris returned to speak with his brother. He wanted to clear the air.

Only, Chris brought a small handgun with him.

His brother was not home—but the girlfriend was. An "altercation" took place between Chris and the girlfriend. A shot was fired by Chris and it hit the girlfriend in the chin.

She lived. Chris was arrested a short time later.

There was a second arrest about ten years hence. It was shortly after the rape allegations made by Jennifer against the two males blew up. Chris was upset because he believed law enforcement had not done enough as far as charging the alleged rapists. In fact, "no charges that I know of," Rachel said, were ever brought against them.

Rachel explained that after "neither of them was arrested . . . Chris became really upset by this."

Chris started to call the perpetrators on the telephone and made harassing threats. He was relentless.

The family pressed charges: stalking. When all was said and done, Chris did another sixty days in prison.

Since then, Chris had kept his life—legally—in order. Maybe moving to Florida had been a good thing, after all.

As for being a father, "Whenever Chris introduced either of us," Ashley McCauley said later, "he always said, 'These are my *daughters*. . . .' People would try to correct him. 'Stepdaughters, right?' And Chris would say, 'No, my daughters!'"

That small-town life in Vermont was something that Chris kept bringing up; how leaving Vermont was a mistake Chris blamed himself for ever since they packed and moved, ultimately winding up in Florida. Relocating to Florida, Chris had felt from day one, was not going to be good for the family. But he understood that Rachel needed to be there for her parents and he supported that decision. The major gaffe Chris kicked himself for was that they moved to St. Pete.

The way Chris later explained it, he and Jennifer didn't start "butting heads" until Jennifer grew into her later teen years while in Florida. Yet, that developing distance between them took on new lengths after she became Hiccup Girl.

It was her cell phone, the individuality that becoming a celebrity ostensibly gave Jennifer, the slow expansion of her ego, a belief that she was somebody she was not—it all contributed, Chris later observed, to the demise of their father-daughter, close relationship.

Misunderstandings the two of them had after the post–Hiccup Girl fame evolved into verbal brawls, slammed doors, insults, and name-calling. They were hurting each other almost every day.

What really fired Chris up was finding those letters Tyrone and Jennifer had written to each other while Tyrone had been locked up. They were graphic and vile, Chris recalled. Tyrone would talk about the sexual acts he wanted to perform on Jennifer when he got out, and it was clear Tyrone was writing to an experienced partner, not a young and innocent teenager. It was also the drug talk from Tyrone in the letters that bothered Chris. It said a lot about how much Jennifer was willing not only to tolerate from the boy, but how far she was willing to dive in with him.

"I even called the detention facility and told them about the letters and how we didn't want him writing to her anymore, but it didn't matter," Chris explained. "They did nothing."

"Jennifer, listen," Chris said one day after reading the letters. "We don't want you two writing to each other anymore. I don't even want you *seeing* him."

Rachel stood by, agreeing. It would be best if Jennifer broke it off.

"You don't like him because he's black!" Jennifer screamed angrily, accusing Chris of being a racist. It was a card she'd pull out from time to time when Chris disagreed with her lifestyle and the people she hung around.

"Look, you certainly don't need to be associated with anybody that is doing and or dealing drugs," Chris said. "*Especially* a guy who wants to have sex with you! He's using you, Jennifer. You're way too young for all of this."

"You're a racist" was Jennifer's comeback.

"I don't like *anybody* from the ghetto," Chris said. Black, white, brown, it didn't matter to Chris, he explained, what color a person's skin was. He was interested in how they acted, how they treated others and his daughter, along with how mature they were.

"Not everybody from the ghetto is bad," Jennifer snapped back.

"I'm not saying they are all bad, Jennifer. But the ones you seem to like and hang out with *are* bad."

Chris didn't even want Jennifer dating, he told her.

"And certainly not *that* element!" He was steaming.

Part of the problem for Jennifer, Rachel later said, was that she didn't understand Chris's condition. Chris had several issues he was dealing with at the same time. He also battled his own demons. The main medical problem was a thyroid condition, which can vary from patient to patient. An adult with a problem thyroid left untreated was prone to mood swings, Chris said, along with fatigue and several other debilitating symptoms. Because of that and other things, Chris had been in and out of the hospital and not at home for the girls all the time. Jennifer saw this as an emotional weakness and often threw it back in Chris's face. His nerves, before he started taking the drug Synthroid to combat the thyroid condition, frayed very easily.

"Especially where Jennifer was concerned," Chris recalled.

"He treated me differently because I was his stepdaughter" was Jennifer's argument.

"When things were good back when we lived in Vermont," Chris remembered, "I never looked at Jennifer any differently. She was my daughter. When the hiccups happened and later when she started to go off the rails, there were times when I felt, 'Why did I even bother getting into this?'"

"You're just my stepfather," Jennifer would say when they had heated arguments. "I have a real father."

"Yup . . . sure thing, and you're just my stepdaughter," Chris would hiss back.

("In a sense, I lowered myself, and it was wrong," Chris explained later. "It would get ugly. I blame myself every day for what happened to Jennifer.")

Chris sometimes viewed himself as the "evil stepdad," he said. A lot of this went on without Rachel around because she worked all the time and took care of her ailing parents after work. Part of Chris could accept that he was the so-called evil stepdad, disciplining the girls the way he saw fit. They were not going to be happy with every parental decision he made. But when Jennifer would call him "stepdad" and tell him his rule and order did not hold weight any longer in his own house because he was her *step*father, it hurt Chris a lot. And he would always react in kind. Words would be exchanged and a battle would ensue. Next thing they knew, Chris and Jennifer weren't speaking.

On top of that, Chris and Rachel had a strict curfew for the older girls: 8 P.M. sharp. No excuses. After becoming a celebrity, Jennifer pushed it, Ashley explained. "She thought she could get away with it—and she did." Ashley knew what Jennifer was doing when she was out, and she often talked with Jennifer about her behavior. But it did nothing. Jennifer was now going to do whatever she wanted to do, and nobody was going to tell her different.

"Rachel," Chris would say when Rachel got home

from work. "I cannot take it. You have to do something. The way she talks to me, the things she says—it *needs* to change."

Rachel would often side with Jennifer after Jennifer lied and said she hadn't done or said anything and Chris was making her out to be the bad person. This caused a tremendous friction between Chris and Rachel. Chris would go off by himself and feel terrible that his wife did not believe him.

Jennifer expressed a desire to be treated as an adult, not a sixteen-year-old. She often talked about how Chris did not know how to take care of any of the kids. And Chris later admitted that his "parenting skills, at that time, in Florida, were sorely lacking. I cannot defend it. I don't believe I took the time, nor did her mother, to sit down and explain to Jennifer, 'This is wrong. This is right.'"

Outside influences were a major point of contention and a serious problem that had, post–hiccup situation, gotten so out of control there was little Chris or Rachel could have done at this point, save for locking Jennifer up.

"She felt we didn't care," Chris said. "She felt that my problems were maybe more important than hers."

And that is the thing about feelings, isn't it? Doesn't matter if the person is right or wrong, but how she *feels* is how she feels. Respecting someone else's feelings and sharing differences and expectations can mend any fractured relationship.

"We never sat down and talked," Chris explained. "It was always an argument. . . ."

The world outside the confines of the Robidoux doors had swallowed this naïve, undereducated little girl, whom Chris, Rachel, and Ashley all described as a sixteen-year-old with the mentality of, at best, a twelve-year-old. Jennifer bought into everything those in her world—including whomever she met online— told her. She believed she was "all that" because she had been on television. She thought she could handle whatever was about to come her way. Yet, what Jennifer never completely understood was that the street, sometimes, can be a merciless abyss of misfortune and criminal activity that one does not realize he or she is immersed in until it's far too late.

Chris portrayed Tyrone, that person Jennifer claimed had initiated her into the "thug life," as a "waste of a life, period."

Sitting at the computer, reading through her Facebook pages, whatever Tyrone had done would pale in comparison to what Chris had just found out. As he'd scrolled through Jennifer's posts, what for him was the beginning of the end for Jennifer living inside the Robidoux household was there before his eyes. On Facebook, Jennifer had bragged that while Chris sat in the living room, watching a football game, on the other side of the wall from where he sat, inside a bedroom she shared with her three sisters—Ashley had moved out by then—Jennifer had brought a "black boy" (not Tyrone O'Donnell) into the house and had sex with him all that afternoon.

And he doesn't even realize it! Jennifer reportedly mocked on her Facebook page, before describing some of what they had done.

It was a bold, subconscious statement to the fact that Jennifer wanted to be taken seriously as far as her being given privacy and more space. She was screaming out emotionally, wanting desperately to be noticed. But she was also sticking it in Chris's face at the same time.

This posting, she had to realize, would eventually be seen by Chris and Rachel.

And maybe that's exactly what she wanted?

"I've never hated her, but after reading that, I was pretty, pretty upset," Chris said, adding, "My fear was one of her little sisters walking into that room while she was having sex with this boy. It was enough for me."

CHAPTER 45

PURE, UNFETTERED RAGE. That was how Chris felt staring at the computer screen, reading what Jennifer had done inside the room opposite him as he watched the New England Patriots football game on that warm Florida Sunday afternoon.

She's got to go, Chris thought.

"I want her out," Chris told Rachel.

"Well, let's talk about it," Rachel said.

"Nothing left to talk about. I'm dealing with this every single day now, Rachel. I cannot do it anymore."

"If I remember right, I said something to Jennifer and it started another fight," Rachel recalled, going back to the moment Chris told her what Jennifer had posted on Facebook. "I remember being in disbelief— a kind of 'what the hell' mode. That she would do such a thing and actually post it on social media, I know was to slap Chris mentally. First having sex, then with a black guy, then under our roof, and then posting it. Talk about spitting venom."

Rachel and Chris were at odds. Not regarding what

to do with Jennifer—but with each other. As Chris saw things, not only was Tyrone O'Donnell the worst-possible scenario for Jennifer to be involved in at her vulnerable age (and it wasn't even Tyrone with whom Jennifer had had sex in her bedroom), but Jennifer was playing Chris and Rachel against each other. Whenever Rachel was around, Jennifer was the sweet little momma's girl, treating Chris with respect. Yet, as soon as Rachel walked out the door, Jennifer's true self emerged: a combative, nonconforming, aggressive know-it-all, who was not going to do anything Chris asked of her, on top of arguing with him and insulting him.

Jennifer was seventeen. It was late summer 2008.

"She was too big for her britches, as my dad used to say," Chris explained. Even though it had been over a year now since her star was born, "she had fallen in love with her fifteen minutes and could *not* let it go. I did not see things getting any better. There was no chance. I only saw things getting worse."

By now, ecstasy, weed, alcohol, pills, and other drugs were a constant part of Jennifer's life. She had an entire new group of friends she hung around. Tyrone was now out of juvenile detention influencing Jennifer and showing her the ropes as far as dealing crack cocaine. Jennifer had fallen into the "hood" lifestyle rather congenially, walking the streets at all hours, carrying dope, having sex, treating those in her life she claimed to love with as much disrespect as she could muster.

"This cannot end in a good way," Ashley would say, trying to talk Jennifer out of the life she was leading. "Please, please, listen to me. . . ."

"We should have shaken her and locked her up," Rachel said later.

Jennifer was the oldest. Ashley had looked up to her all their lives. But now, with Jennifer falling off the deep end, Ashley was greatly concerned and trying to act like the big sister herself.

As far as a reality check, or her integrating back into the real world of everyday, adult life, Jennifer wanted no part of it. She wanted to be *the* Hiccup Girl everyone noticed, paid attention to, and whispered about. She yearned to be that overnight celebrity everyone treated differently and gawked at. But it was over. And had been for quite some time.

Then Chris realized that Jennifer was actually trying to get *him* kicked out of the house. She wanted to rule the roost. If he was gone, she could have the run of the place while her mom worked.

"You're a racist!" Jennifer screamed at Chris.

It was "just about every day," Chris recalled.

They continued to swear and yell at each other, never having a moment of peace.

If what Chris had seen on Facebook wasn't bad enough, he logged on to Jennifer's Myspace pages and was horrified by what he saw there. How had she gone from such a little "sweet" girl to this "thug" wannabe, a "gangsta" chick who talked about hustling and guns and "makin' money" on the street? It was beyond anything Chris could have comprehended in the years prior to the hiccup phase.

He shook his head.

Why isn't Rachel seeing any of this?

Rachel was, actually. Part of her, she said, didn't want to accept how bad it was, while another part of her had been busy working and taking care of her parents, so it was easy to avoid—deny—the obvious and overlook all the outward signs that Jennifer's life was crumbling.

It went from Chris feeling as though he could maybe reach Jennifer and steer her back around to Jennifer hating him and everything he did. She had taken her entire life and pushed the blame on Chris. He was the fall guy for everything bad that had happened. There was nothing he could do or say that was going to change who she had become or where she was headed.

"I would guess her promiscuity and acting out," Ashley later commented, "was based in the fact that she was raped." Ashley had been a witness to the rape and the threats made by the males. She felt Jennifer was locked emotionally back in that space where they had raped her repeatedly for "two years, at least." Jennifer never grew beyond that innocent girl who was sexually assaulted and threatened. And here she was now, acting out on all of those feelings she had stuffed down so long ago.

"She did get treatment," Rachel said. "I did bring her to a therapist to deal with being raped."

"She dated only black guys, she told me," Ashley later recalled, "because she did not trust white men after being raped by those two for all that time."

Chris and Rachel had been slowly drifting to either side of the argument, holding ground, both unwilling to compromise. Chris had seen it coming. Most likely Rachel, too. And if one was to look at the situation objectively, it's clear that Jennifer had a lot to do with the problems between Chris and Rachel, along with Rachel not being around because she had to work all the time to support the family financially.

In his mind, that Facebook post was the "final straw" for Chris. He realized when he saw it that he and Jennifer had nothing left to say to each other. Their relationship had dissolved so completely that it could never, Chris surmised, be put back together. But he held on until the summer, hoping like hell something would change.

Nothing did.

"I'm leaving," Chris said one day. He had thought long and hard about his decision. He needed a break from Jennifer and his marriage to Rachel, too. The separation would do everyone, Chris hoped, some good. He could not deal with what was going on inside the house any longer.

Rachel cried. She had known for a while that a separation was inevitable.

"It was very hard," Rachel explained. "I was torn between the two. Jennifer wanted all my attention and I feel she would use me to get what she wanted, even if Chris had already said no. In return, it caused major friction between Chris and me. I felt with the way the two of them were at odds, I needed to compensate and give in more [to her]. Looking back, I'm still not sure where or when it started, but often wished it was different. It was very hard to be in the middle of two people you love who don't get along."

This was a major decision on Chris's part for a number of reasons. By this time, Chris had found a place for the family in Spring Hill, Florida, two hours north of St. Pete, just south of Gainesville, "in the country," as Chris put it. The house there had four bedrooms. There was room for everyone. It was out of the city ("and away from the ghetto," in Chris's words), and so there was this one last chance to set Jennifer on the right path. Still in St. Pete, they had plans to move out to Spring Hill in the near future.

Chris had friends and family in Tennessee. He would move there and see how things went. No promises. The only absolute was that he could no longer live in the same house with Jennifer, at least not under the terms they had been dealing with.

"You really need to work things out with Jennifer" was a common comment from Rachel whenever they spoke on the phone after Chris moved out.

"I know, Rachel." Chris was terribly saddened by it all. He was torn and didn't know what to do.

It had been a month since Chris left. He'd had some time alone to think about the family situation with a more open and clear head. He liked the way he was feeling. A lot of that daily stress was gone. The constant bickering with Jennifer, yelling and screaming, and then the disagreements with Rachel when she got home—it all suddenly stopped.

Jennifer did not want to move to Spring Hill. All of her "peeps," her contacts, and, one could argue, her business were located in St. Pete, where her life had been. She would be bored in the country. That small-town girl from Vermont was gone. She was a city chick now. More than that, the plan was that Rachel would stay in St. Pete during the week with her parents, which would leave Chris (if he moved back) with all the kids, including Jennifer, and his brother, up there in Spring Hill. There was even talk of Jennifer going back to school after the move.

With some downtime in Tennessee, Chris could clearly figure out what he wanted to do. That move they wanted to make to Spring Hill, if he decided to go back, was going to be mandatory. Everyone needed it. Everyone would benefit from it.

"Just start talking to her," Rachel pressed when she and Chris connected via phone one day. Chris had been gone almost two months by this point.

Chris called and got Jennifer on the phone.

"We need to break bread, Jennifer," Chris said on that first day they had spoken in some time. "We really need to patch this up." Chris explained that he wanted to work together with Jennifer, if not for their sake, for the rest of the kids and Rachel.

Jennifer was quiet. Then: "Why would you *ever* come back?"

Chris knew right there that nothing on Jennifer's end had changed.

"Jennifer could make me pretty speechless," Chris said of those days. "And not many people have been able to do that with me. She was one of the best."

As Chris sat in Tennessee and thought about it, his mind went back to the feeling that it wasn't as though he'd met Rachel when Jennifer was ten or a young teen; she was eighteen months old. For Jennifer, Chris was all she ever knew as a father figure. He had been in her life for fifteen years. Was the guy willing to throw all of it away?

Jennifer and her biological father had grown closer. Rachel said that Jennifer never knew it then, but her biological father had spent time in prison for a major felony. Jennifer knew he had gone to prison, but she did not know the crime and wasn't interested. All she wanted to do was start over with him. Yet, as Chris thought about it, he was totally taken aback by how quick Jennifer was to give the reins of her life to this man she never knew until he saw her on *Today* and then to treat him as a parental figure. Chris surmised it was likely because Jennifer's biological father—someone Chris knew personally from his days in Vermont—was simply telling Jennifer everything she wanted to hear and siding with her on every level.

Still, there was nothing he could do to stop it.

After two months of living apart from his family, Chris felt for the sake of all the girls and Rachel, he needed to set aside his ego, any hurt feelings he still harbored, any concerns about the future, and try like hell to work things out with Jennifer.

Rachel knew and understood how hard it was for Chris.

"This family was fractured badly," Chris said pointedly, "and I needed to repair it. I didn't want to throw in the towel. I was prepared to go out of my way to be nice to Jennifer."

The guy loved his wife and kids and wasn't going to give up.

So he moved back. Chris made it clear that anything hurtful he had said to Jennifer, anything he had done that might have made her hate him, he was willing to change, and wanted to be a better father. Chris wanted things the way they were back before the hiccups, and back before Jennifer had become this person nobody seemed to know anymore.

You look at photos of this family on vacation, on day trips to Disney, family outings, and you see one guy and a group of females standing, hugging, smiling, and loving one another. There's not a spiteful gaze among them. Jennifer, in addition, was the one child smiling the brightest. She appeared so happy to be part of a family. In one photo of Jennifer and her sister Ashley, shot in 2006, they appear to be two harmless, young schoolgirls dressed in costumes, getting ready to celebrate one of the most popular kid holidays of the year: Halloween.

Chris yearned for that innocence that had somehow been lost to be there when he returned.

Before heading back, Chris asked Rachel to make sure Jennifer understood that she should be willing to change, too. There had to be some compromise between them.

"She will, Chris. . . . Just come home."

Chris thought about it and decided it was time to reunite with his family.

CHAPTER 46

JENNIFER AND ASHLEY were at home, sitting on Jennifer's bed, talking. A few of their siblings were in the room, too. They had moved to Spring Hill by this point, a big, old house Rachel and Chris had rented. Jennifer hated being there. She was so far away from the life she had built in St. Pete. She felt as though she was entirely out of touch with everything she wanted and that they had brought her out to Spring Hill as a way to tame her and keep her from her friends. As for school, Jennifer enrolled in the local high school. Yet, no sooner had she started than Rachel received a letter from the assistant principal. Jennifer had been "referred" to the vice principal for poor attendance, low grade point average, and/or insufficient credits. It was clear from the letter that Jennifer was not going to school, and the principal wanted to know if she was quitting. If so, Jennifer needed to file a Declaration of Intent to Terminate School Enrollment form. She couldn't abandon the responsibility of attending every day. There was also some mention in the letter whether Jennifer had been "identified with a disability" and needed an "Individual Education Plan."

Ashley had sat and watched her sister give up on school, but also be in so much pain as she held her stomach, cried out for Rachel, and hiccupped incessantly during those weeks when Jennifer's entire world was her condition. It was agonizing for Ashley to sit by and watch her sister, whom she considered to be her best friend, hurt so much and also quit school—which was what Jennifer ultimately decided. They were so close in age that they got along like twins.

As Jennifer stopped hiccupping, was diagnosed with Tourette's, and began taking medications, Ashley saw a new personality emerge for her sister on some days. It depended upon which medications Jennifer was on. It was strange. Jennifer was not herself.

"What's going on with you?" Ashley asked one day as they sat chatting.

"I see a family . . . ," Jennifer said. "A husband, wife, two small kids."

Ashley wondered what Jennifer was talking about. Jennifer was staring at the wall inside the room.

"The family is all bloody," Jennifer added. "The walls are all bloody."

When Ashley later talked about this incident, she spoke of how Jennifer appeared to be "delusional" on that day. Yet, as they researched things more, Ashley claimed, "Come to find out, the house [we rented] was [supposedly] haunted. A family had died in the house.

A mother had put her kids inside a car inside the garage with the car turned on. The mother then shot the husband and shot herself."

CHAPTER 47

RACHEL HAD KEPT as close an eye as she could on Jennifer while Chris had been away. During that time, she'd noticed some of the changes in the girl were not entirely rooted in her fragile ego, her attitude, and overall outlook on life. Something was up with Jennifer beyond all of that. By then, Rachel had heard about the "bloody wall" conversation and how Jennifer had thought she'd seen the ghosts of a family that allegedly had been slaughtered inside the rented home.

"You okay?" Rachel asked Jennifer one afternoon.

"I'm seeing things . . . hearing voices. . . ."

It was the medication, Rachel knew.

Jennifer was scared. The medication had changed her so much. On some days, she couldn't function. It's unclear if Jennifer was also using other drugs along with the prescribed medications. Nonetheless, the meds were doing a number on her psyche.

Rachel took some time off from work and brought Jennifer to a hospital in St. Pete, and then found a facility closer to their home in Spring Hill. They checked her into the psychiatric ward for evaluation. It was the first time Rachel felt that Jennifer might be having a nervous breakdown.

"She wasn't there very long," Rachel explained,

"maybe four days or so, but the medicines that they had put her on in the months prior had made her not only gain so much weight, but messed with her mind. It was such a rough time mentally for Jennifer."

She seemed to be losing her mind.

Rachel said she often wondered if the medication kept Jennifer from focusing on her school work as she was being tutored, so Jennifer decided to take the easy road of quitting school altogether.

"I don't know how she ever made it through that time in her life because of those medications," Rachel concluded. "The hiccups, her problems with Chris, the meds, I don't know how she did it."

One thing was clear, however: Jennifer Mee was ill-equipped to go off on her own and begin a life away from the family. As it was, she was barely home, anyway, often staying with friends, at motels, or finding somewhere to crash for the night. And yet, that's what Jennifer was thinking about as the summer of 2009 progressed and she prepared to celebrate her eighteenth birthday with word that Chris was coming home.

CHAPTER 48

FROM THE MOMENT he walked in the door and set his suitcases on the floor inside the living room, greeting most everyone with hugs and saying, "I missed you so much," Chris realized nothing had changed where

Jennifer was concerned—but had perhaps even gotten worse.

Jennifer gave him the cold shoulder. She was not happy Chris was back.

"Hope beyond hope" was what Chris had as he stepped back into the family fold. He wanted to "fix things" with Jennifer, Chris explained later on.

That wasn't going to be the case, however.

From the onset, Chris felt Jennifer did not want him there. And, indeed, for the lifestyle Jennifer had gotten used to since Chris had left, his presence was a direct threat to her freedom and ability to be able to come and go as she pleased and do whatever she wanted. Jennifer could get things over on Rachel, because Rachel had spent a lot of time outside the home. While Chris had been gone, Rachel watched the kids on most nights (when she didn't stay at her parents' house), while Chris's brother helped out when Rachel wasn't around. For Jennifer, doing her thing was easy. But Jennifer knew she could not get anything over on Chris. Her lifestyle had changed a bit after they moved north, but she was still hanging with the same people and doing drugs and involved in the "gangsta" lifestyle back in St. Pete.

What played a major role in the demise of the family the first time was that "Jennifer never did anything insulting to me in Rachel's presence," Chris explained. "That played a big part in all of this."

When Rachel was in the house, it was "Hi, Dad! How's it going? I love you."

Chris would roll his eyes. He couldn't get Rachel to understand that it was all an act. To Rachel, "Jennifer was trying . . ."

When Rachel wasn't around, Jennifer would tell Chris, "Look, you do your thing and I'll do mine." She drew a clear line: *"Stay the hell out of my way. I'll stay out of yours."*

That worked out well for Jennifer . . . until it backfired one afternoon. Jennifer was in the living room. She didn't realize Rachel was home. Jennifer and Chris got into it.

"Look, you're not going to school," Chris said. He was appalled that nothing had changed since his departure. "You're not doing much of anything to help out around here. You're not doing your chores. I don't know what to do with you! You need to at least do your chores."

"You go fuck yourself," Jennifer said spitefully. "I'm not doing *any* of that."

Rachel was in the other room. She heard it.

"Excuse me?" Rachel said, walking into the living room.

Jennifer turned white, the blood draining from her face. Her "sweet girl" image had been exposed for what it was: a farce.

Jennifer took off.

Rachel and Chris talked. Afterward, Rachel called Jennifer and explained. It was hard for Rachel to accept that it had come to this, but she had to do it. "You have to move out," Rachel told Jennifer.

Jennifer was seventeen, just about to turn eighteen.

"Fine! I don't want to be here, anyway," Jennifer said.

As Rachel thought about it later, she realized that when they asked Jennifer to leave, Jennifer felt the leash Rachel had kept on all the girls being so short, so taut, that it contributed to Jennifer wanting to cut that cord and go out on her own. Rachel was constantly asking Jennifer, and all the girls, actually: Where were they going? Who were they going to be with? What time they'd be home?

"All of what Jennifer did then," Rachel said, "she was looking for the attention I wasn't giving her. I needed to work my butt off to pay the bills." It wasn't an excuse, Rachel suggested, it was a necessity in order for the family to survive. "Chris was unavailable for Jennifer, partly because there were five kids he had to spread his attention out to and she was being extremely rebellious. . . ."

By then, Rachel had filed for disability/Supplemental Security Income (SSI) on Jennifer's behalf and it was just about to begin coming in. Interestingly, in the paperwork Rachel provided spelling out the application process, Jennifer's "disability" is described as starting on January 23, 2007—the day she started hiccupping. If she received the subsidy, the state/federal government would share responsibility and pay for her apartment, give her Medicaid, food stamps, and also a check in the neighborhood of $700 per month (spending money, in other words). Jennifer loved this idea. She could move back to St. Pete and be off and on her own. It was scary for Rachel (and Chris) to have to think of Jennifer entirely on her own, but what could they do at this point? They had three small children to raise, and the move to Spring Hill, in order to make a good life for them, was still there.

"Jennifer made her own decisions," Chris later said.

Rachel agreed.

Jennifer loved taking part in church activities and going on day trips with her family.
(Photos courtesy Rachel Robidoux)

Jennifer Mee spent her childhood years in New England, enjoying small-town life.
(Photo courtesy Rachel Robidoux)

As she grew, Jennifer harbored a dark secret about her childhood —
one that, according to Jennifer, would change her forever.
(Photo courtesy Rachel Robidoux)

Halloween was one of Jennifer's favorite holidays. Here is Jennifer with
her sister Ashley McCauley in 2006. *(Photo courtesy Rachel Robidoux)*

Jennifer and her family moved to St. Petersburg, Florida, when she was thirteen. *(Selfie courtesy Jennifer Mee)*

At fifteen, Jennifer was active on social media, frequently posting selfies in various situations. *(Selfie courtesy Jennifer Mee)*

Jennifer had an innocent side — and she was a beautiful young woman. *(Selfie courtesy Jennifer Mee)*

Rachel Robidoux remained supportive of her daughter throughout Jennifer's five-week bout with the hiccups and later, after Jennifer was arrested on first-degree felony murder charges. *(Photo courtesy Chris Robidoux)*

Jennifer is shown here with her stepfather, Chris Robidoux. *(Photo courtesy Rachel Robidoux)*

After Jennifer Mee's lengthy bout of hiccups made her
a media sensation and international celebrity, she began to rebel
and do things her parents felt might one day hurt her.
(Selfies courtesy Jennifer Mee)

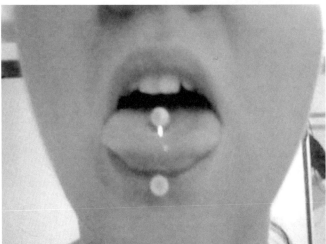

Jennifer frequented popular social media sites, such as Facebook, Myspace, and MocoSpace. She would dress up and post selfies, hoping to attract a certain type of man.
(Selfies courtesy Jennifer Mee)

Jennifer's social media pages indicated that she had become immersed in the "gangsta" lifestyle. *(Photo courtesy Jennifer Mee)*

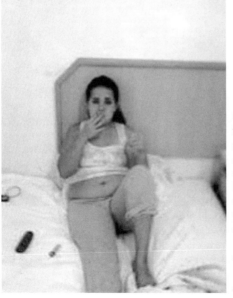

On medication for Tourette's syndrome and a psychiatric condition, Jennifer Mee became depressed after gaining weight and feeling "doped up" all the time. *(Selfie courtesy Jennifer Mee)*

Jennifer fell in love with then twenty-year-old Lamont Newton
and began living with him shortly after moving out
of her family home in 2009.
(Photo courtesy of St. Petersburg Police Department)

Lamont Newton's best friend, described as his "blood brother,"
was nineteen-year-old Laron Raiford.
(Photo courtesy of St. Petersburg Police Department)

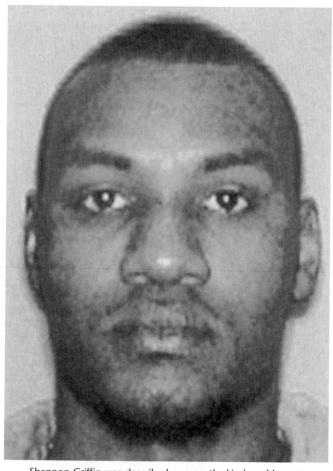
Shannon Griffin was described as a gentle, kind, and honest young man. On October 23, 2010, Shannon went out to meet Jennifer Mee, whom he had met on MocoSpace.
(Photo courtesy of Florida Department of Motor Vehicles)

This renovated, vacant house in downtown St. Petersburg, located just three hundred feet from where Lamont, Laron, and Jennifer Mee were living, became the scene of a brutal crime. *(Photos courtesy of M. William Phelps)*

A flip-flop sandal was found on the street in front of that vacant house. *(Photo courtesy of St. Petersburg Police Department)*

Shannon Griffin's scooter, which he drove that night
to meet Jennifer Mee, was found parked across the street
from the vacant house.
(Photos courtesy of St. Petersburg police Department)

In back of the vacant house, police recovered a sneaker, a baseball cap, a flip-flop sandal, a firearm, and other items spread around victim Shannon Griffin's lifeless body. *(Photo courtesy of St. Petersburg Police Department)*

The firearm used in the murder of twenty-two-year-old Shannon Griffin. *(Photo courtesy of St. Petersburg Police Department)*

EM# Item	Measurements:	
1 LEFT SLIDE	4' 3" WEST OF CURB	8' 7" SOUTH OF WALL
	SE CORNER OF HOUSE / WALL	
2 RIGHT SLIDE	6" EAST	5' 10" NORTH
3 LEFT SHOE	2' EAST	3' 2" NORTH
4 GUN	2' EAST	4' 9" NORTH
5 NEWPORT PACK	2' 3" EAST	5' 9" NORTH
6 RIGHT SHOE	5' 2" EAST	6' 1" NORTH
7 BASEBALL CAP	2' 8" EAST	16' 8" NORTH
8 WHITE PLASTIC TUBE	1' WEST	7' 10" NORTH
9 CONDOM WRAPPER	4' 1" WEST	AGAINST WALL
10 STRAW	4' 3" WEST	10" NORTH
	EAST OF 7TH ST / SOUTH OF EARLE AVE	
11 WATER BOTTLE	13'	23' 7"
12 CIGAR TIP	7'	19' 10"

These charts of the crime scene show where the evidence collected was located — including a condom wrapper (#9), which would prove to be a contentious issue during Jennifer Mee's trial.
(Photos courtesy of St. Petersburg Police Department)

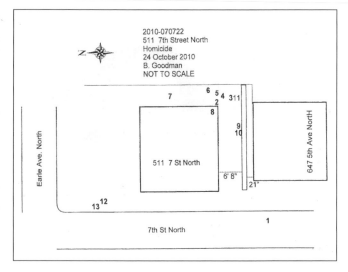

St. Petersburg PD detective Dave Wawrzynski became the lead investigator in the death of Shannon Griffin. *(Photo courtesy of St. Petersburg Police Department)*

Attorney John Trevena, a respected, high-profile trial lawyer, took on Jennifer Mee's case pro bono. *(Selfie courtesy of John Trevena)*

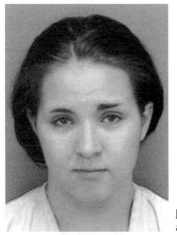

Jennifer Mee, Lamont Newton, and Laron Raiford in 2013. All three are serving life sentences for the murder of Shannon Griffin. *(Photos courtesy of St. Petersburg Police Department)*

Jennifer moved into an apartment in downtown St. Pete. In what would become a worst-case scenario, Tyrone was out of jail and on the streets. Jennifer decided to have him move in with her.

"He would take her state assistance check," Chris said.

Jennifer didn't mind. She felt somebody loved her, she later told me. Tyrone treated her as though she was the only girl in the world who mattered to him.

"I do believe there was a time when he did love her," someone close to Jennifer later said.

Ashley would stop by to see her sister every chance she could. Knowing what Tyrone and Jennifer were both involved in, Ashley was deeply troubled and concerned for her sister's well-being. She'd seen how Tyrone treated her. He'd love her one minute, but beat her the next. Ashley was there on that day, both Jennifer and Ashley later claimed, when Tyrone backed Jennifer up against a door and punched her in the stomach, allegedly causing her to have a miscarriage.

"I don't know for sure if [Tyrone] knew she was pregnant," Ashley said, "but he beat her ass."

Jennifer curled up on the couch and cried. Ashley told her, "You have to get out of here. You *have* to leave him. You cannot live like this."

"Get your ass in here!" Tyrone yelled from the bedroom.

"I have to go," Jennifer said through tears. "He needs me."

Jennifer got up and walked into the bedroom.

CHAPTER 49

CHRIS WAS UPSET. He kept beating himself up about Jennifer and how the two of them had taken a loving and caring father-daughter relationship and turned it on its head; they were enemies now. Chris continued to blame himself for much of it. He worried constantly about Jennifer being off on her own, knowing that she couldn't take care of herself without help from him and Rachel. It had been so hard to let her go. But there was nothing they could do.

One of the prickliest issues for Chris and Rachel had been Tyrone and his influence on such an under-developed, easily manipulated young girl out on her own for the first time. Chris despised Tyrone. He had no use for the boy. He was a criminal, and he spent Jennifer's state money and dealt drugs. There was nothing neither Chris nor Rachel could say to change the way Jennifer felt about him. The harder they pulled to one side, the harder she pulled to the other: an emotional tug-of-war. Jennifer would turn over the racist card whenever Chris mentioned how bad Tyrone was for her, and all Chris could do was shake his head and walk away.

On her own, Jennifer called the house "pretty much daily," Chris and Rachel said. She lived in a little efficiency. Like vampires, Tyrone and Jennifer spent their days sleeping, living for the night. They never had any money; family sources later said both spent what little money they did have on drugs, cigarettes, partying.

"He's using you," Chris would tell his daughter when she called. "It's that simple."

Jennifer wouldn't respond.

As time passed, Chris heard that Jennifer and Tyrone had been kicked out of the apartment she had rented and were living in a sleazy motel hell somewhere in St. Pete. It was almost as if Jennifer's life had followed some sort of scripted trajectory toward the final place she would end up: jail. She had traveled from home to a small apartment, which the state paid for, to a motel—all because her former landlord could not put up with her and Tyrone. Was living on the streets not far away?

Chris decided he wanted to find the hotel and stop in to check on her. Chris loved Jennifer. She might have given up on him and their relationship, but he was not going to give up on her, or stop caring.

Chris soon found the motel room. He knocked on the door and Jennifer let him in.

She seemed okay. She was nervous and anxious, but otherwise better than Chris had expected.

"[Tyrone's] not here," Jennifer said.

That was probably a good thing.

As Chris walked into the room, he noticed a bunch of Styrofoam-looking white material all over the table. There were small chunks of what Chris believed was crack cocaine.

"What . . . the . . . hell, Jennifer?" Chris said, pointing to it.

Right out in the open.

"Don't you touch that. Don't think about throwing it away!"

"What is it, Jennifer?" The closer Chris looked at

it, there seemed to be something strange about the material. It appeared to be crack, but then again, it didn't.

"It's . . . fake crack," Jennifer said.

"It's called slapstick," Chris said later.

He was stunned.

"Don't touch it," Jennifer warned.

Tyrone had taken off-the-shelf sandwich bread and molded tiny portions of it into rocks of a crack cocaine–like material. He'd wet the outside of each "rock" with a numbing agent that many adults and parents of teething babies use for toothache pain. That way, if a user tasted one of the slapstick "rocks," he or she would get a numbing sensation and believe in that moment he was buying the real thing. This was a dangerous business model—junkies don't like to be tricked when it comes to their dope. If Tyrone couldn't get real crack to cut up and sell, he was out there (according to multiple sources) selling fake crack made out of bread and teething gel.

Jennifer too.

(Important to note here: all before she ever met Lamont Newton.)

"If he wasn't doing that," Chris said, "Tyrone would go out at night and do 'hit and runs'—knock people over and take their cash."

Chris made a point later to say talking to Jennifer was like communicating with a twelve-year-old child. As she spoke, you got a sense that there was this little girl on the inside who had never grown up. She came across as someone who could be easily told what to do. When she had said to Chris not to touch the fake crack, she meant it. The comment was coming from a place of experience. Chris sensed that she'd been threatened by Tyrone that if anything happened to his project on the table, while he was out, then when he got back, she'd better watch out.

Chris didn't know how to respond. He had found his little girl. She was living in a motel with a crack dealer.

Could it get any worse?

Driving away from the hotel, Chris turned the focus inward. Nearly in tears, he wondered, *What have I done? Where did I go wrong? How can I fix this?*

"I started to hate myself. I started to hate Rachel's parents. I started to hate my brother," Chris said. "Why? Because I knew partly where we all went wrong."

It was the move to Florida, Chris felt. Rachel had to move to Florida to take care of her parents and Chris now hated them for it.

"I blame myself for everything that happened to Jennifer in her entire life."

Chris felt they should have moved out of St. Pete sooner. He also went back to the rape, a time in Jennifer's life where, he believed, "Jennifer lost faith in *everything*. It changed her completely."

It was as if Jennifer's soul had been left behind in that place where she was allegedly assaulted and the two males systematically extracted her self-esteem, self-confidence, dignity, and any will she might have had to live a happy, healthy, complete life, one devoid of the trappings and emotional confusion the trauma of PTSD can bring later.

As the fall of 2009 was on the horizon, Jennifer Mee was headed for a collapse, one she never saw coming.

CHAPTER 50

RACHEL WAS HOME one day when a producer from *Today* called and explained that the Hic-Cup Ltd. company, which had paid Jennifer to mention the Hic-Cup cup, had taken several screenshots of Jennifer from her appearances on *Today* and posted them on its website. The assumption, from Rachel's viewpoint while looking at the site, was that Jennifer had been taken on as the company's spokesperson, who would be doing sales pitches for them.

Rachel was stunned. This was something they had not agreed to. According to Rachel, she and Jennifer had signed a deal to take the cup on the *Today* show and mention it. They had not signed on to do anything else.

"They even wrote us an official letter after [*Today*] saying they didn't need her anymore," Rachel told the *Tampa Bay Times*.

In that same interview with the *Tampa Bay Times*, Rachel claimed they had been compensated for those appearances and that was supposed to be the extent of Jennifer's connection to Hic-Cup Ltd.

Rachel said the TV producer gave her the name of a lawyer and told her to give the attorney a call. She did.

After Rachel spoke to the lawyer, the firm agreed to take on the case.

"We found out about the lawsuit from a local reporter and the Associated Press," Michele Ehlinger later told me. "The reporter called me and told me about it, and I was stunned because I had not heard anything about it."

Hic-Cup Ltd. removed the screenshots from its website immediately. It was not a big deal to them. They never once felt Jennifer was any type of spokesperson for the company—in fact, the opposite was true. Since the cup had not worked on Jennifer while Michele was in Florida, and Jennifer and Rachel mentioned it only in passing on *Today*, why would they ever contemplate the notion that Jennifer could help their company? It was an absurd assumption as Michele thought about it later.

In the lawsuit, which "the matter in controversy exceeds, exclusive of interests and costs, $75,000," Rachel and Chris alleged that *[Hic-Cup Ltd.] contacted [Jennifer and Rachel] . . .and received correspondence from [Michele and her husband] offering a free Hic-Cup along with an offer for a "generous and lucrative contract for a television commercial" including "a large and immediate cash signing bonus."*

According to the lawsuit Rachel and Chris filed: *The Robidouxs would "retain complete control over Jennifer's participation and script."*

Beyond that, Rachel and Chris were suing because they believed there was "no agreement" in place with Hic-Cup Ltd. to use Jennifer's name or image in "any other form of advertising or marketing of the Hic-Cup." The company, however, the lawsuit alleged, used Jennifer's name and photographs in sales brochures, advertisements, the Internet, and commercials on radio and television. Rachel and Chris felt this was an "invasion of privacy" and a "misappropriation of name and likeness, and breach of contract." They also perceived it as "unjust enrichment from using Jennifer's name and image."

Hic-Cup Ltd. released a statement after the lawsuit went public, stating: *[Rachael had] "explicitly" permitted the business to allow Jennifer "to provide television and media product testimonials for the Hic-Cup cup that would be used in marketing and advertising."*

Michele and her husband spent "thousands of dollars" hiring a lawyer to fight the lawsuit and it nearly bankrupted the company. She met with a lawyer several times.

"We did not think we could afford to get out of it," Michele recalled.

Michele handed the entire case over to the law firm they hired and forgot about it.

"The lawsuit," Rachel said, "ultimately went nowhere."

CHAPTER 51

ALLISON BALDWIN HAD stood by and watched her friend go through serious changes. To Allison, these transformations consumed any goodness Jennifer had left in her otherwise warm, caring, and generous soul. Allison saw various people walk in and out of Jennifer's life, many of whom "were not good for her." Some of those people, Allison added, "changed who Jennifer was. . . ." There was little Allison could do, however, in talking Jennifer out of this life she was now totally immersed in. Jennifer Mee *was* her own person at this point, which was what she had always wanted to be.

Nobody was going to convince Jennifer that what she was involved in was anything other than her own choice.

It was the hiccups, too, and all of the attention Jennifer had gotten used to, Allison went on to note. That period of Jennifer's life had taken a young and blameless child and totally destroyed any purity she had in her. Jennifer was defenseless and weak against all that came her way during and after her star rose and fell. When it came to urges and choices, she lacked any type of self-control. She seemed not to understand there would be serious consequences for the choices she made.

"Not a good decision," Allison told Jennifer one day after Jennifer explained how she and Tyrone had broken up and now she was romantically involved with a twenty-two-year-old man, Lamont Newton. Tyrone had gone to jail after another arrest, this time on charges of robbery and possession of a deadly weapon (a gun). He was going to be down a long time, and Jennifer was telling everyone in her circle she was finally through with him.

Allison made an articulate observation later when she spoke of Jennifer's overall outlook on relationships: "You know, when you're young and *think* you're in love, you are not going to change your mind for *anybody.*"

That certainly summed up Jennifer's attitude toward the men she dated.

"Don't go back with [Tyrone]," Allison had told Jennifer more than once after he beat her or stole her money and Jennifer decided to take him back.

"Oh, don't worry," Jennifer would respond. "He's changed. He loves me. I love him."

"She'd go back and things were even worse," Allison recalled.

So when Jennifer was finally finished with Tyrone, it was a step in the right direction, Allison assumed. But here was Lamont Newton, someone Allison felt was ultimately going to disappoint Jennifer in every way, though Allison admitted she did not know Lamont until Jennifer began dating him.

"We believed Lamont was better than [Tyrone] for Jennifer," Rachel said later. "That much we *thought*, anyway."

"A lot of people might claim to *know* Lamont, but few did," his brother, Earnest Smith, explained. "Lamont was not someone to hang around big crowds."

Lamont Newton had worked at a local Subway sandwich shop at that time. He earned his way. "He was quiet and stayed to himself. He spent most of his [free] time in the studio." Rap music was Lamont's love. Although St. Pete was not known as a mecca for new artists within the rap industry, Lamont fashioned himself as a fairly decent rapper who might have a career ahead of him one day. "He was not someone who messed around with guns or anything. . . . He was a working man."

Lamont found out later, according to Earnest, that when he had first started dating Jennifer, Tyrone was still coming around when Lamont wasn't with her. So she had never really severed ties with Tyrone—that is, until the prison got hold of him and he was gone for good.

Earnest saw his brother as a "loving, caring person who had gotten mixed up with the wrong crowd." Part of that "wrong crowd," Earnest explained, was Lamont's BFF, Laron Raiford, a twenty-year-old St. Pete native.

Moreover, Earnest added, "Lamont never messed with crack cocaine—he sold a little weed, but that was before he met Jennifer. . . . If Jennifer was selling crack, she was doing all of that before he even met her and after, selling it on her own."

True, it was Tyrone who indoctrinated Jennifer into the world of selling crack cocaine. Jennifer later admitted this herself.

His growing up in St. Pete, Lamont later told me, was "both good and bad." Lamont never had his "real dad" around, though he yearned for a connection of some kind with him. "I always wanted [a relationship with] him, but he had other plans." This was not in any way a diss, Lamont intoned, on his stepfather, who was a caring soul who "showed me how to be a man, mentally and physically."

Lamont described himself as someone who didn't "talk a lot." But he balanced that by being a "good listener" with a "good personality" and a "good heart." Like most kids, he'd seen his share of heartache, having been close to his grandmother only to watch her pass away. If that wasn't traumatizing enough, Lamont explained, "Down the line, my heart [broke as] the love of the family, my mom, at thirty-four years old, [died]." Lamont was there. "I seen my mom pass right before my eyes and I still think about it today."

After losing his mother in 2004, Lamont said, it was then that he looked up to and depended on his brother, Earnest, to fill that void of a role model and close family relative to lean on during times of distress.

It was 2008 when Lamont met Laron, who lived next

door to Lamont's brother at the time, and they became best friends.

"We got tight, going to clubs together and making music together—we chilled a lot." It was Jennifer, Lamont said, who did not want Lamont to hang out with Laron every day, as Lamont would have liked. And Lamont said he respected Jennifer's wishes.

As time moved forward, and she got to know Lamont, Allison made several obversations about Lamont and Jennifer's relationship that showed how close they became. She watched as Jennifer, for example, "tried to raise Lamont's child as her own," Allison said. "She was absolutely in love with Lamont. They had the child all the time."

Lamont grew up in a family of two boys and three girls. There were never any problems in the house, Earnest said. "My mom always took us out. We had family get-togethers."

Lamont later talked about a family split apart by death and other problems he did not go into detail about. As for goals, Lamont said he once saw himself playing football. "But I didn't really have goals. I just wanted to make it in life, give to the poor, get my family back together, have kids. . . ." His family had not always gotten along and Lamont dreamed of that quintessential, maybe even clichéd, Southern family image of having barbeques, Sunday dinners with everybody around the table, and big holiday celebrations. Normal things that every human being desires, perhaps.

When they were children, Lamont would always tell his big brother that he was going to be a rapper someday.

"He looked up to me because I am in the music

industry, and anything having to do with music, Lamont was into. He loved rap."

As far as Earnest could tell, whenever he saw Jennifer and Lamont together, "the bond they had, I really do think he did love her. I mean, he was always with her."

Jennifer now lived in a second efficiency apartment in downtown St. Pete with Lamont. It was another small, one-room residence with little to no space. The only door inside the residence was for the bathroom. Allison went over at the apartment a lot, she said, and was able to watch as the relationship between Jennifer and Lamont progressed. What she felt later was that, at best, it was one-sided.

"Lamont did *not* love her. I know he didn't."

Again, it was as if Jennifer was being used, she knew it, but had accepted it as a by-product of being in a relationship. Because Lamont did not hit her, Jennifer viewed this as a loving gesture.

"Jennifer never thought she deserved any better," Allison said, nearly in tears as she looked back on her friend's life. Like many who knew Jennifer Mee, she was frustrated that she was unable to stop what was a fast-moving train from going off the rails.

The first time Allison met Lamont and hung out with him and Jennifer, it was spring break, 2010. Jennifer and Allison had picked up Lamont and drove out to the beach. They met up with some other friends, including several of Lamont's.

"Everything seemed cool," Allison remembered. "They were nice," meaning Lamont and his friends.

"They were boys, of course," which meant they were a bit crass and sexual in their comments and overall attitude. Besides smoking some weed and drinking alcohol, which Allison said she herself did not take part in, Lamont and his boys were okay. Everyone got along. Jennifer was beaming, Allison recalled, when she was with Lamont on that day. Just the look in her eyes: Jennifer believed she was in love.

According to Lamont, he met Jennifer through a friend who had hooked up with Jennifer on MocoSpace. "He went on one date with her, the second date, he did not go," Lamont shared. "So he told me to get with her, because she wasn't his type of girl."

Lamont soon learned that Jennifer was loose. She'd slept with lots of guys Lamont knew, even one of his cousins.

As he got to know her, Lamont claimed, he became "attracted to her personality." He was not the "type" that "cared about looks." And as he and Jennifer grew closer, he couldn't understand why she had gone back with Tyrone again and again. Lamont would hear from Jennifer's own sisters that every chance she got, she would bed down with Tyrone. What unnerved Lamont most was that Tyrone would hit her, he said, and sleep with other girls around town, yet she'd still take him in.

After Lamont and Jennifer moved in together, Jennifer's life took on an entire new level of smoking weed, popping pills, doing X and alcohol, according to several former acquaintances. Lamont never hit her, Jennifer and several others reported.

The state paid for Jennifer's apartment and she continued to get her monthly disability check. Although the apartment was close to downtown, and some might consider the area a bit "ghetto," as Rachel called it, "in Florida, you could be in the ghetto driving around, and one mile down the road are million-dollar homes. Just beyond that are suburbs. A mile from there, you'll see prostitution and drugs," Rachel explained.

No sooner had Lamont and Jennifer moved in together than they began to have the same problems with the landlord that Jennifer had when she lived with Tyrone in the other apartment. They were "playing music too often and too loud in the middle of the night," Rachel later said.

There was that, but other issues became relevant, too. Soon Jennifer was being kicked out of this new apartment because of "suspicious behavior" by her and Lamont. The building's owner, Art DeCosmo, approached Jennifer on October 1, 2010, and asked her to leave. "She just didn't really want to conform," DeCosmo later told reporters. "We were getting calls because of loud music, her sitting out front with different people. It appeared they were not doing the right thing. . . ." A few days would go by and DeCosmo would let it slide and try to look the other way, but he'd receive additional calls about the sketchy behavior and loud music. Jennifer was always cordial, he claimed, and "she always apologized" for the behavior, but she refused to change her ways. So DeCosmo was forced, essentially, to kick her and Lamont out.

Lamont wasn't living with Jennifer officially; he was more or less hanging his hat at her apartment on most nights. Lamont had introduced Jennifer to an entire new group of people, one of whom was Jenni Charron, a rather pretty twenty-one-year-old with brown hair and curly bangs, brown eyes, and sharply painted-on eyebrows, distinctive and check-mark-like. At five feet five inches tall, 185 pounds, Jenni was a strong, tough, streetwise chick, a girl to be reckoned with. Jenni Charron's boyfriend was Laron Raiford, Lamont's best friend, hence the connection. Laron was the biggest of the bunch at six feet four inches tall, a skinny 165 pounds.

"Charron was a good person in my eye," Lamont recalled.

When Jennifer and Lamont were finally tossed out of Jennifer's efficiency during the second week of October, Laron and Jenni stepped up. They lived together at 610 Fifth Avenue North, a little place between man-made Round Lake and Mirror Lake. There was room, Laron told Lamont, and so Jennifer and Lamont moved in.

From the first moment they lived together, someone close to the four explained, "They (Lamont and Laron) had Jennifer selling drugs." Further, this source (who hung out at the apartment) added, "It was Jennifer's *job*. They had Jennifer, at all these weird hours of the night, walking around downtown St. Pete, by herself, selling drugs for them. . . . She'd be hustling on the street—alone."

This is, at best, an exaggeration; Jennifer was selling drugs on her own at this time, she later admitted openly. Jennifer had taken to the job congenially, as if she had found a street calling of some sort. It turned into a release for her. It was a way to spread her "bad girl" wings and fly a little bit on her own. Perhaps she unconsciously did this more because she knew how bad it was going to make Rachel and Chris feel if they found out—a sort of punishment for the way she believed she had been treated due to the problems between her and Chris.

As for Lamont putting her out on the streets, this, too, sounded like it was something Jennifer Mee told the people in her life because the opportunity was there to blame someone else for her own choices and misfortunes.

LOL, Lamont wrote to me when I asked about this. *I don't know any woman that'll sit on the block and sell her man's dope for him.*

Lamont said Jennifer was "into a lot of things" when he met her. He wrote that *[it was] not like when she met me this all started to happen! . . . I didn't make a "good girl" go bad, that is not the case.*

All of the available evidence supports this.

In addition, Lamont wrote about his intention: *[I wanted to] show Jennifer love, something she didn't have from any of her boyfriends. Now it's true I did go to the club and make her stay home, but I didn't make her do anything she didn't want to do.*

Further, Lamont could not stop her from dealing the drugs she had been dealing since before meeting him (and according to Jennifer since she had been thirteen). Lamont seemed to be a scapegoat on whom Jennifer could blame a shitty, criminal life.

One of Jennifer's biggest "problems," Lamont said, was that Jennifer never liked "chilling with girls." Instead, she "liked to chill with guys."

The reason why, Lamont said, people would claim he might not have loved Jennifer was because he never committed his heart completely to her for the sole reason that he knew as soon as Tyrone was on the block, Jennifer would run out and sleep with him.

Later, Lamont claimed, he learned Jennifer was

even "sleeping with Laron" when he and Jenni Charron were not around.

Even more telling, Lamont learned, as he and Jennifer began living at the apartment, "Jennifer and Laron was setting up dates and robbing people."

The implication from Lamont was that Jennifer Mee would go online and lure a guy by promising him a romantic meeting. When he showed up, Laron would be there waiting to roll him.

CHAPTER 52

JENNIFER MEE COULD not run from the fact that she was a country girl from Vermont, who became an internationally known, fifteen-minute, disposable celebrity. In a brief amount of time, she had changed radically. She had morphed from a sixteen-year-old child with the hiccups, who smoked some weed, into a streetwise teen who dealt a bit of cocaine and had sex with Tyrone and other guys. From there, she further transformed into a nineteen-year-old hard-core, street-hustling drug pusher, who was sleeping with Laron Raiford and, according to Lamont Newton, planned and staged robberies. Was this all part of Jennifer's "gangsta" mentality and the life she shared on her social networking pages?

What's clear about Lamont and Jennifer's relationship was that it had been open. Both were "seeing other" people, Lamont said. Both knew it. And both respected the other enough not to "text" and "call" their other lovers while spending time together.

"Jennifer made me look like a bad person," Lamont said. "She made it look like I was the one that had been doing the things she was already doing."

Regardless, Jennifer was now out by herself, walking the streets with drugs (cocaine, pills, X), and users would come up to her and buy. It was extremely dangerous, and so unlike anything most who knew Jennifer would have expected from her. When Allison Baldwin heard what was going on, she immediately told Jennifer she needed to stop it and get herself a different life: dump Lamont, move out of that apartment, forget about Tyrone O'Donnell, and change her ways.

"Attention," Allison Baldwin assessed, looking back. "This girl just wanted attention."

Something Jennifer Mee was about to get—once again—in a big way.

CHAPTER 53

ONE OF THE most difficult things for Allison Baldwin to face was how dangerous a life her friend was leading. Nothing seemed to scare Jennifer anymore. And as Allison watched Jennifer slip further away from the young and naïve girl Allison once knew, Allison took several steps back and disengaged from not only the friendship, but the world in which Jennifer was so deeply involved.

Allison said she never saw Lamont "get violent" with

Jennifer. "But I have seen him get violent with other people."

What Jennifer explained to Allison one day, talking about what she and Lamont wanted to do, seemed so out of touch with reality (even for Jennifer), that Allison wondered after the words came from Jennifer's mouth if she was hearing them correctly.

"We want to build an empire," Jennifer told Allison. She was referring to her and Lamont selling drugs (though Lamont was not there and had never acknowledged this same dream). It was as if she had watched *Scarface* one too many times and believed that was how the real world of selling dime bags of weed and $10 rocks of crack cocaine worked.

The crowd Lamont hung around was absorbed in the "rap lifestyle," as though they were going to become big recording stars one day. Lamont was playing small gigs at some of the downtown clubs on occasion.

"Jennifer thought that was the lifestyle she should be living, because that was the lifestyle her boyfriend was living," Allison explained.

Only, Jennifer was taking it to the extremes.

One interesting point Allison made was that she believed Jennifer never really wanted the fame she received from the hiccups "in general." And that she was "absolutely not" disappointed when her star crashed and burned out. "Once it started happening (that fame), she was going to have to get used to it, either way. I honestly think she would have done it all *without* the fame, if that had been an option. . . ."

At one time, Allison lived with Lamont and Jennifer inside that little efficiency that they were booted from before they moved in with Laron and Jenni. It was hard for Allison to have to sit and watch from such a close viewpoint. Seeing up close how Jennifer's new life unfolded had given Allison an entire new perspective regarding how deeply Jennifer had become immersed in the streets.

"It was the worst decision of my life, moving in there for a couple of weeks," Allison explained. "A lot of bad things happened to me. I witnessed the drug selling and realized how people get caught up into that life so fast."

"How can you walk miles like this with drugs, knowing something bad could happen?" Allison asked Jennifer one night as Jennifer prepared to head out and sell dope. Allison had gone with Jennifer because she didn't want Jennifer out alone. She was scared something might happen. "And so, while I was living there, I wasn't about to allow her to go out there by herself."

Jennifer didn't respond. What could she say?

"Your boyfriend is in the club chillin', and you're out doing . . . drug-dealing work?" Allison said.

The only answer Jennifer could offer was a shrug.

As they walked the beat that night, a "weird car" began to follow closely behind them, so they ran back to the apartment and stayed in.

"Are you actually making money from this?" Allison asked Jennifer. She figured that had to be part of the allure, the main reason why Jennifer was doing it. You look at her Myspace and Facebook pages during this period and Jennifer had photos of money and talked of how much she was making.

"Kind of, I guess. . . . I'm making enough to pay *some* bills."

Allison shook her head. What was the point? If she wasn't making all this money she had bragged about, why do it?

Allison soon had an epiphany. Sitting one night inside the apartment, she told herself: *I know what I deserve in life, and it is not living in this little apartment, watching all that is going on. . . .*

She took one last look around.

"It was scary and so I left," Allison said.

Sometime after Allison had moved out of the efficiency, Jennifer called and explained how she had "moved out, and with Lamont moved in with Laron and Jenni." She didn't mention, of course, that she had been thrown out.

"Where's my stuff?" Allison asked. She had left so quickly and under duress that she hadn't taken all her belongings with her.

"It's with me here [at Jenni's and Laron's]," Jennifer said.

"We're gonna come and get my stuff," Allison said. She had, in the interim, gotten back together with her boyfriend and alluded to the fact that she was bringing him with her. Allison didn't want a hassle or any trouble. She just wanted her stuff. There had been a falling-out between Allison and Jennifer when Allison left, and she wanted Jennifer to understand she didn't want any trouble.

"Okay," Jennifer said. She sounded unsure. There was hesitation and doubt about whether Allison should come over or not.

Allison and her boyfriend drove over to the apartment Jennifer was now living in with Lamont, Jenni, and Laron. It was October 20. By now, Jennifer had changed so much. Her online social presence of that "gangsta/hustla" chick was so vastly different from the person she had been back in the day, Allison didn't know what to expect. She also wanted nothing to do with Jennifer and that life anymore, as long as Jennifer was staying involved. She'd help her friend anytime she needed it, Allison made clear, but that was about the extent of the relationship from this point on.

Laron answered the door. He looked upset and angry. Jennifer might have said something to him, Allison speculated.

"Fuck do you want?" Laron asked angrily, walking out of the door and pushing Allison. "You, mother-fucker," he added, directing his attention to Allison's boyfriend. "Fuck your punk-ass gonna do?"

Laron and Allison's boyfriend pushed and shoved each other back and forth, insults and vulgarities coming out of both of them. Allison's boyfriend wasn't about to allow Laron to disrespect her and talk to him that way without giving it back to Laron. All they wanted was Allison's personal property. It was supposed to be simple.

Jennifer walked out and saw what was going on.

"What the hell, Jennifer?" Allison asked.

Jennifer started acting like a badass, spewing venom at her so-called best friend.

"We actually got into it," Allison said later.

"I don't want any problems here, Jennifer. What the hell . . . I just want my stuff. I just want to go back to *my* life."

Laron stepped aside for a moment and, without warning, pulled out a .38 revolver handgun. He then proceeded to empty the chamber of its bullets in a slow and methodical manner. While he did that, Laron gave

Allison and her boyfriend a clear warning: "Next time you motherfuckers come over here like this . . . talking shit . . . I'm gonna shoot both of you in the mother-fucking head—you got that shit?"

"Whatever," Allison said. "You can keep my stuff, Jennifer!" She wanted to get her boyfriend out of there. "But I'm telling you this, Jennifer. . . . Something is going to end up coming your way . . . karma, some-thing like that. You hear me?"

Allison and her boyfriend left.

"Obviously, if you've ever had a conversation with Jennifer," Allison explained later, looking back on the way things happened, "or received a letter from her, I don't mean this in a bad, demeaning way, but she is kind of illiterate. . . . She's not . . . Well, she has learn-ing disabilities, that's absolutely clear"—which made Jennifer Mee, Allison concluded, an easy mark to manipulate and mold into whatever an emotionally stronger person wanted.

In the days before this incident, Jennifer's sister, Ashley, later reported, Laron did the same thing to her and her lover: pulled out that gun and threatened them with it one day when they showed up to see Jennifer.

Behind the back of Lamont and Jenni, Jennifer Mee was sleeping with a man who was out there robbing people that Jennifer had purportedly set up online. It was clear from his actions that Laron was unafraid of brandishing a weapon as intimidation—a handgun, which Jennifer Mee, according to her sister and friend, knew Laron Raiford had and would use anytime he felt he needed it.

PART THREE

CHAPTER 54

IT WAS ONE of those postcard-perfect autumn weekend nights in Florida. The moon reflected off Tampa Bay, the impeccably clear and crisp air breezing in gusts from the east. As Jennifer Mee sat inside the apartment waiting for her new friend, Jenni Charron, to return home from work, every once in a while a car beeped just outside the window. The street was busy with passersby, people hanging out on their front stoops, talking and laughing. All of this, mind you, juxtaposed seamlessly against the backdrop of those common city sounds any Saturday night in downtown St. Pete produced.

It was close to nine o'clock at night, on October 23, 2010, when Jenni Charron walked in the door of the apartment on Fifth Avenue she had shared with Laron and, for the past few weeks, Lamont and Jennifer. It had been a long night's work. Jenni later admitted in court that she was a dominatrix and fetish expert working for a local "spa," and had been paid to "have sex" with clients. It wasn't that she was proud of what she did for a living, but Jenni wanted to be honest about her life.

And so she was.

On this perfect fall night, Jenni planned on taking

a shower, and then heading out with Laron, Lamont, and Jennifer to the local IMAX theater downtown to see the latest installment of the *Paranormal Activity* films. They had talked about it earlier that day. They had made plans to all meet after she got off work.

After walking in and putting her keys down on the table, Jenni noticed that Jennifer was wearing a rather sharp-looking dress. She thought it was a bit much for the movies, but hey, whatever. Jennifer looked nice when she dolled herself up like that. Maybe she wanted to wear a dress for Lamont.

"Yo, Jen?" Jenni said.

"What up?" Jennifer responded. She was putting on her shoes, Jenni later remembered. Jennifer Mee had Laron's cell phone in her hand. She seemed to be waiting for a call.

This was a fairly common sight for Jenni during the time Jennifer and Lamont lived at the apartment. Neither Jennifer nor Lamont had a cell phone of their own, and both were constantly borrowing Laron's and Jenni's.

Over the past several weeks, since Jennifer had moved into the apartment with Lamont, she and Jenni had gotten "to know each other" fairly well, Jenni said. Jenni would take her and Laron's dog for a walk around the neighborhood and Jennifer would tag along. Jenni's little sister would stop by sometimes and the three of them would go out shopping and commence to, as Jenni later labeled it, share "girl talk."

"We were two girls staying in a house," Jenni later said after being asked to recall the relationship she had with Jennifer. Jenni also had a secret she wasn't sharing with many people (she was going to be a mother), but Jennifer knew.

"Jenni Charron was real cool and laidback when I met her," Jennifer told me. "The first time I ever met her, Lamont and I went to the [apartment] to chill—we had popped some ecstasy pills and was smoking and drinking. Just vibin'. Then after that night, we just started chilling on a regular basis."

As far as Jenni knew, Lamont and Jennifer were not going to be staying at the apartment much longer. They were supposed to be looking for an apartment of their own.

"She gets a check at the beginning of every month," Laron had told Jenni one day when they talked about how long the two new roommates would be there. It was not a big enough apartment for a dog, cat, and four adults. "She and Lamont will be leaving soon."

It wasn't that Jenni didn't like Jennifer or Lamont, but she wanted to be alone with her boyfriend. They were going to be parents.

The movie was set to start just after ten o'clock, so there was no hurry after Jenni arrived home. They could drive to the theater in ten minutes, get their popcorn, candy, and soda, and then get comfortable.

"Where you going?" Jenni asked Jennifer. It was clear Jennifer was preparing to leave the apartment and run off somewhere. She also seemed even more anxious, waiting and anticipating a call.

Jenni said she then watched as "Lamont and Laron"—although only one of them could have done so—grabbed a backpack out of the closet.

Were they leaving, too?

"It's a little early to be heading out to the movies, isn't it?" Jenni asked. She thought they were all getting ready to go down to the IMAX. She wanted to shower and change. Wasn't there enough time?

Lamont and Laron looked at each other.

"What are you going to do?" Jenni asked Jennifer.

"I'm going out to get some money," Jennifer said.

(Jenni would later recall: "All I heard, I . . . They left with a gun." So Jenni knew the three of them were leaving the apartment and one of them had a gun, apparently.)

Lamont said that Jennifer Mee told him, "'I'll be right back.' [She] got Laron's phone and left." This was before the boys took off. Laron had just told Lamont, according to Lamont's recollection, "Hey, bro, come with me so I can get this money." Lamont had a "show" later that night, and it was $100 to get in. Laron didn't have the money to go, but he wanted to.

As Jenni headed for the bedroom to get undressed for her shower, the only thought that had occurred to her was: *They're going out to handle something?* Not that they needed the gun for any particular reason, or they were on their way to do something she knew much about. According to what Jenni later said, she had no idea exactly what they were planning to do. Jenni was no dummy. She understood Laron and Lamont and Jennifer sold drugs. She didn't ask; they didn't tell. It was good that way. Another way she put it was that she had "no indication" as to what they were all planning. As she went into the bedroom to get ready for her shower, "I didn't give it a second thought. . . ." It was just another night in the apartment. This was what they—Lamont, Laron, and Jennifer—did.

As Jenni took off her shoes, she heard Laron take a phone call on her phone. Laron used Jenni's cell phone when Jennifer or Lamont used his.

It was Jennifer Mee, who had since left the apartment and went off by herself.

Laron and Lamont took off after that. Laron had the backpack around his shoulder. Inside the backpack was that revolver he had waved in front of Allison and her boyfriend's faces just days before, threatening that if they came back, he'd use it.

Jenni had been home a total of five minutes.

CHAPTER 55

LAMONT NEWTON LATER told police that he and Laron, as well as Jennifer Mee, went down to "the park" close to the apartment with a plan in mind.

"Well, we were sitting at the park and someone rolls up, says something to [Jennifer Mee]," Lamont said, adding it was a "black guy," who arrived on a scooter.

To me, Lamont said, after he and Laron left the apartment, "we went to one of [Laron's] friends' house." Lamont waited outside. Laron went in. When Laron came out, he and Lamont walked "to Seventh Street . . . and that's when I see Jennifer [Mee]."

"My friend wants to buy some weed," Jennifer explained to Laron and Lamont at that time.

Just then, Lamont recalled, the phone Jennifer was holding—Laron's—rang.

It was six-one, 185-pound, twenty-two-year-old Shannon Andre Griffin on the other end of the line.

From there, Lamont's later description to the police of what happened next became vague, and he skipped over a lot of detail. Although, Jennifer Mee gave a rather telling account within the second statement she gave to police.

That second story Jennifer told went like this:

"I spoke to [Shannon] and he had wrote me on Moco talking about he wanted some weed."

"Come and meet me [at the park]," Jennifer told Shannon over Laron's telephone.

Jennifer had gotten dressed up, waited, and then took that call from Shannon on Laron's phone while at the apartment—most of this Jenni Charron later backed up with her story of walking into the apartment that night and observing what was going on.

"Where can we meet?" Shannon asked Jennifer, who was down on the block then, with Lamont and Laron by her side.

"Grove and Seventh Street," Jennifer told Shannon. Grove and Seventh wasn't a park; it was a two-story, stucco-type house that had been turned into four separate apartments, recently renovated and put on the market for sale. The windows had red trim around them, against a cream-colored exterior. The neighborhood wasn't bad; it was off the beaten path, and the main drag was right around the corner, approximately three hundred feet, from the apartment where Laron, Jenni, Lamont, and Jennifer lived. Incidentally, there was a major hospital, St. Anthony's, just three blocks west of where Jennifer had told Shannon to meet her.

"I'm already at the Coliseum," Shannon explained to Jennifer. Jennifer could hear the noise in the background as he rode on his scooter toward her. The Coliseum was close by, merely one large block south and two small blocks east from where Jennifer stood with Lamont and Laron. Shannon was essentially right around the corner. By this time, Jennifer had let Laron know that Shannon was on his way and would be there any moment.

"When he told me he was already at the Coliseum," Jennifer later told police, "I told him just to come to . . . My Playground . . . off Fifth and Seventh."

Shannon pulled up and parked on a sidewalk across the street from the two-story house where they had agreed to meet in the first place, and Jennifer was there to greet him.

"Hey . . ."

"Follow me," Jennifer said. By then, Lamont and Laron had taken off.

Shannon did what he was told.

Jennifer told police, "I had walked the man to the back of the apartment—the house, whatever the hell that shit is."

That "shit," as Jennifer called it, was a death trap set up for Shannon Griffin to walk into.

As soon as Shannon rounded the corner in back of the house, either Laron or Lamont (probably Laron) said, "Do not say anything!"

Jennifer never recalled which man said this.

That was when, according to Jennifer, Mont, as she referred to Lamont, grabbed Shannon by the neck and choked him (Jennifer claimed she saw this take place) as Laron came around the front of Shannon. With the revolver brandished, Laron "put the gun to his head."

It was game on.

Jennifer knew all this because she was standing there, witnessing the entire confrontation go down. Jennifer later admitted that beforehand she knew there was going to be a robbery and that Lamont and Laron were going to roll Shannon Griffin.

As the altercation ensued, Jennifer did not run

away. Instead, "When I walked off," she explained to cops in a second statement, "I was to the corner and I heard the first gunshot."

It was after that first gunshot, she added, "I ran and went home. . . ."

Lamont said he never saw Laron walk up to Shannon and grab him, nor did he admit to choking Shannon. "When they started fighting and shit, I . . . That's when the other Jen walks to the house, and then I'm going after her, following her, and then soon as I get, like, two houses down, I hear the shots and take off running."

When I asked him, Lamont told a similar story. He said, "The plan was to sell him some weed. Why would I rob someone for fifty dollars if I can make that with one person coming to buy some weed?" Lamont continued, adding that Jennifer "walked him to the back [and told us] she was going to look out." Lamont said he then told Laron to give Shannon the weed.

"So Laron goes in the bag and pulls out the gun!" Lamont claimed.

If we take this scenario and look at it, within the picture Jennifer Mee painted for police, two very important facts in this case that would become argumentative issues for Jennifer, her family, and her lawyer later on became utterly clear: One, Jennifer lured Shannon Griffin to that spot, carefully explaining where they were to meet, knowing that Lamont and Laron were waiting around the corner with that backpack slung over Laron's shoulder; and two, Lamont and Laron were waiting there to roll this poor soul and take whatever cash he had on him and, most important, that Jennifer Mee knew Laron kept his gun inside that backpack.

However, at this point in the plan to rob Shannon Griffin, despite why he was there (and who he was there to meet, both of which would become argumentative issues later), Laron Raiford never expected that Shannon, a big guy who could take care of himself, would resist and fight back.

CHAPTER 56

ALONE INSIDE THE apartment, with just the dog and cat to keep her company, Jenni Charron wondered where everyone had run off to and when they'd be back. They needed to leave for the movie theater. It was close to 10 P.M. and Jenni worried they'd be late for the showing. Like most movie patrons, Jenni liked the previews and didn't want to miss them—sometimes it was the best part of the movie theater experience.

Jenni later said she knew Laron and Lamont had a gun—but she had no idea that on the night of October 23, 2010, they had it with them. It was sometime before that night, while she was outside, in front of the apartment, hanging out with the dog, when Laron and Lamont came home and one of them—she could not recall who—had a backpack slung over his shoulder.

"Lamont's brother got shot at," Laron said.

"What?"

"Yeah, someone shot at him," Lamont said.

Inside the backpack was a .38 revolver. They showed it to Jenni. The weapon was unloaded then, but as time went on and they kept it inside the apartment, each one of them (including Jennifer Mee), Jenni explained, handled the gun, loaded it, and waved it around.

As Jenni was just about to make a call to find out where they had gone off to and when they were coming back, Jennifer Mee came running up the stairs toward the apartment front door. She was screaming something Jenni could not make sense of.

"I heard gunshots. . . . I heard gunshots," Jennifer said, over and over, as she got closer to the doorway and Jenni could hear her clearly now. Jennifer was out of breath; she was overwhelmed and frantic.

"What? Where are Lamont and Laron?" Jenni asked.

"I don't know. . . . I don't know," Jennifer said quickly. She was shaken to the core. Something had happened, Jenni could tell.

Something very bad had just gone down.

Jenni went back into her room and put her work clothes and shoes back on: "To go see where the boys were."

Both girls were now in what Jenni later agreed was "rush mode."

What's more, pregnant with Laron's child, Jenni could only think that Laron was no flight-by-night boyfriend. They had a future. She considered herself his fiancée. She was having his child; they were building a family, a life. On top of that, Jenni considered Lamont one of her closest friends. "Bro" was what she and Laron called Lamont—not as a euphemism, but to mean "brother," someone whom they respected and cared for as deeply as family.

Jennifer Mee was "extremely disturbed" and trying to catch her breath. She paced. It was clear to Jenni that Jennifer had been running.

"She was in a panic state."

Asked about Jenni Charron later, Jennifer Mee said: "She was very chill. I remember she would [be] very secretive . . . and also seemed very creepy. I know that when me and Lamont moved in with her and Laron, she worked at some 'spa,' but I had never been to her job. One thing I do remember, she dressed very promiscuous."

Overwhelmed by what she had heard on the street, Jennifer Mee did not know what to do with herself inside the apartment. It was as though she knew what had happened, but did not know the outcome. She had asked Shannon Griffin to follow her to the back of the building, watched Laron pull out a gun, and as she ran away, she heard gunshots. It wasn't hard from there for Jennifer to make out what had happened. As far as her dealings with Shannon, Jennifer later told police, Shannon had sent her a friend request on MocoSpace about a week prior.

"We were talking, and the first time I had met him, he also wanted some weed, but I didn't follow through with it, and . . . I finally followed through with it and gave him Laron's phone number and told him to call me when he was down this way."

A controversy would ultimately surround this case claiming that Jennifer Mee had set up a "date" with Shannon and lured him to the meeting spot with the promise of a romantic encounter. Shannon's cousin later said that Shannon was going out that night under the assumption he was meeting a female for a date. He was dressed up and excited to meet a girl he had been talking to online for some time. But according to this interview Jennifer gave police—her second—the entire meeting was built around Jennifer selling Shannon Griffin some weed.

During his first interview with police, Lamont Newton would further confuse the situation by telling detectives Shannon became "pissed" when he showed up and saw that "Jen's boyfriend" was there with her—meaning Laron. Even the cop interviewing Lamont said, "That's the kind of scenario that we thought. It was just something that when he rode up there, he was simply asking to speak to Jen [Charron] . . . and it just didn't go over because [Laron] was there."

The feeling was that Laron, who had an explosive temper, Lamont said, and could go off for no reason at times, "snapped" once Shannon showed up and asked for "Jen." It was as if Laron had no idea that "Jen" and Shannon were meeting.

CHAPTER 57

JENNI CHARRON TOOK off out the door while Jennifer Mee stayed behind inside the apartment by herself. Jenni could no longer wait, especially after what Jennifer had said while running into the apartment, out of breath, clearly in a frightened state over whatever had happened.

But Jenni didn't make it down the stairs entirely before she saw Laron running up the stairs toward her. He was wild and screaming.

But where was Lamont?

Jenni turned around and high-tailed it back into the apartment.

Laron rushed in behind her. He was sweating, even more panicky than Jennifer Mee, his heart racing.

Jenni looked at him. First thing she noticed, "Where are your damn shoes, Ron?"

Laron looked down. He wasn't wearing the same Michael Jordan flip-flop Slides he had left in. They were gone—as were the backpack and baseball cap he had on when he left.

More shockingly, Laron did not have the gun.

But Laron did not care about those items. He had one thing on his mind.

Lamont.

Laron screamed, "Bro . . . he was shot and is dead. . . ."

Jennifer Mee and Jenni took this to mean what Laron believed at that time: Lamont Newton had been the one who got shot in what had turned very quickly into a melee in the darkness behind that newly renovated house. Punches were thrown. Words shouted. Gunfire. It had all happened within a few seconds in the darkness and Laron had no idea what had transpired, who actually got shot, or why Lamont wasn't behind him. The only deduction Laron could draw from it all was that he had shot his best friend and killed him—which, right there, put the weapon in Laron's had by his own admission.

The last thing they expected when they confronted Shannon Griffin with a weapon was that the guy would fight back. But that was what Shannon had done. He swung at Laron, hit him, and grappled with Laron on the ground.

"When Shannon realized it was a robbery, he tried taking the gun from Laron," Lamont told me later. "By the time I was about to help Laron, that was when a shot went off. I didn't touch Shannon or the gun. I didn't take his money. His keys . . . It happened so fast I didn't have time to do anything if I wanted to."

Laron was nearly in tears now, crying out, "Mont got

shot. . . . He's dead!" He walked over, in a fit of rage,
and punched a hole in the Sheetrock inside the living
room near the door. All of them inside the apartment
were staggered by this revelation, scared and upset. It
wasn't supposed to happen that way. Nobody was supposed to *die*. The gun was for intimidation. It's even
clear that Lamont, according to what he told police,
had no idea that Laron was bringing the weapon with
them to the meeting with Shannon. The way Lamont
put it, he and Laron weren't a couple of thugs walking
around town at night, looking to shoot and kill people.
At best, they were two-bit, budding thieves stretching
their wings to try and turn over a new gig: rolling
people. Drug selling hadn't been all that lucrative.
Why not set up potential buyers and then roll them? It
had seemed like such a great, easy-way-to-make-money
idea.

On paper—that is.

But now this.

Laron thought quickly. He went over and dead-
bolted the door. Punching his fist through the wall
again, he shouted, "Bro is dead! Bro is dead!"

Lamont.

Damn.

A minute went by.

Then two.

Laron heard footsteps coming up the outside stairwell.

Someone was outside the door and now heading
into the apartment, banging . . . and banging.

Laron looked at Jenni and Jennifer.

Shit.

The cops? Already?

CHAPTER 58

LARON BACKED AWAY from the door slowly. He had to figure out what to do. He was certain the cops were on the other side of the door and about to barge in any second and take him away. He had to make a move.

Quickly.

Jenni ran over and opened the door out of instinct.

Lamont, holy shit!

Alive and well.

"Bro! . . . Motherf . . . you're alive?"

Lamont looked exhausted. Beads of perspiration poured off his face like a sweating glass of ice water. He, too, had been running. His chest heaved in and out. Lamont was in a state of absolute alarm.

Holy shit, holy shit! What just happened out there?

It seemed like a blur. They had set out to roll some dude and were now certain they had killed him. How quickly a situation could turn deadly when a gun was brought to the party.

"If I knew it was going to be a robbery," Lamont said to me, "Shannon would have never gotten shot." And that, in and of itself, Lamont suggested, proved he had no idea Laron was planning to rob Shannon Griffin, indicating that any plan to roll Shannon was between Jennifer Mee and Laron. He explained further how it was two against one. "We didn't need a gun. . . . Laron took it upon himself to have a gun and rob Shannon. I didn't know he had the gun in the bag."

If Laron and Jennifer planned this robbery together, what Lamont said would become very important.

Jenni took a look at Lamont as he lay on the floor and noticed he had "cuts and bumps on him."

Shannon had given the boys quite the fight, apparently. Laron and Lamont were both banged up fairly well. Laron lost his shoes, his hat, the backpack, and the weapon.

"When both the boys came in and you took a good look at them," Jenni said later, "it looked like both of them had gotten pretty physical at some point with someone. It looked like they kind of had their butts handed to them."

Lamont took a few steps into the apartment and was so fatigued—emotionally and physically—that he collapsed on the floor. His condition scared Jenni so much, she thought maybe he had been shot, which was why she rushed over and searched Lamont to see if he had any bullet wounds. There was some blood, but she learned that was from the scuffle with Shannon and a later fall Lamont took while running back to the apartment.

Laron paced. What were they going to do? They needed to leave. Go somewhere else. Get out of the neighborhood.

Still, none of them later reported hearing any sirens or cops rushing to the scene. As it was, Shannon was gravely injured from being shot multiple times. He was lying on the ground in back of that building, possibly still alive and bleeding to death. A simple call to 911 might have saved the guy's life at this point, but time was running short.

Of course, no one called 911—the four of them inside the apartment were more focused and certainly more concerned about themselves. In fact, as Lamont lay on the floor trying to catch his breath, Jenni stripped him of his clothing and tossed all of it, along with whatever Laron was wearing, into the bathtub. She then filled the tub with water, pouring bleach over everything.

Jenni said later, "[It was to] get rid of any physical evidence that may have been on the clothes."

The cover-up had begun for them.

After putting on fresh clothes and talking it through with everyone, Lamont determined that the cuts and bruises he had were from falling on the tar as he ran toward the apartment away from the crime scene. He had also scraped the side of his face on a fence near the apartment as he made his way up the stairwell.

"I think I shot him," Lamont later reported Laron saying inside the apartment as they stood around and talked about what had happened and what the hell they were going to do next.

"*I think I shot him. . . .*"

CHAPTER 59

AS JENNIFER MEE stood inside the apartment, listening to the others, she had to realize that what she was involved in, beyond any crime she had ever committed before that night, was about as serious as things could get. A man had been shot, and there was a damn good chance he was dead. Jennifer had been there and had a view of this murder. She'd witnessed the attack, even set it up, and heard gunfire cut through the clanking of the city night as she ran away.

Lamont was a guy, Jennifer later explained, who had not steered her in any wrong direction since they had met and (arguably) had fallen in love.

Where do I start? she wrote to me after I asked her to explain her relationship with Lamont. *He just was . . . damn . . . he was so sweet and sexy. Yes, I loved him with all my heart. He claimed to love me. He never showed or said anything to make me think differently.* This was written years after the Shannon Griffin incident.

Jennifer then added that the child she used to take care of, Lamont's kid whom she loved "like he was my own child," as it turned out: *[Lamont] got a DNA test and it came back that the baby wasn't his—we were both really hurt, we loved him dearly.*

"She kept a lot of things from me," Lamont said of his time with Jennifer. Ultimately she would take Lamont away from his son, he claimed. Also, Lamont believed that Jennifer was the driving force behind planning the robbery. "I would say nobody coached her. . . . Only a woman knows what to say to a man to get him to come up[town]" to meet her.

Although others who knew her and hung around with Jennifer claimed Lamont (and Laron) had sent Jennifer out on the block to sell dope, Jennifer disagreed, explaining to me, "Really, I wouldn't go anywhere. I sold dope out of my house or . . . a hotel room. I really never had to run the street to sell dope. I left that up to the boys." If a "junkie" was in desperate need of a purchase, Jennifer explained, and couldn't make it to her place of residence, only then would she embark out into the wild streets of St. Pete to meet him or her, but it was rare. "No, [Lamont] never made me do anything. If there was something I wasn't comfortable doing, he would do it." Then this: "I never really ever faced any trouble with Lamont."

One important fact Jennifer mentioned was that she would often, before meeting Lamont, engage in sex with men for money. I had asked if either of the boys had ever asked her to prostitute herself. There was some indication from a source that this might have occurred. (It definitely did not.)

"Lamont was never down with the pimpin' or trickin' shit," Jennifer told me. "I remember when I told him about me doing it. He was like, 'You don't know what type of shit these muthafuckers carry.' Hell no, I would never trick for anyone."

CHAPTER 60

LAMONT NOTICED THAT Laron was becoming more aggravated and maybe even desperate as time passed inside the apartment and the inevitable happened: the cops busting in through the front door and taking them all away.

"We *have* to go! We *have* to go!" Laron said a number of times. "You *have* to take me somewhere."

Jenni mentioned going back to the crime scene to look for those items Laron had left behind. Her reasons were pragmatic and rather simple, Jenni later claimed: "To retrieve items that the boys left behind, including the gun [and] anything that would have put them there. . . ."

Help cover up a murder, in other words.

"I have no idea where the gun is," Lamont said.

"You are *not* going back there," Laron told Jenni.

Jenni asked them where it happened.

They wouldn't tell her.

Jennifer Mee kind of stood off by herself during this time, not saying much of anything, not offering any advice those there could later recall. Jennifer, the consummate follower and people pleaser, was going to go along with whatever the others decided. That was her nature. That was her routine. That was her role within this foursome.

After calling a friend, Jenni later said, a car showed up. Who it was the boys had called for a ride was someone she did not know.

They all got into the car and took off to "South St. Pete," heading toward an apartment a few friends of the boys lived at. Jenni said later she had never been there before that night.

Jenni got scared. She didn't want to hang out anywhere the boys could be tied back to, because of the obvious heat that was about to be cast upon them as soon as Shannon Griffin's body was discovered. By now, all of them felt and agreed Shannon was dead.

So Jenni called a cab and decided to take everyone to her friend's house. No one would suspect they'd be hiding there.

Something bothered Jenni: her fingerprints on the gun. She had handled the weapon while it was inside the house. All of them (with the exception of Jennifer Mee, Jenni later testified) had held that gun at some point. She was worried the gun would be recovered and she would be brought into a murder she'd had, by her admission, nothing to do with. What's more, her so-called fiancé had been involved in an armed robbery that had resulted in a murder—she wanted to protect him. He was the father of her child. She had no idea, of course, that behind her back, Laron was having sex with Jennifer Mee whenever the opportunity arose.

Jenni called her friend on the way to her apartment. She lied: "Hey, is it okay with you if I bring the boys over with me? We got into a little argument with the landlord and we kind of need a place to stay for the night until everything calms down."

"Yeah, sure, I'm leaving, anyway . . . going over my boyfriend's. My house is your house, Jenni."

Jennifer Mee, Jenni, Lamont, and Laron stayed at Jenni's friend's apartment on that Saturday night, while her friend stayed at her boyfriend's house. While they were there, Jenni later said, all of them, at some point, talked about what they were going to say to the police if and when they came around asking questions.

They needed to get their stories straight.

They needed a narrative they could all agree on.

And they also needed to get rid of all of Shannon's belongings that one of them had taken from the crime scene (though no one ever later took responsibility for grabbing the items), all of which Jennifer Mee had placed inside a supermarket shopping bag back at the apartment and had brought with them to Jenni's friend's home.

CHAPTER 61

HE LIVED IN a section of downtown that local St. Pete residents referred to as historic uptown, right around the corner from 511 Seventh Street North. He had moved into the apartment just a month before that tragic night of October 23, 2010.

A lawyer with his own practice, Jason Brazelton had been up later than usual on this night. He was out taking his girlfriend's toy poodle for a casual walk around the neighborhood. It had been such a pleasant night, so peaceful and serene. The weather was nearly ideal by native Floridian standards. And yet, Jason later noted, he felt something odd that night—something different and even strange.

After walking into the house, after walking the dog, as Jason got settled, he had heard what sounded to him like fireworks coming from a direction nearby, sounds that Jason later described as a "rock . . . hitting a tin roof."

Who thinks *gunshots* when they hear pops in the dead of night in the city? Our brains are trained to go right to car exhaust backfire or fireworks—casual, everyday noises we're used to hearing—but gunshots?

Not a chance.

After going over what just occurred in his analytically trained mind, Jason reasoned that someone was trying to break into a garage he had disconnected from his house and that person had possibly broken a piece of wood, hence the popping sounds.

So Jason ran out of the house and had a look around.

"But I didn't see anything," he said.

Thinking back to that noise, Jason added, "It was very . . . loud, obviously, and I remember it because the repetition of it sounded like gunfire, but the noise itself sounded like something else. . . . My first instinct was I thought someone was trying to break in. So . . . I went outside and kind of walked around the house."

Jason decided to take a close look around the building and immediate area. He was curious and needed to know where the noise came from.

He grabbed a flashlight and began searching. Having already experienced what Jason thought to be a "weird night altogether," it wasn't long before he pointed the flashlight toward the back of a nearby vacant home for sale and came upon "somebody laying there."

Homeless person, Jason thought immediately. Some poor soul, with nowhere to go, passed out on the ground, sleeping off his latest Mad Dog 20/20 binge. The house the man was behind had been vacant, Jason knew, so it was likely a hot spot for area homeless to frequent.

With his light directly pointed at the guy, Jason turned it off quickly, not wanting to startle him awake.

When Jason got back home, he told his girlfriend what he had seen.

"Well, you should probably call the nonemergency police line and report it," she suggested.

So Jason called the police to report a homeless man sleeping off a bender behind a vacant house near Millennium Youth Park.

Fifteen minutes later, Jason looked out his window and saw lights flashing around the scene.

The police had arrived.

CHAPTER 62

THE FIRST COP on the scene used his department-issued flashlight, and, with another cop in tow, both made their way to the back of the building on Seventh Street North. The rear of the home was cave dark and a tight squeeze around the fences and concrete barriers if you didn't know where you were going. As they approached what one of them later referred to in his report as "the sleeping man," they nearly stumbled over "two sneakers" and a "sandal on the ground," along with a "firearm (revolver) that was pointed in the direction" of the man.

The man was lying on the south side of what appeared to be a concrete retaining wall. He had no shoes on and his hands were "extended over his head." His eyes were "glazed over and half open." A small amount of blood inside his mouth and nose was visible. He wore a red Ralph Lauren Polo shirt. The cop with the flashlight shined it on the center of the man's chest and detected what was a circular bloodstain pattern. So he lifted the man's shirt to see if he could verify any wounds.

There they were: *three small entrance wounds in the center of [his] chest.*

The cop knew for certain that "the subject" was dead and called for backup.

The troops came out, including the SPPD's Homicide Division.

After yellow police tape was spooled around the scene and curious onlookers began to gather, Jason Brazelton walked out of his house and noticed there was far more activity at the scene than would normally be for a homeless guy rousted out of an alcohol-induced nap and then told to take a hike. So Jason walked over to the police tape fencing the entire area off to see what was happening.

"I'm the guy who called it in," Jason told a cop standing by the yellow tape.

By now, Jason realized it was much more than a homeless man sleeping off a drunken night.

Somebody was dead.

CHAPTER 63

THE SPPD CRIMES Against Persons Homicide Unit mans one shift: 8:00 A.M. to 4:00 P.M., Monday through Friday. This might sound like an ordinary office job, but each and every detective in the unit is on call twenty-four hours a day, seven days a week. There is no rest for those who investigate murder.

Homicide detectives rotate cases as they come in, meaning one detective takes a case, and the next homicide that comes in goes to the next cop in line, and so on. It's random. On Sunday, October 24, 2010, Detective Dave Wawrzynski was next up. It was early morning, as daylight began to illuminate the city streets, when Wawrzynski took a call and was first told about the death of Shannon Griffin. As for any observations from those at the crime scene already, Wawrzynski was informed that it appeared to be a robbery that had resulted in a death. Traditionally, St. Pete had between eighteen and twenty-five homicides per year.

"Sometimes," Wawrzynski said, "we've been as high as fifty, and . . . I believe one year we had it as low as nine."

Wawrzynski was the lead on this case, not by choice, but by luck of the draw. In what would become an issue for some later after Wawrzynski was accused of focusing his case strictly on Jennifer Mee because of her celebrity and her running in front of his car back when she went missing in June 2007, Wawrzynski perceptively pointed out that as far as him becoming the lead detective in the Shannon Griffin murder investigation, it had simply been his turn at the wheel.

The first thing Wawrzynski did whenever he encountered a homicide scene was try to figure out if it needed to be expanded beyond what had been already established and cordoned off by first responders. At times, and by no fault of their own, those on patrol first arriving to assess a scene don't realize that potential evidence might be scattered farther out from the parameters that have been contained by the yellow tape. As Wawrzynski walked up behind that vacant house on the morning of October 24, 2010, he looked around and made a call to extend the crime scene. There could be evidence as far away as the street out in front of the house, and possibly even on the opposite side of the street.

At six feet, 195 pounds, with his shortly cropped salt-and-pepper hair and Floridian-tanned skin, Dave Wawrzynski cut an imposing, professional figure. He looked the part of detective: from his general blue dress shirts against dark slacks and sport coat to match, to the gold shield dangling from his neck and firearm strapped to his side.

Coming upon Shannon's body, Wawrzynski considered that the area wasn't particularly a known drug hangout or dope-selling region of the city known to cops. It was sort of away from the main path and tucked away in back of a fairly nice home.

"As much as the media wanted to make it out as one, it wasn't," Wawrzynski recalled, speaking to a later idea that Shannon Griffin had been murdered in a drug-saddled neighborhood. "Anywhere in the city can be a drug area today."

Standing over Shannon's body, studying what they had, Wawrzynski made the determination immediately that Shannon wasn't dressed as someone who had gone out to buy dope. Shannon wore nicely pressed, new jeans and a white tank-top T-shirt underneath a new Polo shirt. Moreover, he had on "clean white socks, because his shoes had come off during the struggle," Wawrzynski pointed out, "and it appeared that his pockets were turned out . . . and his pants were unzipped and pulled down just below his undergarments."

That evidence by itself told the detective this didn't seem to be a hasty robbery-gone-wrong situation. There was some organization to the crime—or at least the after party Shannon's killer or killers had at the scene.

He was going somewhere else became Wawrzynski's first observation. *Why he is behind this renovated, vacant building, it doesn't add up.*

"Either before or after he was dead, somebody went through his pockets," Wawrzynski said to a colleague, standing there, trying to wrap his mind around a motive.

"Rabbit ears," cops call it when a victim's pockets

are turned inside out. It's a common phenomenon in the city.

"What would come up later," Wawrzynski said, "during trial, was why did he have his pants down? Well, that's a very common thing nowadays when people rob people."

As a perpetrator, you come upon a potential victim, you demand he take off his shoes and either pull his pants down or ask him to take them off completely, so when the robbery is over, the victim has to basically re-dress before chasing after you.

"Could it be indicative of a sexual act taking place?" Wawrzynski asked rhetorically. "Sure," he said, answering his own question, "but it's just as indicative of a robbery."

Homicide cops have to look at all possible scenarios.

Everything Shannon might have had on him was gone: phone, wallet, watch, and jewelry. He had been stripped of all his personal possessions.

"And so, you look at this, and we're back to robbery," Wawrzynski concluded.

Turning, checking out the scene around where he was standing and what was left behind, as Wawrzynski put it, "Somebody gave us a big gift."

The murder weapon.

Wawrzynski walked over to the southeast corner of the building by a white fence, and there on the ground was the weapon sitting on top of the concrete walkway, a yellow evidence card next to it.

How 'bout that!

Next to the gun was a pack of Newport cigarettes, a "right shoe" (a red-and-black high-top sneaker), a "right slide" (flip-flop), a matching left sneaker to the other one, left closer to the fence, but still near the body, and an empty water bottle. Several yards north of those items lay a baseball cap. Heading directly west of the body and all of that evidence was a small alley, about seven feet wide, separating 511 Seventh Street North and the house to the right of the crime scene, 647 Fifth Avenue North, with a small garage between them. In that alley, around the corner from the body, maybe forty feet away, was a "condom wrapper" and a straw. Out on Seventh Street North, police located the left "slider" and a second water bottle.[13]

The obvious note Wawrzynski took away from staring at all of this was that the victim had certainly been lured or forced back into this area of the vacant house, either under a ruse or he was overpowered. Otherwise, there would be no other reason for him to go back there in the first place.

"It wasn't a transient walkway or anything like that," Wawrzynski commented. It wasn't a place walkers would cut through, either. "It's a fenced-in area with a decorative wall, and so there was no reason to be back there unless you went back there for a specific reason."

Moreover, it was a corner lot, with Earle Avenue North, running along the north side, and Seventh Street North, parallel to the east. It was unlikely someone would simply wander back there. But let's say you wanted to bring someone back there and rob them; then it was the perfect space: dark and out of view from the main street.

One of the flip-flops had been left close to Shannon's legs; the other one in the street out front. Wawrzynski deduced from that evidence that the sneakers were likely Shannon's, while the slides had fallen off as his murderer either struggled with him, fled the scene, or a combination of both.

As far as homicides go, this one wasn't planned or thought through all that much; it was clear from the evidence that it happened in the moment and had perhaps been a crime of opportunity.

Yet, that being said, as Wawrzynski considered what evidence he had at this point, why was the victim here? He had to have come to this location for a purpose. Did he live in the area? Did he know someone from the neighborhood? What was it that brought this man here on this night at the time he arrived?

The next move for Wawrzynski was to set the boys out to recanvass the neighborhood, knock on doors, ask questions, and see what they could come up with. Patrol had done a partial canvass right after arriving on the scene. But it's one thing for patrol officers to walk around and find out what the neighbors saw or heard; it's quite another for Homicide detectives, after studying the crime scene, to then go out and ask pointed questions.

As they did that, almost immediately, something became apparent: the scooter that had been parked on the opposite side of the street throughout the entire night and into sunup did not belong to anyone in the neighborhood. The SPPD could account for all the vehicles parked up and down the street. However, this black-and-white Peace Sports VIP scooter, standing up on its kickstand across the sidewalk, its front tire actually in someone's driveway, did not have an owner.

So whose was it?

"I bet that's how our victim got here," Wawrzynski said.

CHAPTER 64

JENNI CHARRON WENT to work the next morning "like it was another day," so as not to draw any attention to her or her boyfriend, Laron Raiford. Laron had been up most of the night, frantically trying to figure out his next move.

Jennifer Mee, Laron, and Lamont were still at Jenni's friend's apartment, where they had spent the night after the murder. Hedging their bets that there was no way the homicide could be tied back to them, they decided to wait it out there. Just before the early hours of October 24 had broken, Laron had second thoughts about staying in town and texted a friend, hoping she could help.

I GOT GET OUT OF ST. PETE MAN, ASAP

Y, the friend texted back.

KILLED SUM1 . . . LETS DO IT

Almost ten hours passed before Laron and the girl exchanged texts again; it was now after nine o'clock on that October 24 morning. The crime scene was bustling with Wawrzynski and detectives from Homicide already making great strides in putting together a victimology on Shannon Griffin to determine the final hours of his life, what he was doing, and, most important, who it was he had gone off to meet.

The SPPD had run the tag on the scooter and had
come up with a hit: Shannon Andre Griffin, a twenty-
two-year-old man from the opposite end of St. Pete.
Just as Wawrzynski had thought, Shannon was far away
from where he lived and had no reason that they could
immediately determine to be in the neighborhood
where he had died.

So the SPPD had a name and an address. Wawrzynski would have done it himself, but he was busy working
another lead, so he sent another detective from the
team to make contact with Shannon's family and let
them know Shannon had been the victim of a homicide. But also, the officer should find out any prelimi-
nary information that could help the case. It was
obvious this would be one of those forty-eight-hour
cases: solve it quick and lock up your man, or wait it
out and suffer the consequences of it going cold.

Doug Bolden, Shannon Griffin's cousin, had lived
in St. Pete for the past ten or more years on the day the
SPPD knocked on his door and relayed the grave news.
Doug was stunned by the death of Shannon as he cried
his way through the initial pain and shock. For Doug,
those tears mourned a cousin who was known as someone who never messed with anyone, someone for whom
doing the right thing was the only choice, and giving
the shirt off his back to help another human being was
how the man had lived his short life.

After the initial shudder of hearing for the first time
that his cousin had been found murdered on the opposite end of the city, Doug explained how happy
Shannon was just about twelve hours before as he celebrated his one-year anniversary to the day of working
for Walmart and had plans to go out. That Saturday

was the start of his first fully paid one week's vacation. Shannon had worked his ass off all year for it.

"He was real bubbly, really excited about earning his first week off," Doug said. "He was planning on going out. We were talking about going to the mall. And then he told me that he had met someone online." Shannon had a smile on his face as he told his older cousin about the online girl he had met. He was enthusiastic about the "date" he had set up with the girl. "I'm going out to see a young lady," Shannon had joyously told Doug.

"So you're blowing me off?" Doug said jokingly.

"And from there, he got dressed and put on his best gear," Doug explained.

What made Doug so certain that Shannon was leaving to go meet the girl he had been speaking to online—someone with whom Shannon seemed to think he wanted to begin a romance—was that Shannon, as he left, "[smelled] like a bunch of cologne— my whole house had cologne in it," Doug recalled.

Shannon stood by the door. "Hey, I'm going out." Again, he said: "I met a young lady!"

He was happy. He was like a high-school kid going to the prom.

Doug Bolden was elated for his cousin, quite excited to see Shannon getting out on the town and meeting new people. Shannon was a guy who never missed work. He was a dedicated employee.

"I was so proud of him," Doug said. "I brought him over here not as just a relative, but as a mentor [for him]. And he came over here—before he came over here, he was pretty much . . . We have a farm in Mississippi . . . and ever since Hurricane Katrina he was shell-shocked. He really went into hisself. He left school. And when I brought him over here, I was real excited to give him the opportunity for a fresh breath of air."

Shannon had been devastated by what he saw during and after Katrina: the homelessness, the suffering of his fellow neighbors, the loss of life and property. It all weighed heavily on this caring young soul. He had given up on most things, becoming quite disillusioned by what life and Mother Nature could throw at you without warning. But once he moved to Florida, under Doug's loving guidance and cautious teaching and genuine encouragement, Shannon had gotten his GED, began working at Walmart, and his outlook on life had changed. For Doug, who was quite a bit older than his cousin, it was "like watching my own son" flourish in life.

Then Doug mentioned the scooter. Shannon had bought it for himself. He took a loan. He worked for it, Doug acknowledged. And so this one night of him leaving, going to see a girl, had made Doug even happier because Shannon had never gone out and treated himself that much.

"I was just so excited," Doug said, again beginning to cry, "to see him . . . meet a friend."

CHAPTER 65

DETECTIVE DAVE WAWRZYNSKI jumped on what seemed to be an encouraging lead early that morning after Homicide investigators realized a business near the murder scene had a security camera pointed at the house where the crime had taken place. What a lucky break it would be if they had video of the murder.

"Actually, we had a lightning strike a few days ago," the woman inside the office explained, "and it wiped out all of our security."

That's the way investigations go: hot and cold. Wawrzynski walked out of the office disappointed, but he knew that even with this setback the murder they were looking into was not going to take weeks or even months of investigation to solve. That was clear from the evidence left behind at the scene.

The more frustrating murders to solve—at least those similar to this one—involved high-risk victims (which Shannon certainly was not), such as prostitutes, drug addicts buying dope, drug pushers selling dope, or the johns frequenting prostitutes. Those types of victims are difficult to pin down because they have access to so many people who are participating in the same types of behaviors that they are. Because of that, the pool of suspects grows exponentially as the case opens up, and generally no one on the street wants to get involved or talk. When you have an upstanding citizen with a good job, a young man who has never been in any trouble and lived with a good family—a man otherwise minding his own business—the list of people he could have come in contact with throughout the course of his night was very small. Not only that, but Doug Bolden already had reported to SPPD detectives that Shannon was a recluse. The deceased had kept to himself.

And he had a cell phone.

"Who they are and what they did in their lives never changes how we approach or treat the victims of a homicide," Wawrzynski made clear. "But it does change our approach as to how we go about investigating and open other alternative options and avenues that make closing the cases more likely, in my opinion."

Wawrzynski was optimistic. The fact that Shannon Griffin was found in a place nowhere near where he lived, in an area of the city where he normally did not visit, gave Wawrzynski some sense that they were going to be able to find someone that knew why Shannon was there on *that* specific night at *that* specific time.

And then the first big break: Doug Bolden provided the SPPD with Shannon's phone number. Homicide did not have Shannon's phone, but Doug told investigators that Shannon had it with him when he left the house and was obviously going to use it to communicate with the girl he had made plans to meet.

So Homicide had department communications contact the phone company and see what they could come up with on short notice.

"And every once in a while, well, you get lucky," Wawrzynski noted.

Within a few hours, the SPPD had a plethora of data to sift through, including the last phone number Shannon Griffin had called, who owned that phone number, the address of that person, the location where Shannon actually was on the street when he made the call, where the other person he spoke to was located when the call had been received, and what time he had made the call or calls.

Basically, the SPPD had a timeline of Shannon's night, on top of the person he was talking to—or, rather, at least the name of the person who owned the phone that was used for the conversation with Shannon.

Sounded like a major breakthrough.

And wouldn't you know it—out popped one name for Homicide investigators when they tracked it all backward.

Laron Raiford.

More important, the SPPD now had an address to go along with that name.

"Obviously, we cannot say [at that time] it was Mr. Raiford on the phone with the victim, but it was *his* phone," Wawrzynski recalled.

Which was as good a place to start as any.

Detective Wawrzynski's focus was now on one suspect.

CHAPTER 66

WHILE AT WORK on that Sunday afternoon, Jenni Charron took a call from someone in Laron's family. At some point before that, Laron and his friend had started to once again text back and forth, picking up their conversation from the previous night. This time, there was a bit more urgency and panic.

THEY LOOKIN 4 ME CALL MY UNZ PLZ, Laron texted his friend at 9:29 A.M. on Sunday.

HW U KNW THAT

THEY CALLIN ME N CAME MY UNKS LOOKIN 4 ME

DAMN

Then Laron admitted for the second time: I KILLED
SUMBODY

Laron's friend didn't respond.

TXT BCK PLZ AM NT LIEIN ... DID U CALL MY UNK,
Laron texted, obviously nervous and concerned, wanting to make it clear that he was serious about what he
had just shared.

No response.

Laron's uncle called Jenni and explained what was
going on.

After she hung up with Laron's uncle, Jenni took a
second call.

"This is [a detective] from the St. Pete PD, Homicide. . . .
We got your number from our investigation . . . and—"

"I'm working right now," Jenni said, "I have to go."
She quickly hung up and called for a ride back to her
friend's apartment, where the others were still hiding.
She then opened the back of her phone and took out
the battery.

"I gotta go," she told her boss. "Sorry . . ."

Along the way back to the apartment, Jenni had the
car stop so she could purchase a TracFone, giving her
a new phone number unassociated with any of them,
allowing Jenni, a girl who had been schooled in how to
survive on the street, to communicate without anyone
knowing who or where she was.

In Laron Raiford, the SPPD now believed it had a
solid, potential person of interest (POI)—or, if not,
someone with whom they needed to speak to immediately and could then lead them to a POI.

"Laron was our focus," Detective Dave Wawrzynski
made clear.

Homicide's number one goal from that moment on
was to find Laron Raiford and question him.

CHAPTER 67

BACK AT JENNI'S friend's apartment uptown, Jenni and Jennifer decided to go out to the corner store and get a few items. The boys wanted new underwear, T-shirts, socks, blunts, and a few packs of Newports. There was no way they were going anywhere near the apartment back down by the crime scene to grab any of their belongings. Laron or Lamont did not even want to go out in public.

Detective Wawrzynski was riding uptown with Detective Joe DeLuca in an unmarked cruiser near this same time. Both cops were driving around a neighborhood about two blocks from where Jenni and Jennifer were walking. Wawrzynski just happened to turn, looked down a side street, and then saw "Miss Charron with another, unknown female."

Jenni had a bag of items in her hand as she and Jennifer reached the corner of the apartment complex parking lot, where they had all been holed up since the previous night.

Wawrzynski had a printout of Laron Raiford and Jenni Charron in the car, which included their photographs. Jenni had been arrested in the past, as well as Laron. After they got Laron's address from his phone records, Wawrzynski and Homicide had gotten Jenni's name from someone in the neighborhood where they lived, and also from a police report.

"That's her," Wawrzynski said, staring down, looking at the photo of Jenni attached to the printout.

The cruiser pulled up in front of both girls as they walked.

"Jennifer?" Wawrzynski yelled out his window. Jenni was dressed in all pink, sweats, and a T-shirt. She looked toward Wawrzynski after hearing her name.

"Yes?" Jenni responded.

Jennifer Mee kept quiet.

DeLuca and Wawrzynski popped out of the vehicle. Wawrzynski took the printout with him.

Both Jenni and Jennifer knew why they were there, of course, but they had made a choice not to say anything.

Wawrzynski held up the printout with Jenni's photo and some information about her and matched it to her face.

"Your last name?" Wawrzynski asked Jenni.

She told him.

They separated Jenni and Jennifer—and, according to what Jenni later said, they handcuffed her. At first, Jennifer Mee told them she had just met Jenni outside the corner store and decided to walk with her.

"I want a lawyer . . . ," Jenni Charron said immediately.

"Whoa," Wawrzynski replied. He walked her toward his unmarked car.

Later, Jenni explained that Wawrzynski and DeLuca played the "whole good cop/bad cop routine" with her. "I had one telling me that I was going to jail for five to ten years for accessory after the fact and hindering and obstruction, throwing all kinds of terms and different charges at me. Then I had another detective come and actually sit in the backseat with me, and he told me he was just trying to locate Laron. . . ."

"Where is he?" Wawrzynski wanted to know, meaning Laron.

"I don't know," Jenni said as she began to "cry heavily and sob with deep gasps," Wawrzynski's report indicated. Then she said, "My life is always so fucked up. . . . I love Laron. . . . I think I'm pregnant. . . ."

"You have no idea where he is?"

"I don't know where he went or what he did last night," she said next.

Wawrzynski stepped out of the car and walked away. DeLuca had talked briefly with Jennifer Mee. Then he went and spoke with the corner-store owner and a neighborhood guy standing around. Both of them claimed Jennifer had walked with Jenni in and out of the store—she was lying. As DeLuca confronted Jennifer Mee with the difference in the stories she was giving him, Jennifer decided to change her story. Now she claimed she had met Jenni on Eighty-Ninth Avenue North, on the west side, and followed her into the store.

Wawrzynski called his boss and explained that he had found Jenni Charron, but there was no sign of Laron.

"I'm on my way," Wawrzynski's boss told him. He was bringing another detective, Gary Gibson.

Gibson arrived with their boss and told Jenni why Wawrzynski and DeLuca had stopped her and Jennifer Mee.

"Can I talk to you for a few minutes about this?" Gibson asked Jenni. It was nonthreatening. All volunteer.

"Sure," Jenni responded.

Gibson made it clear that she was not under arrest. "And she agreed to go back to the station to answer some questions."

As a patrol officer who had arrived on the scene to transport Jenni back to the SPPD was placing Jenni into the backseat of his patrol car, he later noted in his report that Jenni "said something unintelligible about guns" as she got in.

"Look, Miss Charron," the cop explained, "I am not familiar enough with the case to discuss it or interview you myself. Could you wait, please, to speak to one of the case detectives? I'm merely here to transport you to the department."

Wawrzynski, Gibson, their boss, and DeLuca now had to deal with Jennifer Mee. At this point, Wawrzynski said later, he did not recognize Jennifer Mee, even though he'd been part of the team looking for Jennifer when she ran away from home years before and had since become known as the Hiccup Girl. To Wawrzynski in that moment, Jennifer Mee was just another girl with Jenni Charron, someone they ran into while looking for Laron, the main target of their investigation.

"This is Jennifer Mee," Gibson said after he had huddled with Wawrzynski and the others and they talked about what to do with her.

The name now rang a bell with Wawrzynski.

"That was the whole total that we knew that Jennifer Mee was involved—that she was *with* Jennifer Charron," Wawrzynski later explained. "When she's found with Jennifer Charron on the street, that's it—but she's still not a suspect. Still, nothing. It's like, 'Okay, oh yeah, I know you.' And that was it."

It was an accurate statement; up until this moment of the investigation, the entire focus was on Laron Raiford. The only reason they had been looking for Jenni Charron in the first place was to find Laron.

Jennifer Mee was free to go. The SPPD had no interest in her. To Gibson and Wawrzynski at that particular moment, she was some girl walking along the street with Jenni Charron, nothing more.

Funny thing was, if they had followed her, Jennifer Mee would have led them directly to Laron.

CHAPTER 68

JENNI CHARRON WAS on her way to the SPPD, sitting in back of a patrol car, watching a row of St. Pete palm trees pass by. Jenni and the cop began a conversation as he drove. She seemed to want to talk. But her true motivation was to ask questions and try and figure out how much the cops knew.

They discussed the TracFone Jenni had on her. She said she didn't even know the number, admitting, "I tossed my other phone after I knew the cops were looking for me."

Asked what she did for a living, Jenni said "self-employed, a housecleaner."

That was one way to put it, perhaps.

"I actually own about four or five different phones," Jenni said.

The ride from Eighty-Ninth Avenue, near Riviera Bay, where Jenni had been picked up, to the SPPD was about eight miles due south on the 275. As they pulled into the SPPD parking lot, Jenni asked if she could smoke a cigarette before going to the second-floor interview suite inside Burglary to chat with detectives.

"Sure," the cop said. "You need some water? Want to use the bathroom?"

Now was the chance to do all that.

When they finally made it upstairs, before she was led into an interview suite, Jenni said, "What's going on?"

"You'll soon find out."

This made Jenni a little nervous. She asked: "Was there two guns or what? Is he laid up in the hospital? Did the dude have a knife and cut him? I just want to know if he's okay! Is Jen [Mee] here?"

They walked into the room. Jenni was told to sit down. "Look, the detectives will be in here soon to interview you. I do not know enough about the case to discuss it," the cop repeated.

Jenni was tired. She wore lots of makeup and had been sweating. She appeared to be worried and, at the same time, somewhat composed, as though she'd been through this drill before. It was hard to gauge how she came across, how she was feeling.

The officer waited with Jenni for about an hour and they talked.

"Does this normally take a long time?" Jenni asked, wondering why the detectives weren't there yet to interview her.

"Yeah . . ."

It was close to four o'clock. Jenni was becoming impatient.

"I have Crohn's disease and need to take my medication," she said.

"Give me a minute," the officer told her. He called Gary Gibson, who was working closely on the case with Dave Wawrzynski and Joe DeLuca.

"I'll be there shortly," Gibson told the officer over the phone, who then relayed that information to Jenni, making sure it was okay with her if they waited just awhile longer. He did not want to keep her from taking her medication.

She shrugged. "I can wait a little bit longer, I guess."

As they sat, the cop later reported, Jenni made several "spontaneous statements." She seemed to state things randomly that seemed to pertain to the case.

"I don't know if he shot someone or someone shot him . . . ," she said. It was unclear if this was a question or a statement. "I hope you all find him before I do, because I'm going to strangle him."

She never said whom she was referring to regarding "him." The cop assumed it was Laron Raiford.

Ten minutes went by.

"Am I under arrest?" Jenni asked.

"No," said the cop.

Jenni became passive and seemed to be weakening emotionally. She said: "I want my mom—that's all I want right now."

CHAPTER 69

AS THAT OFFICER kept Jenni company until detectives arrived to speak with her, Dave Wawrzynski and his colleagues had good reason to be running a bit late. Once they sent Jenni off to the SPPD and Jennifer Mee back on her way, they developed a solid bead on Laron, who had been tracked by Homicide back to an apartment on Eighty-Ninth Avenue North, near the Pinellas and St. Pete–Clearwater International Airport region of the city, right near where Jenni and Jennifer had been walking when detectives stopped them. They didn't know then, but that apartment was rented by a friend of Jenni's.

Hours before they had stopped Jenni and Jennifer on the street, DeLuca and Wawrzynski had gone to Laron's father's house. Laron's dad said he wasn't there. "He might be over at his uncle's place, though," Laron's dad had said, giving them the address.

The uncle had no idea where Laron was, he claimed. "He has a girlfriend. But I'm not sure of her name or where she lives." He could not offer anything more.

From there, they went back to the SPPD and did some additional research on who Laron Raiford was and where he had lived throughout his years. One address stuck out to the detectives. An old police report the guys dug up had listed Jenni's and Laron's names. The report was maybe a month old. So DeLuca and Wawrzynski decided to follow up on the address Laron and Jenni had given—which just happened to be across the street and down the block from the homicide scene.

After banging on the door to that apartment, it was clear no one was home. So they canvassed, asking questions about Laron and Jenni to anyone they ran into around the area. Several people in the neighborhood gave them information.

According to Wawrzynski, he then got Jenni's cell phone number from someone she knew and he had one of his investigators call her.

"We had a fight last night," Jenni had said. "They left," meaning Laron and a friend. Jenni didn't sound as though she was trying to raise any alarms. "They went to a hotel."

The SPPD had no idea where Laron was or who he was with. But as luck would have it, as DeLuca and Wawrzynski were back inside the SPPD planning their next move with Gary Gibson, an anonymous tip was called in. The tipster noted that she had seen Laron at that uptown apartment, near Eighty-Ninth Avenue North, thus the reason why DeLuca and Wawrzynski headed up that way and were cruising around the neighborhood where they had spotted Jennifer Mee and Jenni Charron walking back from the corner store.

"You are close," the tipster had said. This led them to believe the caller knew that Wawrzynski and DeLuca had stopped Jenni and Jennifer. "Those two guys involved in the shooting are still in my friend's apartment," the caller shared. "The police are close by. . . ."

The female tipster gave them the apartment address, and it was not far away from where Jenni and Jennifer had been stopped.

After sending Jenni back to the station with a patrol officer, DeLuca and Wawrzynski let Jennifer Mee go and then called in backup and put several officers on the Eighty-Ninth Avenue apartment complex. Concurrently several investigators went door-to-door, knocking, in search of Laron. There was a good chance that Jennifer Mee had gone into the apartment and explained to Laron and whoever else was inside what had happened as she and Jenni made their way back from the store.

A call was then made to the tipster to find out which apartment, exactly, they needed to search for Laron.

The tipster said once again, "You're close. . . . Go

just to the west of Fifth Street North—that's where my friend lives, to the left of the first breezeway."

Wawrzynski and his team knocked on every door on the west side of the building. Every resident answered and allowed them in to search for Laron—that is, except apartment number seven.

They found out the name of the person renting that apartment. It was Jenni's friend. They called the female tipster back and asked if she knew a person by that name.

"I guess you just figured it out," the tipster said.

But there was no answer when they first knocked.

Wawrzynski assembled a team around the perimeter of apartment number seven. They had their guns drawn and the door covered. Another detective went and got a set of keys to the apartment from management. While that happened, Wawrzynski made contact with Jenni's friend who rented the apartment; she gave verbal consent for them to go in and conduct a search.

The gun had been left at the scene of the crime— but that didn't mean Laron would not have a second weapon inside the apartment.

Once they were all set up, Detective Gary Gibson— keys in hand—knocked on the door one last time, announcing, "This is Detective Gibson from the St. Petersburg Police Department—we need anyone inside to exit the apartment immediately, with their hands in the air."

As he listened closely, Gibson could hear movement on the opposite side of the door.

Something was about to go down.

CHAPTER 70

GIBSON HEARD A voice from beyond the door: "We are coming out!"

"Make sure your hands are up and come out slowly. . . ."

Anything could happen. An ambush might be waiting for these cops on the opposite side of the door.

The door creaked open and out walked a "tall, thin black male."

Wawrzynski recognized him as Laron from the photo printout he'd had with him most of that day. He held his weapon on Laron: "Walk toward me. . . ."

"I don't want to die," Laron said, with his hands above his head. He began to cry. "I don't want to die."

As Laron walked out, he turned his head and spoke to Lamont, who was standing directly behind him, a few yards away. "I love you, man," Laron said to Lamont. "Stay together."

"Lay on the ground—now!" Wawrzynski told Laron. He did as he was told.

"Name?"

"Laron Raiford."

"You know why we're here, Mr. Raiford?"

"Yes."

Laron was taken into custody without any resistance or fight. The dance was over and Laron knew it.

Wawrzynski took Laron by the cuffs, helped him up off the ground, and led him to a patrol car. As he was doing that, officers escorted Lamont out of the apartment.

Jennifer Mee walked out by herself and sat on the

trunk of a detective's vehicle in the lot nearby while everything went on around her. She chain-smoked cigarettes. It took about three hours to get everything sorted out. The tipster had told the SPPD that the "second male inside the apartment was the shooter." Laron was there when it happened, but "it was the other male that shot the victim." Wawrzynski presumed that second male to be Lamont Newton. Although, as Lamont was being walked out of the apartment and was asked for a name, it was the first time Wawrzynski had heard Lamont was associated with this case.

As officers walked Lamont toward a waiting vehicle, Jennifer jumped off the trunk of the cruiser and asked if she could say good-bye. "He's my boyfriend."

"No problem," said one of the detectives.

Jennifer kissed Lamont and told him not to worry.

Lamont had $26 on him, which he asked the cop if he could give to Jennifer.

After Laron and Lamont were taken away, Wawrzynski conversed with his colleagues and they agreed that Jennifer Mee might be helpful in their investigation. After they asked, Wawrzynski said, Jennifer volunteered to take a ride down to the station and talk to them.

"We still have no idea of her involvement," Wawrzynski later explained. "All I know at that point is that the second guy, Lamont Newton, who I don't know anything about yet other than his name, who is *also* alleged to be involved, has a girlfriend who is Jennifer Mee."

The reason they wanted to talk to Jennifer, Wawrzynski added, was because if she had been Lamont's girlfriend, "maybe he told her something—that is our *only* interest in her at that point."

Jennifer Mee, same as Jenni Charron, was considered a witness—someone who might be able to help cops solve a homicide.

CHAPTER 71

JENNI CHARRON WOULD not stop talking as she sat in that interview suite inside the Burglary Division of the SPPD. She and a patrol officer waited for the detectives to come in and formally interview her as a potential witness. As Jenni sat, she looked out into the hallway and watched as Laron was escorted past the interview room, an officer walking him toward another room nearby.

"I feel much better," Jenni said, "knowing that Laron is okay. Can I strangle him now?" she asked, somewhat laughing.

"I'm gonna call my lawyer as soon as I get out of here," Jenni said next.

The cop was curious: "Your lawyer?"

"Not for me," Jenni said. "No. For Laron."

No sooner had a detective arrived to sit with Jenni and chat was Jennifer Mee walked into the same room. As Jennifer sat down, she looked at Jenni and said, "Just tell the truth about what happened. . . ."

They sat for a few moments. No one really said much. Then Jennifer Mee—whom Jenni referred to as "Jen 2"—was escorted to a separate interview room. Soon after, Jenni Charron was asked to take a walk to yet another interview room, where a detective was sitting with Laron Raiford. Laron looked rather beaten. Not in a sense that someone had hit him, but that he'd lost a race. About an hour had passed since Jenni had watched them escort Laron by the room where she had first waited. She now believed she knew why she had waited so long. They had wanted to put her and Laron together.

"Look, your boyfriend has already told us what happened," the detective explained to Jenni—Laron sat, listening, not saying anything—"and now we need to hear the truth from you so we can see if it matches up to what your boyfriend here has already said."

"Jenni, just tell them the truth, okay," Laron encouraged.

Jenni started crying. She was "visibly upset," according to a report of the conversation.

"What happened?" the detective asked.

"Blood . . . went bad," Jenni said. "Dude started fighting back. All I know is they—Laron, Lamont, and Jen—was going to rob someone. I wasn't there." She was crying harder, looking down, looking at Laron, searching the detective's face for an answer. "I didn't hear the gunshots."

"Who had the gun?" the detective asked.

"I don't know which one had the gun in the backpack. . . . Lamont said he was the one who had it."

"All right, what did Lamont say when he got back?" Laron sat in silence.

"'The dude's dead,'" Jenni said Lamont had told her. "They wrestled over the gun and it set off, and Lamont was worried that if he didn't shoot, then *he* was going to be the one dead."

From this first statement Jenni gave, it was clear she and Laron had talked about what to say—and both were now blaming Lamont, the same person they had called Bro.

"Take her back to Burglary," the detective told the officer.

Jenni was still bawling as they walked her out of the room and back to that same interview suite in Burglary she had first waited in.

CHAPTER 72

THE SPPD NEEDED a formal statement from Laron Raiford. Detective Dave Wawrzynski had spoken to Laron and gotten an admission out of him, but Laron hadn't given them a complete narrative, locking himself down to facts (as he saw them, naturally). In a separate interview room nearby, Lamont Newton had told his version, giving up Jennifer Mee and Laron as co-conspirators and partners in the crime, but adding that those two were the driving force of the operation.

With that in place, the SPPD needed a recorded statement from Laron.

Laron was a wreck. He was "visibly shaken"; he had expressed several times after arriving at the SPPD that he had to vomit. Wawrzynski removed his handcuffs and asked Laron if he needed a drink of water.

Laron waved him off and, before answering, ran to the garbage can, leaned over, and dry-heaved into the bucket several times. This was a good sign for Wawrzynski. With Laron so scared and nervous that his body was physically reacting to what was coming, he was ready to talk and probably make a complete confession. It wasn't food Laron was trying to vomit out of his system, but guilt. He needed to dump whatever weight he'd been carrying since Shannon Griffin was murdered.

At times, Laron would weep like a child, tears streaming down his face; at others, he'd calm himself, be okay for a time, only to start crying all over again. When he wore his glasses, Laron had the look of a bookish professor type. He dressed fashionably per the times. He spoke in terse sound bites, not complete sentences. He used street slang a lot. It was just after six o'clock on Sunday night, October 24, 2010, when Laron sat with Detective Joe DeLuca, who ran the interview, and Detective Dave Wawrzynski, who sat back and listened. For the most part, Wawrzynski piped in when he felt Laron was getting off track. It had been some time since they had picked up Laron. It was clear by this point that Laron had composed himself enough in order to be able to go through the murder step-by-step.

Shortly after he arrived, Laron had given up his rights to have a lawyer present, and he did it again on record and also signed a waiver.

He needed to do this and do it quickly.

DeLuca asked if Laron felt he had been treated fairly, up until this point.

Laron was calm. He had stopped crying and had gotten hold of himself. He balked: "No . . . ," he said softly, stretching the word out.

"What do you mean?" Wawrzynski asked.

"'Cause the one that's talking now," Laron explained,

meaning DeLuca, "is trying to accuse me of killing the dude that I didn't kill."

Wawrzynski took a breath. When the detective had talked with Laron after Laron had first been brought in, Laron had already admitted to him that he was part of this. Was he now, on the record, going to make this difficult and deny it all?

"Other than *that*," DeLuca clarified, asking Laron if he had been "*physically* hurt" by any cop at any time.

"Ah, no."

They then went through the normal rigmarole of cop lingo and rights.

DeLuca encouraged Laron to explain what happened to "the guy . . . Shannon," and asked if Laron was willing to do that.

"Yes," he answered.

"Go ahead."

Laron brought "the girl Jen" into the crime right away. He could not have meant Jenni Charron, or he would have referenced her as his girlfriend. "[Jen] met him (Shannon) off of MocoSpace. She gave him my phone number. He calls my phone. Jen talks to him. Said he wants a half an ounce. So we decided that we was going to take the money from him."

We.

Not me. Or they.

But *we.*

As he continued, Laron explained how his girl came home before the robbery, meaning Jenni. When she walked in, Laron said he took her phone and "gave Jen [Mee] my phone."

Shannon only had that one number—Laron's.

The SPPD could back this statement up with phone records they already had.

So far, so good.

Laron said they left the apartment and walked "toward Seventh Street and Grove." There was some confusion when they got there about where they were going to rob Shannon. "So me and Lamont walked back behind the house. . . . We're waiting, and Jen and the dude comes around the corner. Jen walks off. I have the"—unintelligible, but it sounded like "gun"—"and then me and the dude go at it. . . . Me and the dude break up. . . . I run. I hear the first gunshot. So I run . . . and hear more gunshots."

Laron said he ran fast, and he quickly found himself back inside the apartment.

"I'm telling my lady and the other Jen that Lamont done got killed. Then, like two minutes later, Lamont runs through the door."

Beyond that, Laron told a very similar story to that of Jenni Charron as she later described what happened inside the apartment. The way Laron talked through it, however, gave detectives the indication that if Lamont had not been shot, then Lamont must have been the one who shot Shannon—because Laron put himself away from the scene as the shots were being fired.

Then, pointing directly at Lamont, someone for whom Laron routinely referred to as his "blood brother," Laron added, "[Lamont] said after I run off, him and the dude was fighting with the gun. The dude shot the first shot, and [Lamont] was saying it grazed his face . . . and he said that on the ground they was tussling and that he ended up shooting the dude."

Laron spoke of them leaving the apartment. Then, interestingly enough, Laron said that while they were at Jenni's friend's apartment uptown, "Lamont's girl shows us the wallet. . . ." So Jennifer Mee had Shannon's wallet, according to Laron, the entire time. Jennifer took out Shannon's driver's license, his credit cards, and his bank cards (all of which would be later verified by Jennifer's fingerprints). As they sat and talked about what to do next, since he did not have "a lot of charges on" his record, Laron told detectives, "They decided they was going to pin it all on me so I can hopefully get less time."

When Jenni and Jennifer went off to the store, Laron explained, he called his ex-girlfriend and asked her what he should do next. He was scared. She told him to turn himself in and explain to the police what had happened.

Not once as Laron talked his way through the entire night, and what they did afterward, did DeLuca or Wawrzynski ask a question or interrupt. They simply allowed Laron to tell his story the way he saw it.

Finally, after Laron paused and then asked himself if he was leaving anything out, Wawrzynski wanted to know about "the dude's belongings." Where did all of Shannon's personal possessions go?

Laron said Jennifer Mee had them in a bag. "They was trying to burn it, but they couldn't burn it."

For the first time, it was then revealed how much money Shannon had on him when he was murdered.

"There was, like, fifty-five bucks, but then they found like five more," Laron said, adding how they took that blood money and Jenni and Jen bought marijuana with it.

Shannon Griffin was murdered for $60. So little value was placed on human life these days, it was sickening for these detectives to sit and listen.

DeLuca asked: "When he was coming there, it was Jennifer, right, you're saying it was Jennifer *Mee,* right, which is Lamont's girlfriend? And your girlfriend is the other Jennifer."

"Yes, sir," Laron stated.

"What's your girlfriend's last name?"

Laron shrugged. "Um, I don't know. . . ."

Guy was living with the woman, had purportedly knocked her up, and he did not even know her last name!

Real catch, that Laron.

"So Jennifer Mee was the one that made contact with this guy?" DeLuca wanted Laron to verify that. This was the first time that detectives had heard of Jennifer Mee's active involvement, essentially.

"Yes!" Laron said.

"She's the one that called him down there. . . ."

"Yes!"

"He was being called down there, and he thought he was buying marijuana?"

"Yes . . . yes."

There was no discussion about Jennifer Mee meeting Shannon for a date. The dope buying was, apparently, part of the "story" Jenni, Jennifer, Laron, and Lamont had all concocted to tell police.

"What was the intention when he came down?" DeLuca wanted to know.

"That Jennifer Mee was supposed to take the money. But it didn't go that way. It ended up being *totally* different . . . 'cause the dude ended up fighting with us."

With or without realizing it, Laron had put it all on Lamont. He claimed again near the end of the recording that he was running away as he heard the first shots ring out in the hustle and bustle of that deadly St. Pete night fewer than twenty-four hours earlier.

Wawrzynski asked if they ever had any weed to begin with. Was their entire "intention" the whole time to take whatever cash Shannon had on him and not provide him with any drugs?

"Yes, sir," Laron said, meaning they never had any dope. The entire plan, from conception to birth, was to smash Shannon in the head and grab his cash.

They discussed where Jennifer Mee was and how she had communicated with them as she waited for Shannon to show up. Jennifer had called Laron to let him know what was going on from his cell phone, Laron explained. Laron had his girlfriend Jenni's phone.

Several more questions by Wawrzynski centered on details back at the crime scene that could not be argued. These were things about that scene that could never change. He centered on those hard facts of the case: shoes, the gun, where they were located.

Laron named each piece of evidence and where it was located at the scene.

Corroboration.

That's what the SPPD wanted to hear. Within any case, there is always an unchallenged truth that could can never be impeached. Laron was speaking to that end of the case and nailing it.

Wawrzynski asked Laron if at any time during the altercation that resulted in Shannon's death if Shannon ever said anything to them.

"Um, all he said was, 'Pussy niggas . . .' That's it."

The interview ended at six-fifty in the evening. Not once during the interview, same as Lamont's interview in a separate room nearby, did Laron Raiford bring Jenni Charron into the robbery, the planning of the robbery, the planning of luring Shannon with a "date," or saying that she knew any of it was going to take place. Yet, he did—same as Lamont—seal Jennifer Mee's fate by telling detectives that she had lured Shannon to that site, walked Shannon around that corner into the back of the building so they could rob him, and then, after doing her job, walked away. Later, both men stated, it was Jennifer who went through Shannon's belongings and, with the others, tried to burn those possessions in back of the Eighty-Ninth Avenue North apartment building, thus helping to cover up the murder.

It was the law that mattered to the SPPD: a homicide during the due course of a robbery—even if none of them had planned it—was a felony charge of first-degree murder, punishable in the state of Florida by life in prison *without* the possibility of parole.

CHAPTER 73

AFTER SPEAKING WITH Laron, Detective Wawrzynski went over and sat down with Jennifer Mee. She was quite nervous. Jennifer appeared dirty, tired, and unkempt, as though she had been awake all night and day.

"I've been staying in a covered bus bench for the past several days," Jennifer told Wawrzynski. "I really don't have a home. I've been staying in several area hotels and apartments."

"You working?" Wawrzynski asked casually.

"No."

"Where have you been staying recently?"

"With Jenni."

Wawrzynski took a breath. In a nonthreatening manner, rather sincerely, he said: "You know you're involved deeply in this matter, and it would be best to tell the truth."

With that, Jennifer wept. She looked toward the floor and wiped her runny nose on the inside of her shirt. Through all that emotion, as tears ran down her cheeks, Jennifer told Wawrzynski, "I called him. . . . I met him on MocoSpace four or five days ago. He sent me a friend request and we shared several messages. I had never met him face-to-face before Saturday night." She paused. Then, between hyperventilating breaths: "It . . . was my idea to meet him . . . and . . . and . . . get money. I used Laron's phone to text him, and [Shannon] agreed to meet near Grove Street."

Jennifer Mee had just admitted to an SPPD detective that she had masterminded the entire robbery.

As she spoke, Jennifer's demeanor fluctuated between her breaking down and bawling and pulling herself together. Wawrzynski wasn't putting any pressure on Jennifer to come clean about everything. More than anything, he simply was trying to tell Jennifer, without coming out and saying it, that she would be much better off in the end if she was honest. Jennifer had no idea, of course, that she was actually admitting to setting up a first-degree murder, regardless if she knew or not that Laron was bringing a weapon with him.

Continuing, Jennifer told just about the same story

as Laron had previously, explaining how she made plans with Shannon to sell him a half ounce of weed for $55, but they did not have the drugs and planned on taking his money.

"Jenni didn't know about [it]," Jennifer said, indicating that Jenni Charron was not part of the robbery/murder in any way.

She then gave a blow-by-blow account of speaking to Shannon and coaxing him to follow her behind the renovated house. She even told him where to park his scooter.

"I knew Laron and Lamont were waiting behind the house."

As they got to the corner of the back of the vacant house, Jennifer told Wawrzynski, that was when Shannon saw Lamont and Laron waiting. "They will give you what you came for," Jennifer said she told Shannon at that point.

He was a bit uneasy about the deal, she said. Shannon sensed something was up.

"I'm going watch out for the cops while you get what you came for," Jennifer said she told Shannon before walking away from him.

"As soon as I walked by the back corner of the house, I could see Lamont grab him by the neck from behind. . . ." Lamont had wrapped his arms around Shannon's neck and had pulled him backward. "Laron put the gun to his head . . . and that's when I ran away and heard one gunshot and then a second gunshot. . . ."

At times, Jennifer was "very emotional," Wawrzynski noted in his report of this initial interview: *She expressed remorse for the victim.*

After they finished, Jennifer Mee seemed very different. It was as if she had unloaded an enormous burden off her fragile psyche. She smiled a lot. She seemed "jovial," Wawrzynski pointed out in his report of the conversation. It was quite a difference from the former person sitting, crying uncontrollably at times, tears streaming down her face, while admitting to taking part in a robbery that had resulted in a murder.

"Can I have something to eat?" Jennifer said a number of times after they wrapped up the interview and she agreed to provide a second interview on tape.

"Sure," Wawrzynski said. He told her that one of the detectives had gone out to get some pizzas for everyone.

"I think I might be pregnant with Lamont's baby," Jennifer said next, kind of just spouting things off the top of her head. "And you know, I consider myself trisexual," she added jokingly, laughing. "I'm willing to 'try' anything!"

Sergeant Terrell Skinner, who had no idea what Wawrzynski and Jennifer had just talked about, brought in the pizza. He put it on a table inside the room where Wawrzynski was interviewing Jennifer. She ate as though she hadn't had food in quite some time.

"Do you remember me from years before?" Wawrzynski asked Jennifer as she ate.

"I don't . . . ," she said.

He explained how she had run in front of his car years before in an alley near her home, "and I had to brake hard."

That made Jennifer smile. "I do remember that."

Near the end of his report detailing this interview, Wawrzynski made one final point: *It should be noted at no time did [she] hiccup.*

CHAPTER 74

JENNI CHARRON WAS not yet finished talking. Sitting, and still not formally interviewed by detectives, Jenni made several more spontaneous statements. Now, though, her comments were, without Jenni knowing, corroborating what Laron and Lamont had shared with detectives in other rooms. If you look at that as a cop, you can only draw one conclusion: the truth was finally rising to the surface.

"I think I'm pregnant with his child," Jenni began this time.

The cop was amazed that Jenni was sharing such intimate secrets.

"It's one of the reasons why we wanted Laron to take the blame—because Lamont has a child. But Laron then decided he did *not* want to take the blame, because I might be pregnant."

It was obvious they had all made up a story in case law enforcement came knocking, but they had now abandoned that tale. They were confident that coming clean was the right thing to do.

Jenni and the cop talked some more. The cop wasn't asking her questions. Jenni was, more or less, working through the situation on her own. At one point, she mentioned how "stupid" the entire crime was and even seemed to blame the victim by asking herself why a person would *ever* go online, talk to someone, and then go out and meet that individual in person. It seemed so dangerous, she said.

"The dude worked at Walmart," Jenni said. "He's never been in trouble." This was an interesting statement, because it meant that Jenni and Jennifer Mee had talked about Shannon, either before the crime or after. Then, without any elaboration or reason, she added, "Little Jen masterminded this whole thing. . . ." Jenni had just verified what Laron and Jennifer Mee herself had talked about by further explaining how they (Laron, Lamont, and Jennifer Mee) were supposed to provide a half ounce of weed and planned on grabbing the dude's cash and running.

"Lamont has gunpowder burns on his temple because he was so close when the gun went off. . . . Laron, Lamont, and Jen 2 were supposed to split the sixty dollars three ways." She paused before adding how "stupid it was" that a man had been murdered for $60.

"I make a good living cleaning houses," she said. "I use the money to pay rent for me and my mother. I also feed and clothe my boyfriend, and I just recently allowed Jen 2 and her boyfriend to move in with us."

Jenni admitted that she had lied when she spoke to a detective earlier. "But, hey, you can't blame me for trying."

The cop then asked, "Why did they take a gun? Couldn't Laron and Lamont just beat him up and take the money? At least, then, nobody would be dead."

"They took the gun because 'other people out there' have guns."

Joe DeLuca and Dave Wawrzynski then took Jenni into a second room and formally put her statement on record. It was a short interview. She summarized what she had been saying. It was important to the SPPD that

Jenni Charron was a witness, not a suspect in the case.
That was very clear from all the evidence.

When she was finished, detectives brought her back
to that initial interview room, where she waited once
again for a ride back to the Eighty-Ninth Avenue apartment so she could grab her keys and head back home
to her own apartment.

In his report of the time he spent with Jenni Charron, Officer Mark Blackwood said, *I was told that the
detectives considered Charron a witness and not a suspect.*

While waiting to be released from the SPPD and
driven back home, Jenni stood outside and smoked a
cigarette with an officer. It just so happened Laron was
brought outside so he could smoke, too. Laron and
another officer stood far way, on the opposite side of
the walkway.

"I love you," Laron yelled after spotting Jenni standing, puffing away. "Come visit me in jail!"

"I love you, too, Ron. Yes, I'll come and see you—
and I'll be looking for a lawyer for you."

When she returned to the interview suite, Jenni
decided to give the cop one more piece of information
she had just remembered, most definitely to take herself completely out of the equation, so the SPPD would
not look at her as a co-conspirator or accessory after the
fact. Jenni made a point before leaving to tell the officer
that it was Jen 2 who stripped Lamont of his clothing
when he came home. And it was Jen 2 who placed all of
Shannon's belongings in a Save-A-Lot bag with Laron's
and Lamont's clothes and then poured bleach on it all,
hopefully destroying any forensic evidence.

CHAPTER 75

DETECTIVE TERRELL SKINNER had been involved in many different tasks as the investigation into Shannon Griffin's death unfolded, both as a supervisor and on an investigatory level. As the sergeant-in-charge of Homicide, Skinner was a hands-on type of boss. He liked to get into cases and look at them instead of pushing paper around, counting beans, and disciplining cops. One of the responsibilities Skinner took on in Shannon's case included sitting down and speaking with Lamont Newton and then, later, Jenni Charron. Skinner had also popped in on several of the interviews the other detectives conducted as they were going on.

Skinner had met with Officer Blackwood outside that room in Burglary where Jenni had been placed after she had first been brought in.

"She doesn't want to talk without an attorney," Blackwood had told Skinner.

Jenni had made it clear that she did not want to participate in any interviews without first speaking with her attorney.

"But she's not a suspect," Skinner had explained to Blackwood. "She's a witness. She does not *need* an attorney."

Skinner stepped into the room and sat down with Jenni. He introduced himself. "Hi, Jenni, listen, I just spoke with Officer Blackwood and he tells me you want an attorney. I want to make it clear that you're not a suspect here. You're a witness, okay? You don't *need* an attorney."

Jenni was comfortable with that and so she opened up. If she was not being viewed as part of the team that had robbed and subsequently murdered Shannon, why not talk about all she knew? After all, back at the apartment, she and Jennifer Mee, Lamont, and Laron had talked decisively about this very moment: what to say and when to say it.

"Can we talk?" Skinner asked.

"Yes," Jenni responded.

Skinner asked Jenni what she knew about Shannon Griffin.

Charron stated she met the victim, Griffin, on a social network site about a week ago, Skinner wrote in his report. *She advised she decided to meet with Griffin because she and Laron got into an argument and broke up.*

This statement was in total contrast to just about everything the SPPD had gotten from Jennifer Mee, Laron, Lamont, and even Jenni up to this point. It was almost as if Skinner's report had mixed up the two Jennifers. And yet it wasn't a typo or a name out of place within the report. The details that Charron (as Skinner named her in his report) spoke of with him came directly out of Jenni's mouth.

"I asked Griffin to meet me at the park in the five hundred block of Seventh Street North," Jenni explained to Skinner, according to his report of a conversation he had with her. "As I was waiting for Griffin at the park, Laron, Lamont, and the other Jennifer that dates Lamont showed up." From there, she claimed, when Shannon arrived, he and Laron "got into an argument and Laron pulled out a gun from a gray bag and forced the victim behind the vacant house. Afterward, I heard several shots."

Based on that statement alone, it appeared that Laron, according to what Jenni Charron had just told Sergeant Skinner, executed Shannon Griffin for meeting up with his lady.

"What did you and Lamont and Mee do when Laron took the victim behind the vacant residence?"

Jenni didn't flinch. She said: "We went back to my apartment. . . . Laron came back several moments later, stating he and the victim struggled over the gun and it went off."

"Did Laron leave anything at the crime scene?"

"The gun. The bag the gun was in. A black Polo hat and his black Jordan sandals."

Skinner said thanks and walked out of the interview room. As he left, Jenni cracked a smile.

She had put their plan in motion.

Detective Skinner went out into the office and found Dave Wawrzynski, his lead detective running the investigation. He then explained what Jenni Charron had just told him. By this time, Wawrzynski had already spoken to Lamont and Laron and had gotten totally different versions from what Jenni had just told Skinner.

"I interviewed Laron," Wawrzynski explained to his boss. "He said it was *Mee* that lured the vic to that area after meeting him online, for the purposes of a robbery he and Lamont were supposed to do. Laron stated that when the vic arrived, Mee brought him to the rear of the vacant house, and he and Lamont proceeded to rob him. . . ."

"All right," Skinner responded. He was confused.

He needed to get to the bottom of what was going on. So he went into the room where they had Laron waiting. Skinner explained to Laron what his girlfriend, Jenni Charron, had told him personally.

"No, no . . . After the robbery, Jen, Lamont, and Jenni decided, without my permission, to come up with the story Jenni gave [you] because . . . I would get a lighter sentence if I took the fall for the entire murder."

Skinner sat and thought for a moment. It made sense.

"Look, his belongings are in the bathroom at [Jenni's friend's house] inside the vent," Laron said, hoping to prove that what he was saying was the truth and that Jenni was only trying to protect him.

Skinner radioed Gary Gibson, who was still on the scene where Laron and Lamont had been arrested. He asked Gibson to check out the vent and get back to him.

Sure enough, there were Shannon Griffin's belongings inside a bag, stuffed inside that vent.

Still, Skinner wanted to be certain. He grabbed Jenni and walked her down to the room where Laron was being held.

Jenni sat down.

"You tell Jenni here to tell the truth about what happened," Skinner explained to Laron.

Jenni began to cry. "I . . . never met him online," she said without anyone twisting her arm. "It was [the other Jennifer] that met him online and set up the robbery, along with Laron and Lamont. I was . . . at home when those three went to do the robbery. . . ."

Jennifer Mee had already given a formal statement to the SPPD. In a brief recorded interview Jennifer had given when she had first arrived, she blamed the others and told that same park story Jenni had told Skinner.

But now, Skinner wanted the truth out of Jennifer Mee. So he summoned for a detective to bring Jennifer to his office so he could talk to her himself.

"You've been lying to us the entire time, haven't you?" Skinner asked Jennifer. "Well, it's time for you to tell us the truth."

Jennifer Mee looked at him. She thought she'd been through this with Wawrzynski already. Tears welled in her eyes. She appeared shaken to the core.

"I will . . . tell the truth," she said through tears.

Skinner called Wawrzynski into his office and told him to get with Jennifer Mee and interview her a second time. Get it on record.

"The results of the Mee and Newton interviews, as well as Raiford, removed Charron from participating in the offense," Wawrzynski told me later. "Their statements were factually consistent . . . with the scene, as well as the evidence collected."

Furthermore, knowing that some would later question all of this, Wawrzynski noted, Laron, Lamont, or Jennifer Mee never brought Jenni Charron into the planning or carrying out of the crime, with the exception of those first stories for which they all later said on record were lies to support a story they had made up.

CHAPTER 76

WHEN IT WAS first conceived in the early 1600s, the autopsy was considered controversial and speculative. To many people, the idea of cutting open a human body and searching inside to see what information could be learned about a death felt medieval, not to mention a terrible insult to the dead and invasion of the soul and spirit. The first recorded autopsy, according to Guy N. Rutty's book *Essentials of Autopsy Practice*, was performed in Massachusetts in 1647.

Nearly 370 years later, the autopsy is one of the only reliable ways we use to figure out medically and scientifically how a human being exactly died. In Shannon Griffin's case, there was no doubt he had been shot and those wounds caused his death. Yet, as the associate medical examiner (ME), Dr. Chris Wilson, found almost immediately by studying Shannon's body, those reports from the three alleged murderers that there had been "two gunshots" fired did not match up with the wounds Dr. Wilson uncovered on Shannon's body.

In no particular order of appearance, Wilson located a gunshot wound on Shannon's "right upper lateral chest near the right shoulder," a second wound "in the upper chest in the midline," a third in his "right upper chest," and a fourth and final wound located "in the right upper chest, immediately inferior" to the third gunshot wound.

Shannon Griffin had been shot a total of four times.

Wilson put Shannon's death at 11:35 P.M. His findings included "multiple gunshot wounds of chest with associated injuries to aorta, lungs, with hemopericardium (bleeding in the heart itself) and bilateral hemothoraces (an accumulation of blood)."

Shannon had been shot through the heart.

He never had a chance.

Dr. Wilson concluded the cause of death to be "multiple gunshots wounds," the manner of death—no surprise here—"homicide."

CHAPTER 77

NOT LONG AFTER Jennifer Mee was arrested, her friend Allison Baldwin was at home with her boyfriend when Ashley McCauley, Jennifer's sister, called.

"Holy shit . . . oh, my God . . . they killed someone. . . . They shot someone. . . . Jennifer's arrested! She's in jail," Ashley said.

"Wait, wait, wait . . . ," Allison responded. "Jennifer would *never* kill anybody. What the hell happened?"

Ashley was crying. "They killed someone. . . . They killed someone. . . ."

After they hung up, Allison called Rachel.

"We don't know what happened," Rachel clarified. "All we know is that Lamont and Laron shot somebody. . . ."

The ties that bind were fraying and would soon break. Earnest Smith spoke to his brother, Lamont, over the phone. Lamont told him Laron had explained to him on that night how they were going down to the park to "sell somebody some weed." It seemed so simple. It was second nature. They had done it so many times before.

"He never even told Lamont that it was going to be a robbery," Earnest claimed Lamont told him. "My brother was going into it blind. You know, they get there and Laron pulls out a gun and starts shooting, so [Lamont] basically didn't know what was going on until the last minute."

"I'm truly sorry for what happened to Shannon," Lamont told me. "I ask for forgiveness from his family. Even knowing I didn't do it or played a part, I didn't do anything to stop it. . . ."

Further, Lamont added, the "evidence" would prove that he didn't have the gun in his hand that shot Shannon. "Evidence don't show that I took [the gun] from Shannon—it is clear that I did not play a part in the robbery."

Earnest Smith had tried to stop Lamont from hanging around Laron: "Because I already knew what type of person Laron was. . . . He used to break into people's houses and all that. I knew about this. I didn't want my brother around it. But, you know, Laron and [Lamont] were like brothers, so what could I do? I couldn't pull him away from Laron."

Late that Sunday afternoon, Shannon Griffin's mother, Shanna, took a call from Doug Bolden's wife.

"I have some bad news," Doug's wife shared. "Um . . . it's Shannon . . ."

"What about Shannon?" Shanna asked.

"He was shot and killed."

Shanna said her "heart just sunk," adding later, "He was a good kid, trusting kid. He would have never expected anything like that (an ambush)."

What would the forensic evidence prove? That it was an ambush by both men, Laron and Lamont? That one or the other actually shot Shannon? That there was a struggle and the gun went off? Was what Laron, Lamont, and Jenni first said—how Laron snapped after seeing Jenni with Shannon at the park—the truth?

Moreover, the SPPD found a new condom wrapper near the scene that would soon prove to have Laron's fingerprints on it.

What did *that* say?

Had Laron come upon a scene of his Jenni and

Shannon, found the used condom wrapper, picked it up, and thought: *What's going on here?*

Did Laron kill Shannon in a fit of jealous rage?

As Jennifer Mee sat in jail, facing one of the harshest charges on the books, Rachel Robidoux, as she learned of the so-called evidence, began asking herself all of these questions.

CHAPTER 78

DETECTIVE DAVE WAWRZYNSKI filed three first-degree felony murder warrants and sat before a grand jury on October 28, 2010. The lead detective testified to much of what SPPD Homicide detectives had uncovered during its rather thorough—albeit brief—investigation. From the SPPD's position, the case was closed; the perpetrators were in jail awaiting the state's prosecution.

It did not take but a few hours for the grand jury to hand down indictments on all three suspects.

With that done, Wawrzynski still had a lot of work to do in buttoning up the case: search warrants, subpoenas for phone records, telephone and text messages, cell towers, and all those intricate pieces of evidence (both forensic and circumstantial), which juries take for granted these days. Wawrzynski expected all of the records he was looking to get his hands on to back up what Laron, Lamont, and Jennifer Mee had admitted to, thus bolstering the state's cases against each defendant.

When Wawrzynski sat back and thought about the case, no doubt shaking his head at how senseless this particular murder had been, he couldn't help but go back to that moment behind the vacant house when things went bad.

"If I had to guess, he was winning," Wawrzynski speculated—meaning Shannon. Which led to an important question in this case that would have many asking why Jennifer Mee and Lamont Newton were charged with first-degree felony murder. "At the end of the day, was there any intent to go and kill Shannon Griffin?" Wawrzynski added. "I don't know if we could ever prove that or how we would prove that. They're going to rob somebody and kill them. Well, I don't think anybody ever discussed that or put that out there. He ended up dead based upon their intent to go rob somebody."

That was the crime the evidence proved, including three statements from three defendants there at the scene of the murder.

"And that's felony murder for us," Wawrzynski concluded.

The SPPD, Wawrzynski seemed to say of his critics, don't write laws. They can only enforce laws.

The bottom line here was that if a gun had not been brought to that robbery, Shannon Griffin would likely still be alive.

Wawrzynski said he might be naïve, but he never once thought that the case would ever become anything but a "typical homicide." He never suspected or expected it to blow up into a media frenzy—the way it was about to occur. The thought he had was that Shannon's murder would wind up on page B-17, a small article in the corner of the police blotter page, and then it would disappear from the public's judgmental eye.

His entire contact with Jennifer Mee, Wawrzynski wanted to point out, "was a microcosm, about ten minutes on that Sunday evening . . . other than seeing her through the windshield of my car as I almost ran her over. I was in her house one time . . . and I don't even think I spoke to a living soul. For me . . . what made [Jennifer Mee] *her* is no different from other people that have lost their way."

The detective said he got the impression that as she admitted to her role in the crimes, sitting and speaking about it all, Jennifer "did not realize how significant a problem all of this was going to be in her life."

Part of what saddened Wawrzynski about Jennifer, Laron, and Lamont was how nonchalant they were after they had finished giving the SPPD the truth. How they all sat around eating pizza while waiting to be taken off to Pinellas County Jail. They seemed so relaxed and unaffected by the circumstances that had put them there. It was as if none of them "understood that they had taken a life."

Of course, they knew Shannon was dead and that they had killed him. But as Wawrzynski listened to each defendant talk afterward, and observed how they acted, joking around and laughing out loud at each other, he emphasized, "I don't think they understood what that meant—the taking of a life!"

Wawrzynski additionally commented, "I could not understand why this case was something the media felt they needed to pick up on—and, like a lot of these cases, the victim, Shannon Griffin, gets lost in it all. For the families involved, it's a life-altering moment."

As Jennifer was brought before the judge and was refused bond, Wawrzynski was there to testify. Afterward, he chatted with someone from *Today,* a producer in Florida covering the fall of Jennifer Mee, aka the Hiccup Girl.

"Can I ask you a question?" Wawrzynski said.

"Sure," the producer answered.

"Why are you guys here?"

"Because she's news."

"No," Wawrzynski intoned, "you guys *make* her news."

PART FOUR

CHAPTER 79

ASSISTANT STATE'S ATTORNEY Christopher LaBruzzo is a bookish-looking man, with curly, receding black hair and short sideburns. He generally wore black, thick-framed glasses and sharp and shiny, likely tailored, suits. A Tulane-educated lawyer, LaBruzzo was an analyst for Loews Hotels before becoming the lead trial attorney for the Felony Division of the Sixth Circuit of Pinellas and Pasco County. He has an articulate and matter-of-fact way of speaking, and there's a nervous tone in his voice. As far as Jennifer Mee's case was concerned, LaBruzzo knew from the moment he took it on that the state had some work to do.

Back in March 2013, ASA LaBruzzo had entered into negotiations with Laron Raiford for a plea deal. The state had offered Laron somewhere near forty years for taking Shannon's life.

Laron declined.

Thus, they were all called into court, where a judge explained to Laron that it was his right to reject the offer and take his case to trial. But he should consider the deal seriously before doing so—because if he took it to trial, he would be facing a life sentence.

"When you're twenty-two years old," the judge explained to Laron as the accused killer stood smug and full of attitude, "sixty seems like you should be in the old folks' home. But when you get there, um, you think, 'Well, that isn't so old.'"

Laron reiterated and rejected the deal.

After taking his case to trial, LaBruzzo and the state convicted Laron Raiford in just a few days; and on August 30, 2013, Laron Raiford was, as promised, sentenced to life in prison.

Heading into Jennifer Mee's trial, ASA LaBruzzo didn't see the same clear-cut case being tried before the court. There were definitely hurdles. Yet, somewhere near nine o'clock on the cool morning of September 18, 2013, after nearly three years of motions, pretrial hearings, and arguments from both sides, Jennifer Mee and John Trevena faced off against LaBruzzo and the state of Florida. Inside the Sixth Judicial Court, room number three, in downtown Clearwater, Judge Nancy Moate Ley sat on the bench and announced the start of the *Florida* v. *Jennifer Mee* trial.

There was one problem as everyone sat and anticipated this long-awaited, high-profile trial: John Trevena was absent.

Just great was the look on everyone's face.

"He'll be about five minutes," Trevena's co-counsel Bryant R. Camareno told the judge. Trevena's second co-counsel was a man by the name of—no kidding—Jesse James.

When Trevena finally arrived, he addressed the court and spoke of an eleventh-hour revelation regarding his client, who had announced to him during jury deliberations the previous day that part of her disability might include her being schizophrenic.

As far as murder trials go, that would be considered a major game changer.

When the judge questioned Trevena about any paperwork he might have to support the new claim, Trevena said he did not have any. It had been only one day since he had found out himself, and he wanted some time to have Miss Mee checked out.

The judge questioned the timing, as likely everyone else in the courtroom did, save Rachel and the rest of Jennifer's family. Trevena had represented Jennifer, the judge smartly pointed out, for "what, for three years," and he was just discovering this incredible, often obvious, psychological disclosure about her *now*? It wasn't as though a person suffering from schizophrenia could hide it.

After a long discussion, including several recesses and a meeting between Jennifer and a court psychologist, it was determined that Jennifer might suffer from a bit "lower than average" intelligence, but she clearly understood what was going on, what the possible outcomes of her trial could be, what sentences she could receive, and why she was on trial, to begin with. In the court's view, Jennifer was no more a schizophrenic than Trevena was.

The judge signed an order finding Jennifer "competent" to stand trial based on the "stipulation of the parties."

Both the state and John Trevena agreed.

Shannon Griffin's family had waited three long years for justice; it was time to move on.

CHAPTER 80

WEARING A PURPLE blouse, with an utter look of *oh-my-god-this-is-suddenly-very-real* on her ashen face, Jennifer Mee sat next to Trevena and his co-counsel. There was a single piece of paper and a blue Bic pen sitting atop an oak table in front of her. Her long, flowing, full-bodied black hair had grown out, thick and healthy. She kept a serious look on her face, indicating that if she had not known in the past that her life was at stake, she certainly did now. Jennifer was a twenty-two-year-old woman at this stage of her life, no longer the innocent teen with the hiccups, or even the "gangsta" wannabe out peddling dope on the street corner. She had gained some weight, but she wore it well. She looked fit, with her face a little chubby in a cute sort of way.

As opening statements began, Jennifer developed a gaze, an almost surreal look of shock and awe that overtook any other expression she might conjure. She stared straight ahead in a stoic gaze, mostly looking at the ground, unflinching, statue-like, her hands at her sides, still as rocks.

ASA LaBruzzo walked to the lectern, with his yellow notebook, wearing a concrete-gray suit. He bit his lower lip, moved the microphone into position, pushed the lectern out in front of himself a bit, then put his hands together into a praying gesture and let Jennifer Mee have it with one simple, riveting opening sentence, quickly and effectively setting the tone of the state's case into action: "She set everything up."

He paused. Jennifer Mee and her table were directly in back of the lectern, so LaBruzzo had to turn completely around to address Jennifer, which he did as he repeated himself while pointing at her: "*She* set everything up."

It was the first image jurors were given of Jennifer from the ASA. Sitting before them was the mastermind behind a murder—at least that was the message. LaBruzzo didn't say that she set the robbery up and a man was murdered during the carrying out of that crime. The way LaBruzzo left it ringing in jurors' ears, it initially indicated that Jennifer Mee had set up and carried out a murder.

An aggressive, damaging accusation right out of the box.

Jennifer Mee, mastermind.

Jennifer Mee, cold and calculated.

Jennifer Mee, murderer.

LaBruzzo went on to tell the story of Shannon Griffin's life and tragic death in an A-to-Z narrative format, speaking about how "they"—"a man named Laron Raiford and a man named Lamont Newton and Jennifer Mee"—"lured" Shannon down to that renovated house under a ruse of selling him a "half ounce of weed."

And during that manufactured drug deal, well, they killed him.

As he continued, using his hands to articulate certain points, LaBruzzo, who could carry his voice rather well, using an authoritative, striking tone, kept going back to "You are going to hear" as a preface in order to put a stamp of evidentiary approval on his case. It was one thing, of course, for LaBruzzo to stand there and bark allegations at Jennifer Mee. It was quite another for him to promise jurors that the evidence he was going to present would ultimately convince them of her guilt in planning and carrying out the senseless murder of a young man just getting started in life.

The ruse was the weed, LaBruzzo implied, but "instead of marijuana," he added convincingly, "they had a loaded thirty-eight-caliber handgun."

He called Shannon's death scene a "dark alleyway." He said it several times, giving the impression that they had lured this man into a deadly setup he never saw coming.

One extremely important piece of evidence LaBruzzo brought up as he got going and fell into a groove was the evidence collected at the Eighty-Ninth Avenue North apartment where the four spent the night after the murder. Here LaBruzzo was smart to bring into the fold the word "forensics," as he knew juries desperately wanted what they saw on television each week: that rock-solid, scientific evidence that screamed, *"Aha! She was there! Her fingerprints are all over the evidence."*

After spelling out where law enforcement had located that bag of Shannon's belongings, LaBruzzo said, "And you're going to hear how forensic techs came and collected . . . all the other evidence in this case, and you're going to hear when they collected the wallet, they fingerprinted this item . . . and they were able to develop a fingerprint that was ultimately identified to Miss Jennifer Mee on the Florida driver's license of Shannon Griffin."

Jennifer had handled Shannon's license. This connected her to him.

And then LaBruzzo answered a criticism that would surely come up during the trial and even in the media trial waged by both sides during press conferences and surprise stoop speeches: *Did the SPPD go after Jennifer Mee?*

"Initially law enforcement wasn't a hundred percent sure of what Miss Mee's involvement in this case was. . . . You're going to hear she *voluntarily* went down to the police station and that she met with law enforcement and she gave a statement." And in that first statement, LaBruzzo added, Jennifer claimed there was a love triangle—same as Laron, Lamont, and Jenni—among Laron, Shannon, and Jenni Charron. But as "law enforcement then continued their investigation" and spoke to Jennifer Mee a bit more, and put together what all of the others were saying, they realized it had all been part of a tall tale the four had made a promise to tell.

The facts, LaBruzzo intoned, were the facts. They would not change. He asked jurors not to be persuaded by anything other than those facts of the case that the state would present. And when push came to shove, the DNA evidence that the state was going to present would back up those statements Laron, Lamont, and Jennifer Mee recorded for law enforcement. After the lies were tossed out and all three told the truth, the case came together rather perfectly; everything seemed to fit. Before that, of course, law enforcement kept coming up with questions that did not make sense because the information they were receiving had been littered with lies.

Finishing up, laying out the law for jurors so each would understand it in layman's terms, LaBruzzo carefully and persuasively explained: "The case that is in front of you is one of felony murder. The court is going to instruct you on the law, but basically what it's going to say is there are certain crimes in the state of Florida by design and by enumeration by the legislature that if you engage in such acts, such as a robbery, that if someone is murdered or killed in the course of that robbery, then you are, in fact, guilty of murder in the first degree."

Jennifer Mee did have "the *intent* that [a] crime be committed. . . . In her own words, *she* set everything up . . . ," LaBruzzo concluded, ending where he had begun.

LaBruzzo thanked the jury and walked back to his table.

"Mr. Trevena," the judge said, "do you wish to give an opening?"

"Yes, Your Honor," Trevena said while standing and walking toward the lectern.

CHAPTER 81

JOHN TREVENA IS a man who owns and "loves" fast and luxuriously expensive cars—"Bentleys, Mercedes, Corvettes, BMWs, Porsches, Cadillacs"—along with those superfast, "cigarette-type speedboats." He fashions himself a "hardworking" and "hard-drinking" man, living his life to the fullest when not in a courtroom facing off against prosecutors and attorneys out to bury his clients, either financially or criminally. Yet, John Trevena's life growing up was anything but a window looking into the glamorous worlds of the rich and famous, which Trevena would come to embrace later on.

"My family was quite poor," Trevena told me. "My father was a one hundred percent World War II disabled veteran, who suffered catastrophic injuries during the war, leaving him mostly blind and quite crippled from bullet wounds to the chest and a large bayonet wound to his liver."

As a disabled vet, Trevena's father provided for his family with only a small monthly pension, which was near the poverty line at the time. Trevena's mother was a loving and caring soul, a housewife that raised his three siblings and Trevena (the youngest) the best she could, with what little they had. It was a difficult life, but not a life devoid of love, affection, and compassion for others.

Through those tough times, Trevena said, whereas some might want to fade into the obscurity of quitting school and perhaps belly their lives up to the local gin mill bar to cry in the bartender's ear and drink away the blows of life, Trevena and his siblings thrived. Each one went on to graduate high school and attend four years of college, all later earning bachelor's degrees.

"I was the only child to receive a postgraduate degree," Trevena said respectfully.

Those lessons in humility he was taught growing up helped Trevena when it came time for him to begin thinking about life after school.

"To pay for tuition, I would work up to three jobs," he said. "I was also awarded an academic scholarship. One of the jobs I worked while attending law school was as a police officer, where I received a great deal of practical experience about the justice system."

His life experiences would all come in handy as Trevena went to work fighting for the rights of his clients. A case like Jennifer Mee's was especially personal to Trevena because he didn't see a vicious, evil killer when he looked into Jennifer Mee's eyes. She certainly was not. He saw a young girl growing up in a family that had struggled, forever living week to week, a family on the fringes of poverty and possibly one hospital stay or car accident away from being broke—much like many Americans today. The Robidoux family members were good people at heart, Trevena felt. They had been trying to work out a winning hand with the cards they'd been dealt. Jennifer, especially, had lost her way somewhere along the path of life. She wound up in a situation she had hard time pulling herself away from. Trevena didn't want to see the rest of her life spent behind bars.

Married for a second time, to a twenty-nine-year-old "Texas beauty queen" he called his "soul mate," Trevena walked toward the courtroom lectern, about to give his opening statement in *Florida* v. *Jennifer Mee.* The defense attorney thought about how young and naïve and ill-equipped Jennifer Mee had been to deal with the consequences of her life. Trevena saw a troubled girl with medical, mental, and educational issues. How in the heck was he going to get her out of this mess? A mess, in fact, that could result in Jennifer spending life (without any chance of parole) in prison. She was so young that if Jennifer was found guilty, by the time her life was over, she most certainly would not recall what it had been like on the outside, in the free world. Indeed, the stakes could not have been higher—and Trevena knew it.

Trevena spoke softly, in a calm and soothing voice. With his salt-and-pepper goatee and shortly cropped black hair—just turning gray along the borders—he came across not as your typical fist-pumping, boisterous, accusation-hurling defense attorney banging a drum of *"she didn't do it."* Instead, more than anything else, John Trevena gave a comforting sense that he was there as Jennifer Mee's legal advocate—the one person fighting for her rights—to jurors and those in the courtroom looking on. He was not about to stand up and rip apart an investigation or condemn a prosecutor for going after Jennifer Mee without supporting his disagreements with the holes he had found in the case. He was defending his client, plain and simple, trying to explain to jurors that Jennifer was being overcharged, by his estimation, and the evidence would prove as much.

He first explained to jurors that an opening "statement" was not evidence; and that by not using the term "opening argument," addressing jurors at this stage of a trial should not be a thunderous, chest-pounding indictment of one side against another. An opening statement in Trevena's mind was a "road map" to guide jurors through the muck of a case and "where," he added thoughtfully, nodding in the affirmative slightly, "the evidence will lead you."

Trevena clarified that opening statements gave "cues" in order to point out certain "testimony that would come later." He encouraged jurors to "evaluate that testimony in light of some of the issues that would" be presented during the course of the trial.

It was a solid strategy. Part of Trevena's job was to coach jurors into understanding that Jennifer Mee was at the wrong place at the wrong time, heavily influenced by her peers, unable to determine right from wrong, and in no way had participated in a murder. Trevena also saw a forceful prosecution based in part on the fact that Jennifer Mee was a celebrity. The high-profile nature of the case, Trevena was certain, played a major role in the state having gone after Jennifer as aggressively as it had.

"Honestly," Trevena told me later, "Miss Mee seemed too dim-witted to be the mastermind behind any criminal enterprise. . . . Intellectually, she just didn't seem to have it together. The state kept using the term 'mastermind,' and I was like, 'Mastermind of what?'"

In Trevena's view, there was a terrible "rush to judgment" in this case. "I thought they were running roughshod over her because of her quasi-celebrity."

Part of what led Trevena down this road, he added, was the fact that the chief of police "did a big press conference to announce her arrest. . . . This was your normal, run-of-the-mill, inner-city crime—however tragic and terribly sad it was for the victim's family—that if it made the news at all, it generally made the back page."

Trevena blamed the SPPD for announcing that they had the Hiccup Girl in custody in the first place and inviting the media firestorm to its doorstep.

"This started by them identifying her as the Hiccup Girl," Trevena remarked.

As far as the two statements Jennifer Mee gave to the SPPD, Trevena made it clear that he had a major problem with that evidence.

"The police department was trying to capitalize on her celebrity status and made it look like they had made this fantastic arrest in such a short time. . . . They were moving so rapidly, that the lead detective didn't even know that another detective had interviewed her and obtained a statement from her, and so he turned around and goes and gets *another* statement from her."

That all being said, however, Trevena also knew the law in Florida and the battle he was up against in that regard was something out of his and Jennifer's hands: the felony murder rule.

"Florida has a very clear-cut felony murder rule. You could be the getaway driver. . . . Two guys come out of a bank, you are waiting, and it could be that one of your *codefendants* shoots a guard and you're on the hook. . . ."

Yet, a second problem Trevena and Jennifer faced was that the state was also alleging that Jennifer set this entire robbery up. It was rather simple. She contacted Shannon. She told him where to meet. She coaxed him behind that vacant house. He was murdered.

Any way one added that up, it came out to the same solution.

For Trevena, "Yes, Jennifer Mee made admissions that they were going to take his money, you know, rip him off . . . and she even used the term 'robbery.'" But in this experienced lawyer's opinion, the missing link was the idea that Jennifer Mee had no clue whatsoever that there was going to be a violent confrontation. She definitely did not know, moreover, that Laron and Lamont would use violent force to steal Shannon's money, much less whip out a .38-caliber handgun and kill the man. "She was unaware that they were bringing a gun and certainly unaware that they were going to use violent force," Trevena told me.

As Trevena continued his opening statement, he turned around, pointed to Jennifer, and said, "Miss Mee sits alone as the only one charged here with first-degree murder. The state must prove to you that she committed first-degree murder. Not that some other party who is not in this room . . . but that *she* is the responsible party for first-degree murder."

It was a powerful statement of the law.

Then Trevena tried to inject some reasonable doubt into the state's case. He explained that the state would have jurors believe that there were only "three people" involved in the crime, and he named Laron and Lamont as the other two.

"But there were really *four* people involved," Trevena told jurors. "We believe the evidence will show that there's a fourth individual named Jennifer Charron . . . and Jennifer Charron, you will learn, was never charged with any crime whatsoever relating to this shooting." There was a certain hint of *"can you believe it?"* in Trevena's voice, over an undertone of *"how dare they?"*

From that pivotal point of his defense, Trevena placed the blame on Jenni Charron, claiming that the evidence would eventually prove it was Jenni Charron who should be sitting in the place of Jennifer Mee inside the courtroom.

Then he broke into a biography of Jennifer Mee and her life, at one point saying, "Miss Mee is known, as you heard from jury selection and from the court, as the Hiccup Girl. Miss Mee was, at the age of fifteen, subject to an extraordinary amount of both local and national publicity because of a medical condition, which caused her to have continuous hiccups. Now, you notice as she sits here today, it's unlikely you will see any episodes of hiccups because she is now controlling that condition through medication. . . ."

The state objected.

The judge suggested a bench conference.

Trevena was then allowed to continue.

As he did, more objections led to additional bench conferences. After sorting it all out, Trevena turned his focus once again on Jenni Charron, absolutely disparaging her character, attacking her former means of making a living.

"Jennifer Charron, you will hear, she is going to testify that she had a considerable amount of money. She was making *good* money. You will learn through the testimony on cross-examination that she was working, essentially, as a prostitute. . . ."

He then explained the living conditions of the four at the time of the murder. He mentioned the statements each gave to police and how different—yet alike—they will sound. He argued that the "cover story" of Jenni Charron being essentially caught with Shannon by Laron was, in fact, the way it happened, and that Jennifer Mee was the scapegoat.

Jenni Charron, according to Trevena, was the state's "star witness," and that's why she was never charged with any crime, not even as an accessory after the fact, a crime that she admitted to and the SPPD was well aware of.

Finally John Trevena encouraged jurors to ask themselves which of the stories they were about to hear during the course of this trial "made sense," and to keep in mind that, when four of six shots were fired that night, Jennifer Mee was nowhere in sight.

"She is *not* at the scene."

Then it was back to Jenni Charron and how the SPPD used Jenni to nail Jennifer Mee.

"It wasn't like it was a deal cut," Trevena said of the detectives and their interaction with Jenni on that Sunday after the murder, and later. "It wasn't like the detective said, 'Miss Charron, you tell us what really happened and we're not going to charge you with a crime.'" For Trevena, it was more complicated than that. Kind of like the detective saying, "Miss Charron, tell us how

Miss Mee *is involved* and then you won't be charged with anything. You're a witness. You're not a defendant."

This was a bold accusation on the part of Trevena, and yet it was allowed to linger without an objection.

Trevena stated that the true motivation here was for the SPPD to gain notoriety through charging the Hiccup Girl with first-degree murder.

ASA Chris LaBruzzo vehemently objected.

"Sustained," the judge said. "Move on."

In the end, Trevena implored jurors to view the evidence with "common sense" and truly take a look at the theories he had just presented of a salivating pit bull attacking a defenseless poodle. They should keep in mind that the state decided to toss the book at a young girl, who didn't know any better, all because of her celebrity.

"I was facing an uphill battle from the start," Trevena said later, defending the bold position he took during his opening statement. "It was really her only chance."

CHAPTER 82

JASON BRAZELTON WAS the state's first witness. To no one's surprise, the attorney briefly explained how he had come upon Shannon's body, thinking he was looking at a homeless man sleeping off a bender.

After Jason introduced jurors to the victim, Officer Kurt Bradshaw took the stand to describe what he found when he rolled up to the crime scene after Jason Brazelton had called it in.

This was textbook, prosecutorial "scene setting" by the state. The best way to present a case to jurors was to begin with the 911 call and then allow the case to unfold from there. Within Bradshaw's testimony, however, that scene setting contained several graphic images displayed for the jury, among them Shannon Griffin's brutalized body. This brought a sense of jolting realism to the trial that had perhaps been lost in all of the Hiccup Girl hoopla leading up to the first few witnesses. Not forty minutes into the trial, jurors had a clear look at the result of a robbery gone bad and the decision a group of three people had made to rob a man of $60. Here was the dead body of a young man who believed he was scootering his way downtown to meet a girl.

After introducing how and where the victim was found by bringing in Jason Brazelton and Kurt Bradshaw, the state produced its first character witness— Doug Bolden, who was going to inject some heartfelt emotion into the trial.

Wearing a yellow dress shirt and black dinner jacket, Doug Bolden walked into the courtroom. Watching him, Rachel Robidoux, who was sitting in back of her daughter, nearly lost control of her emotions. As her chest heaved in and out rapidly, she dabbed her eyes with a tissue. Rachel's display of raw emotion was infectious and sincere.

A handsome man, like his cousin, Doug Bolden spoke clearly and articulately. Here was a guy who had lost a cousin he viewed (and loved) as a son. The loss had been devastating to Doug, his wife, and the Griffin family as a whole. Shannon was a guiding light, a bright star within the family. He had simply been looking to make a life for himself in Florida after experiencing the horrible effects of Mother Nature at her worst. Listening to Doug Bolden, one got a sense of just how pointless and meaningless this murder had been.

The state had Doug go through that night Shannon was leaving the house: how happy he was, how cheerful his spirits were, and how it was all based on the fact that Shannon was going to meet a female. Nowhere in Doug's account did it seem as though Shannon was going out to score a small amount of marijuana. Regardless of what all the others had said, to Doug Bolden, Shannon was heading out on a date.

ASA Janet Clack Hunter-Olney, LaBruzzo's co-counsel, questioned Doug Bolden with an affecting genuineness and candor, asking at one point: "Okay, how long had he lived with you here in Pinellas County?"

"It was almost two years."

"And was that the last time that you saw Shannon?" she asked next, referencing that night Shannon had left the Bolden household so happy and excited to go meet a girl.

"It was . . . It was the very last time."

"What is the next thing that happened?"

When Doug spoke, he smiled at times and looked down at others, no doubt calling up the imagery associated with the memories he was sharing. It had been such an alarming blow, and those moments before Shannon left the house were etched in Doug's mind as if they had happened the previous day. How could a man forget the final moments with someone he loved? How could Doug Bolden ever rid from his memories the idea that his cousin had been taken from him and his family for nothing?

"He told me," Doug continued, "like I said before, he was like, 'Hey, I'm going out. You know, I met a young lady.' Personally, I was excited for him because he was someone who *rarely* ever went out. I mean, he was someone that went to work. . . . I was so proud of him."

As his testimony continued, Doug spoke of a man he had mentored into getting his GED. He talked about how the two of them walked down to the Walmart together so Shannon could get a job application. Then when Shannon got the job, the sheer happiness Doug saw on Shannon's face came across as though the young man had hit the lottery. To Shannon, the simple things most people took for granted were things he relished. He was grateful for so much in so many ways. It was a joy just to watch him grow and live, Doug suggested.

ASA Hunter-Olney showed Doug several photos of Shannon's scooter and asked him how long Shannon had owned it.

"I want to say about six months."

Hunter-Olney stopped the testimony at that point and asked the judge if she could approach the bench. Soon all the lawyers were standing around the judge, talking.

There was a problem.

Jennifer Mee was Hunter-Olney's issue. As Doug talked through Shannon's life, Jennifer had begun to cry. It was very animated and loud. It was as if the floodgates of emotion had let loose after Jennifer suddenly realized that a real life had been snuffed out and that she had been part of it. She sat staring blankly straight ahead; at times, her lower lip was quivering. She sniffled and wiped away what were, no doubt, real tears. The look on her face was grave, sullen and dramatic, an upside-down smile.

This was problematic for the state. As the trial moved forward, there was going to be plenty more emotional testimony and scores of graphic photos. Jennifer had to be strong, prepared for all of it. She couldn't sit through the trial and cry. LaBruzzo, in a statement to the judge, wondered if it was "not proper" that Jennifer was displaying so much emotion.

"So you're asking me to do something?" the judge asked him during the sidebar, out of juror earshot.

"Yes," said Hunter-Olney.

The judge wanted to know what the state wanted, exactly.

"We would like you to instruct her that she needs to get a grasp of her emotions."

As they talked it through, Jennifer folded both hands in front of herself on the table, twiddled her thumbs nervously, and was on the brink of totally losing it.

Trevena's co-counsel had a short chat with Jennifer, encouraging her to be tough, hold tight, and try to get a handle on herself. If she needed a break, they could take one.

Hunter-Olney then continued with Doug Bolden, showing him several pieces of physical evidence he recognized as Shannon's personal belongings. It was a difficult moment. Doug looked down at Shannon's wallet and, of course, saw his cousin again standing inside that house, saying good-bye, smiling, happily going about his life, coming out of his shell for the first time. It was a lasting image, sure—but also a final one.

The state ended its direct examination by having

Doug explain how the SPPD notified him of Shannon's death by a knock on the door and the shocking revelation that his young cousin had been murdered.

John Trevena began by asking Doug Bolden about Walmart. Wasn't it considered a "drug-free workplace," and would that be something that Shannon knew?

Doug said sure.

After a few additional questions, Trevena asked Doug if he knew "Shannon to be a marijuana smoker?"

"No."

Trevena then asked the same question several different ways, alluding to the idea Doug had presented that Shannon was going downtown on a date, *not* to buy some weed. This was all part of Trevena's argument bolstering the theory that Shannon and Jenni Charron were hooking up.

As they continued talking back and forth—Trevena had to tread carefully on the memory of the victim— it was clear Doug Bolden believed Shannon had met a girl online and had made plans with her for a date that night. There was never any discussion between the two about Shannon going out to buy weed. And there was never any discussion about the girl's identity.

After establishing that Doug had a computer in the house that Shannon often used to go online, Trevena said he was done.

They took a break.

At about 2:45 P.M., testimony resumed.

CHAPTER 83

ON THAT SAME day, September 18, 2013, as the afternoon session began, the state brought in its forensic technician, Brent Goodman, a fifteen-year SPPD employee. This was the state's *CSI* man. He was the guy who had arrived at the crime scene with his criminal tackle box, latex gloves, flashlight, and tweezers to sift through whatever evidence had been left behind by Shannon's murderers. Goodman had a master's degree in forensic anthropology and was qualified in blood spatter analysis, drug lab work, and arson investigation.

Quickly, as LaBruzzo questioned Goodman, the forensic tech dismantled any images the jury might have had of a Gil Grissom–like television character walking around the scene, investigatory light bulbs going off in his head, questioning witnesses, solving crimes in sixty minutes, in between commercial breaks.

"Do you have the ability to arrest anyone, or do you carry a weapon?" LaBruzzo asked.

"No, sir, I do not."

Goodman's job was to collect evidence and study it. He didn't make distinctions or judgments about how important or not a particular piece of evidence was to a case. He collected what he found, bagged and tagged it, maybe analyzed it back at the lab and made a report. He also took crime scene video, which the jury was now going to get a chance to look at, taking each one of them into that dark back alleyway on the night of the murder.

Another reason for having a witness of Goodman's caliber on the stand was to introduce the physical pieces of evidence the SPPD had collected during the course of its investigation. This took time and explanation, and a witness like Goodman could bring the trial's momentum to a standstill. Thus, over the course of the next hour, the state had Goodman introduce one piece of evidence after the next that had been collected from the scene and Shannon's body.

LaBruzzo and Goodman went through all of it: the shoes, the flip-flops, the cigarette pack, the condom wrapper, the plastic water bottles, that .38-caliber weapon. Photos were introduced, giving the jury a clear perspective of the scene and where each piece of evidence had been found. When one took all of this in, and looked at it under the light of the testimony accompanying it, a picture of Shannon's last moments—parking his scooter, walking across the street to meet up with Jennifer Mee, her leading him behind the vacant house, two men attacking him, Shannon fighting violently for his life, a gun discharged, a young man dead—came to mind.

Jennifer looked on and cried. Here were the remnants of what she had run away from. Perhaps it was the first time for her to imagine what happened as it all unfolded in the wake of her quick getaway.

The other part of Goodman's testimony was to explain the scene at the apartment where Laron and Lamont had been arrested and where they had found Shannon's belongings.

The murder team of Jennifer Mee, Laron Raiford, and Lamont Newton had tried to get rid of Shannon's belongings by burning and then hiding them. Yet, as Goodman explained, he also found a bleach bottle and other items associated with trying to clean up evidence. So although the team tried to get rid of the evidence, they had not done a good job disposing of the items.

Goodman had also collected buccal swabs of DNA from the suspects. That evidence would, of course, tie into any additional evidence collected at both scenes.

As murder trials go, this was a classic A-to-Z narrative of presenting the evidence and building a case for jurors. As the testimony continued, witness after witness, each piece of evidence after the next, all seemed to lead to one conclusion: Jennifer Mee—despite how she felt now, and what she had first told the SPPD—was at that scene, had participated in a cover-up afterward, and, by the law, had admitted to taking part in first-degree felony murder.

Trevena had only a few questions for Goodman. What could he get out of the guy in the end, really? Goodman was presenting cold, hard, and mostly scientific facts. It was best to allow them their place in the trial and move on.

In Jennifer Mee, Trevena had a client, he said, "who just didn't get it. It's sad, really. She never understood the severity of this. . . ."

Another factor Trevena talked about later, one he said he could not go anywhere near during the trial, was the "race issue" and the idea that Jennifer Mee had dated only black males. Sad as it was, there were some people in the world still living in the 1960s racist South, Trevena knew. He had to take that into consideration and go into the trial with the honest realization that Jennifer Mee would be judged on her life choices, whether anyone in that courtroom would admit race was an issue or not.

In looking at all of the complications Jennifer Mee faced, aside from the wealth of evidence against her, Trevena felt the best way to defend his client was to focus on the back end. Go through the trial recognizing the worst might happen (Jennifer would be found guilty), while hoping for the best (an innocent verdict, manslaughter, or some other result).

By "back end," Trevena meant an appeal. He'd win the case on appeal. He'd done it before. "You see, initially, our goal was to try to work out a plea deal. We tried and tried and tried." The state, Trevena maintained, was uninterested in any sort of realistic plea deal, at any time. "And I shouldn't say they *wouldn't* do it," Trevena added with a bit of sarcasm. "But the numbers they gave us seemed really unreasonable for someone so young. We came as high as fifteen years and we were told that even twenty would likely be rejected."

To sit down and begin talking about a plea deal with Trevena, the state wanted somewhere near "twenty-five [years] and upward," Trevena said.

There was no way Trevena could "stand there in good faith," he explained, "and take a girl at that age, with her mentality, and tell her, 'Okay, now, you're going to spend the next quarter century in prison.' It just didn't make sense to me."

On the flip side, however, most cases similar to Jennifer's were routinely pleaded out and a trial avoided, Trevena maintained. The state hardly ever prosecuted an inner-city robbery resulting in a murder. And a quick cursory search of cases in Florida backed up Trevena's statement. It was the most cost effective and better for all involved if a plea was reached by both parties in these types of cases.

"The state would have cleared this case *but* for her status," Trevena was convinced. "Another defendant that had no notoriety or celebrity would have easily been able to plead it out. I've done it myself in many other cases—but not this one! They *wanted* that trial."

CHAPTER 84

AS THAT TRIAL, which John Trevena was certain the state was using to showboat its prosecution of a quasi-celebrity, continued on September 18, 2013, twenty-five-year SPPD veteran Melinda Clayton was called as the judge announced that Clayton was going to be the final witness of the day.

Clayton, a latent-fingerprint examiner, was dressed professionally in a camo-green blazer and black slacks, which echoed nicely against her long, naturally beautiful gray hair. Clayton was an important witness for the state. She was set to tie up a few evidentiary loose ends with unimpeachable scientific evidence.

After Clayton explained how fingerprints work and how effective they can be in connecting a particular person unequivocally to a piece of evidence, she broke into a narrative about the specific work she had done in this case. One interesting fact the jury heard right off the bat was that even identical twins do not share the same fingerprints. Clayton's testimony bolstered the fact that fingerprinting is a science that we have used for over a century and will continue to use as long as there is a crime to solve. It was an old-school investigatory tactic that worked.

The major piece of testimony the state was looking for out of Clayton came a few minutes in. The state asked if Clayton had fingerprinted Jennifer Mee and also had found fingerprints on Shannon Griffin's license.

She said yes to both.

Then ASA Hunter-Olney asked if Clayton had analyzed both sets of the prints and drawn a conclusion.

Clayton had.

And what was that?

"My conclusion was that the print that was obtained from the front of the driver's license was the right index finger of Jennifer Mee."

Jennifer Mee had held Shannon Griffin's license at some point. That was a devastating and damaging image for jurors to have in their heads regarding Jennifer Mee.

The state had no further questions for Clayton.

Defense attorney John Trevena asked a few nonessential questions, and after several redirect questions from the ASA, Clayton was cut loose. The day concluded with the thrust of the judge's gavel.

CHAPTER 85

A CELL PHONE buzzed on one of the courtroom tables as the judge worked on a laptop computer at the bench. People filed into the courtroom on September 19, 2013, as firearms expert Yolanda Soto, a state witness, prepared to shift the government's case into cruise control.

What the state did flawlessly was not belabor any one particular issue or witness. This was a lot harder to do than it might seem. At times, murder trials can get bogged down by expert analysis and from expert witnesses who are forced to carry on, and on, by a prosecutor that has never heard of the quote "less is more." Here, LaBruzzo and Hunter-Olney asked only those pertinent questions of their witnesses and did not allow them to ramble on. They'd put their experts in the seat, have them list their credentials briefly, and then asked them to provide their particular piece of the puzzle. That was it.

For Yolanda Soto, her role in this trial was to identify the murder weapon as being the same gun in the photos and in the video the jury had seen and then describe how that weapon worked. This gun was not an automatic handheld killing machine of any sort, a sort of rapid-fire weapon that went off on a hair trigger. It was a "single-" and "double-" action revolver, a .38 Special. It took effort to fire in that single-action mode, and even more effort in double-action mode.

"Three and one-quarter pounds" of pressure, to be exact, in single action, Soto told jurors, and "nine and three-quarter" pounds in double action.

The implication was that a .38 Special was not a weapon that fired easily. One school of thought with this testimony would be to pooh-pooh any sort of notion that the murder happened accidently.

Soto explained how the strands of steel being cut as a bullet exits a barrel leave those telltale marks a ballistics expert uses to compare a particular bullet to a particular weapon.

Long story short, the rounds found inside Shannon's body matched the barrel of the weapon found at the scene, Soto explained.

And after that, the state said it was finished questioning Yolanda Soto.

Trevena stuck to the same line of questioning, having Soto explain further single- and double-action weapons. He spent some time asking about the pounds of pressure needed to fire the weapon and was able to get Soto to admit she had no idea whether the gun was fired in single- or double-action mode during this particular crime.

As they chatted back and forth, it became clear that Trevena was trying to make a point that the weapon *could* have been fired accidently and not on purpose, providing the finger behind the trigger was powerful enough.

Why he was interested in this was anybody's guess. But after a few moments of questioning, Trevena indicated he was done with Soto.

A second forensic expert was called: Janel Borries. She told jurors she was the assistant director for the Pinellas County Forensic Laboratory, supervising the DNA section of the lab. Because her expertise was in DNA sequencing and the measurement of DNA strands (the ladder part of the popular DNA animation strands), it took some time before Borries began to explain her role in the investigation. However, when she did, the questions and answers were rapid, each coming one after the next.

"Did you have an opportunity to examine the items in that envelope?"

"Yes, I did."

"And what are those items?"

"They were represented as swabs from shell casings and [a] gun."

"And I am showing you what's been entered into evidence as State's Exhibit 20—did you have an opportunity to examine *that* piece of evidence?"

"Yes, I did."

"And could you please tell the jurors what that piece of evidence is?"

"It's a condom wrapper."

The ASA asked about another piece of evidence from the scene. "Did you have an opportunity to examine that?"

"Yes, I did."

"And what are those items?"

"They are swabs that are represented as being from the hammer of the gun, the trigger of the gun, and the grips of the gun."

Borries then talked about swabs taken from Jennifer, Laron, and Lamont that she had analyzed, before the ASA had her explain how the lab protects itself against contaminating evidence. It was a necessary departure from the quick back-and-forth exchange, because with DNA and blood spatter and so many evidence packages came the possibility that some could be mixed up. The state wanted jurors to understand that this was no Keystone Cop organization; these were lab professionals that followed strict guidelines and policies and procedures to guard against any type of contaminant.

When all was said and done, neither Jennifer Mee's nor Lamont Newton's DNA "[could not] be excluded" from being contributors to the items they had discussed (the condom wrapper and the weapon), but Laron Raiford's DNA was an unmistakable match found on both.

He was there, in other words.

As Borries checked the clothing—Lamont's, Laron's, and Shannon's—she found a "mixture of the three individuals'" DNA on all of it. In addition, regarding a tank top T-shirt (Laron's or Lamont's), it was determined that "the major profile could be determined . . . [and was] consistent with the buccal swabs from Jennifer

Mee." Jennifer must have, at some point, handled or worn the shirt.

Borries said she also found the presence of a chemical that had been used to try and wash away forensic evidence.

The ASA asked if she had an idea what that chemical might have been based upon her scientific analysis.

"Bleach," she said.

Other clothing from Shannon Griffin's body included DNA from all three (Shannon, Lamont, and Laron), in addition to another donor that was unidentified as being Shannon, Laron, Lamont, or Jennifer Mee.

All of this testimony firmly locked into position for the state the idea that all three charged in this case had been at the crime scene, had handled Shannon's belongings, while Laron was the one that held the weapon. The science, unmistakably, backed up the statements given to the SPPD by Jennifer Mee, Laron Raiford, and Lamont Newton, with small discrepancies in each.

The state's case was beginning to come together.

Trevena's co-counsel did not have much for Borries. Again, it was hard to argue with science.

Associate ME Chris Wilson took the oath next and put the notorious exclamation point on how terrifying and painful death had been for Shannon as he endured round after round into his chest. It was not a fast death. Shannon knew what was happening and suffered. As Wilson talked through the autopsy, the state produced several photographs of Shannon's body, displaying his wounds for jurors. It was striking and gruesome and illustrated how senseless this crime had been.

Jennifer Mee, passive and still, could do no more than, at times, turn away from the images and cry.

Wilson described entrance and exit wounds, internal injuries, and what actually killed Shannon: a bullet to his aorta.

When given his crack at the medical examiner in this case, John Trevena zeroed in on a potential "rush to judgment" argument he had waged in his opening statement. The first question Trevena asked the doctor was based on the time of the autopsy being just a day after the murder. Trevena wanted to know if this was typical.

The doctor said they received bodies twenty-four hours a day and generally conducted autopsies the same day that a body came in or the following day.

"Now, I heard the state's attorney ask you about alcohol and drugs in the victim's system, and I believe you said there were no drugs in his system, correct?"

"That *we* could determine," Dr. Wilson said.

"Let me ask you about marijuana, for example. In general, marijuana has a tendency to stay in the system much longer than other drugs?"

"I'm not a toxicologist. I really cannot answer that question."

"You have not had that issue before dealing with the longevity of marijuana in a person's system?"

"No."

"And have no knowledge of that?"

"Correct."

What at first seemed like an important fact Trevena was able to get out of the doctor—that there was no "stippling" around any of the gunshot wounds on Shannon's body—soon lost any impact it might have had on jurors when the doctor further explained his answer. No stippling indicated that shots had been fired from some distance away from the body. Stippling is a black residue found around a gunshot wound on the skin or perhaps even on the clothing. The presence of it tells the expert the barrel of a weapon had likely been placed directly on the skin/clothing, or at least very close, and then fired. Picture the end of a gun barrel spraying black powder out of its nose and that hot powder burning the skin around the entrance wound like a brand.

Wilson answered by saying that he could not really agree with Trevena's explanation because Shannon's clothing had been removed from the scene and so he had to conclude an "indeterminate" finding regarding how far away or close the shooter was to Shannon at the time the weapon was fired.

In the end, they decided on about twelve inches or less as a possible measurement for the weapon barrel and Shannon's skin. What this had to do with Jennifer Mee did not become entirely clear as Trevena concluded his questioning and the court recessed for an afternoon break. But the one thing it did say was that whoever fired the weapon that killed Shannon held it at least a foot away at the time.

CHAPTER 86

ROBERT SCHOCK HAD spent thirteen years with the SPPD's Homicide Unit, but the last twelve of his twenty-five-year career in law enforcement with the state's attorney's office as a special investigator. The reason why the ASA had called Schock was clear from the start of their conversation.

"I'd like to ask you some questions about what's been . . . called a 'jail call,'" LaBruzzo said, before urging the investigator to talk about the telephone system inside a jail and how an inmate makes a phone call to the outside.

This was a precursor to what the state had viewed, undoubtedly, as one of its most detrimental pieces of evidence against Jennifer Mee: her alleged "admission" over the phone to her mother during that first call Jennifer had made back on the day she was arrested on felony murder charges. It was a conversation that Rachel Robidoux had lived with and thought about ever since her daughter had been arrested.

"I often ask myself why I even asked her to explain what happened to me, over the phone," Rachel said later.

What Rachel and others later clarified was that Jennifer Mee was not articulate in any way, and thus her explanation of what she did on that night should not be taken literally—it was Jennifer's way of expressing what had happened to her.

Robert Schock had found the call between Rachel and Jennifer after the state's attorney's office asked him to check out all the calls made by Jennifer Mee from the jail.

Playing devil's advocate, one might conclude: *Well, there you go. They went after her, looking to take out of context a telephone call between a mother and her daughter and nail her child for murder!*

But this investigation tactic was standard procedure for law enforcement when looking at a murder suspect's behavior. By the time they'd decided to look at this, Jennifer Mee had been charged with felony murder. The state was simply building its case.

Then, as LaBruzzo started to talk about the call, Trevena asked for a bench conference, saying he was going to object to the call, its relevance, and its admission into trial. Trevena explained to the judge that he felt the state was going to introduce the call as an "admission," and Trevena did not think the call rose to the level of an actual confession. He was concerned that jurors might see it that way if they heard the call.

LaBruzzo said he was not planning to submit the call as evidence through Mr. Schock; he wanted to use another witness, on another day, in that regard. The only testimony he wanted out of Schock regarding the call was verification that he had located the call and how. Through that testimony, LaBruzzo could then provide documentation about the call to the court.

The judge wanted to hear the call.

The jury was asked to leave the room.

LaBruzzo played the call.

Judge Nancy Moate Ley asked Trevena to wage his argument.

"Your Honor, the first ground would be relevancy. It is not tantamount to an admission against interest such that it should be introduced in this case, particularly considering ground two of the objection that any probative of that recording is substantially outweighed by the prejudicial effect of playing that recording to the jury."

From where John Trevena saw things, the call itself said "very little" and was "of great concern" to him if it was allowed by this judge to be introduced.

"One other concern I have . . . ," Trevena continued, "is this is a free call that an inmate gets upon their arrest. Correct me if I'm wrong, but the normal admonition against anything you say may be recorded in this call." He explained how he could not "recall hearing that" in the recording. "Under Florida law, to record a conversation, it either has to be the beep, which I heard no beeping, or there has to be an oral, verbal, warning indicating that the phone call is being recorded, which the court and I have heard probably hundreds, if not over a thousand, of these calls over the course of many years of practice."

Trevena talked about hearing "repeated warnings" throughout those other calls, such as "This call may be monitored."

"Well," he told the judge as LaBruzzo listened, "I don't recall hearing it all throughout the call."

They argued back and forth about the warning. However, the matter at hand, effectively, was whether the judge was going to allow the jury to hear the call at all. Without that call being introduced, those warnings would not matter. And if that call did not make it into the trial, Jennifer had a chance.

After LaBruzzo and Trevena talked it through in front of the judge, hammering each other's arguments, the judge, perhaps a bit too nonchalantly, said, "All right. They (the tapes of the calls) are both admitted."

And that was it.

Since the matter was fresh, LaBruzzo thought what the heck, now was as good a time as any to hear the calls. And it wasn't long after when the jury was brought back in and the tapes were played.

* * *

A lot of it was common conversation between first a granddaughter and her grandfather, and then a mother and her daughter. The exchange everyone would be talking about in the coming days was a minute or so into the tape: "Who'd you kill?" Rachel had asked.

"I ain't kill nobody."

"Well, then, how are they charging you with . . . murder?"

"Because I set everything up. It all went wrong, Momma. Shit went downhill after everything happened, Mom."

With LaBruzzo finished with Schock soon after the jury had heard the call, Trevena questioned Schock about the process of the calls and how the recordings were made. Trevena's argument felt weak and shallow compared to the riveting missile LaBruzzo had launched with that phone call being placed into the record. There was no unhearing those intensely self-incriminating words from the woman on trial for felony murder.

"Because I set everything up."

Within the context of that one sentence alone, Jennifer had seemingly admitted not only to setting up the crime, but, more important in the state's case, taking part in it all.

When Trevena realized he wasn't getting anywhere with Schock, he quickly passed the witness.

Gary Gibson, Terrell Skinner, and then Dave Wawrzynski would be next. They were the state's three SPPD investigative witnesses. Gibson and Skinner were textbook state witnesses, coming in and giving a blow-by-blow account of the investigation from their different, albeit similar, perspectives.

Trevena tried unsuccessfully to get both Gibson and Skinner to give a little bit of a jolt to the idea that Jennifer was targeted, but neither took hold of the live wire. And to that end, Trevena was not too concerned. His focus was on Dave Wawrzynski—whom Trevena saw as a lead detective out there targeting his client with a net, looking to catch her up in a felony murder charge after realizing who she was.

CHAPTER 87

AS HE SAT back and thought about all these little pieces of the evidence puzzle building a picture of the state's case, John Trevena could not help but think back to that darn call. Hearing his client say—in an open courtroom to the jury—that she had set "it" up was a devastating blow they were going to have a hard time coming back from.

"It was quite agonizing to sit there and watch it unfold, really," Trevena recalled. "We kind of knew where it was all headed after that. Because unless the jury would nullify" that call, a task attorneys could not ask them to do, Trevena felt they were going to lose the case.

Trevena's only hope at this point was that the jury looked at the case and decided the law was too harsh as it applied to Jennifer "and cut her a break and cut her loose."

Yet, that was so rare, so unheard of, it was unlikely to happen.

As he searched jurors for any type of indication as to what they were thinking or feeling, Trevena felt most members of the jury were "horrified" by the stakes and the job they had in front of them. It was written all over their faces throughout the trial. They shifted in their seats and looked sullen and sad at times. The trial was definitely an emotional tax many in the jury box were paying every hour.

In "combat" mode as the trial carried forth, Trevena developed a strategy that included him "trying to lay the groundwork" for an appeal during the trial itself. His thought was that the state's eagerness to prosecute Jennifer Mee this time would subside if they faced a second trial—a retrial. So Trevena had to do whatever he could to interject grounds for an appeal during the trial itself.

There were, of course, no surprises as Dave Wawrzynski sat and testified for the state during the ASA's direct line of questioning. Wawrzynski, as the lead investigator, talked jurors through what turned into a rather brief investigation that, in Wawrzynski's opinion, was thorough and solid to the core. He explained how one lead pointed them in the next direction and the dominoes all fell together as that day—Sunday—unfolded. The key, the detective said, was that anonymous tipster with the courage to phone in and report what she knew, who she felt was involved in Shannon's death, and where those individuals were hiding out.

From there, Wawrzynski hit on all of the key aspects

of the SPPD's investigation, with him not only leading the charge, but also supervising it.

Walking the crime scene.

Shannon's body.

The evidence at the crime scene.

Doug Bolden and a victimology campaign.

The idea that the bottom of Shannon's socks were clean, indicating to Wawrzynski that his killer or killers had removed Shannon's sneakers, on top of pulling the pockets out of his pants and dropping them slightly, told the detective that this was a common type of snatch-and-grab robbery he had seen many times before.

He spoke about:

- Viewing Shannon's wounds at the scene
- How his investigators did a thorough canvass of the neighborhood
- How the scooter led them to identify Shannon
- How, at first, they had developed a person of interest—Laron—and no one else
- Getting Laron Raiford's name into the system and the SPPD, and ultimately coming up with the name Jenni Charron
- How uncovering Jenni Charron's name led to Lamont, who led to Jennifer Mee
- The arrests at Jenni's friend's apartment
- Phone records
- His interview with Laron
- The three admissions
- How all of the evidence corresponded with what Wawrzynski had heard from Laron, Lamont, and, eventually, Jennifer Mee

Wawrzynski discussed his interviews with Jennifer Mee and how she had admitted to him that she'd first lied about Jenni Charron and Shannon and that park. It was a story they had all made up—and that it was she who had actually set up the meeting with Shannon through MocoSpace.

As they arrived there, ASA LaBruzzo played the tape of Jennifer's second interview, where she had admitted to everything. As the tape played, and Jennifer talked about MocoSpace, crying during that portion of the interview, she sat motionless inside the courtroom, staring down at the oak table in front of her. Her shoulders were slouched; her face drooped. Tears once again were streaming down her cheeks as her chest heaved in and out every so often.

Wearing a white blouse, with her hair tightly pulled back into a bun, her skin pale, Jennifer looked tired and worn down by the trial process. It was almost as if she knew where this was all heading and could do nothing more than slowly accept it, witness after witness. Trevena had already explained to Jennifer and Rachel that there was zero possibility that Jennifer was going to testify on her own behalf. It just wouldn't be prudent to put her on the stand and watch her fall apart emotionally while retelling everything she had explained to the police once already. LaBruzzo would bury her.

On the reverse end of things, the taped interview jurors heard helped John Trevena establish the argument that most of these cases were pleaded out because they were typically slam dunks, once the suspect was brought in and he or she started to talk.

Of course, Jennifer did not know she was admitting to first-degree murder. She believed that by telling the truth she was taking herself out of that part of the crime.

Wawrzynski did a fair job of explaining how the SPPD didn't take a confession or admission and then

close a case. The evidence had to corroborate the
admissions or it wasn't yet a closed case from their
point of view. Pertaining to the notion of Jennifer,
Laron, and Lamont telling that story of Jenni Charron
down at the park meeting Shannon, the SPPD could
not find any corroborating evidence to support it. But
once the suspects coughed up the truth, all of the
other evidence the SPPD had uncovered—namely,
telephone records—fit into that truth like a finely
machined piston into its corresponding cylinder. The
case came together without any effort; everything,
effectively, made sense to detectives after that.

An important fact that Wawrzynski made during this
final part of his direct questioning was that the phone
records taken from Laron's account matched up to what
Jennifer Mee and Jenni Charron and Laron were telling
the SPPD. All of them had said that Jennifer Mee borrowed Laron's phone and used it that night. This was
significant in the context of the phone records. Because
when the SPPD went back and checked out Jenni Charron's phone records—working on the idea that perhaps
the first story was true and would be challenged later
on—they did not find any connection whatsoever to the
case as it had been described for them by the suspects.

"And I looked at Miss Charron's phone," Wawrzynski told the court as his direct testimony wound down,
"which is a phone that was also identified to us. . . .
That number doesn't show on Mr. Griffin's phone log.
But on Mr. Raiford's phone log, there are six phone
contacts between that phone number and Mr. Raiford's
phone number, all during that time period starting
around [eight-seventeen] and ending at [nine forty-
three at night.]"

How damaging was this testimony? Unimpeachable

phone records showed that Jenni and Shannon had never spoken through their own phones—Jenni would have had to be using Laron's phone if she spoke to Shannon on that night. Each suspect and the SPPD's witness, Jenni Charron herself, at one point or another, had said it was Jennifer Mee using Laron's phone. But what's more, Laron had borrowed *Jenni's* phone—another fact established by all the suspects—and had spoken to Jennifer Mee between the time Shannon left his house and when he arrived at the crime scene. This shattered any argument that could be made for Jenni and Shannon hooking up. It was clear that Jennifer Mee (using Laron's phone) was discussing Shannon's trip up to the crime scene with Laron (and Shannon), just as they had all (including Jennifer Mee) told the SPPD in their statements.

Beyond that, when one looked at Shannon's phone records, there was Laron's phone calling and communicating with him.

CHAPTER 88

AFTER A "COMFORT break," called by the judge, John Trevena stood and began his cross-examination of Dave Wawrzynski. He asked the detective how many years he had been with the SPPD.

"It will be ten in October," Wawrzynski said.

A softball—the last one hurled at the detective from John Trevena.

Then Trevena asked if Wawrzynski had heard of

Jennifer Mee before he met her in 2010 as part of the Shannon Griffin murder investigation.

Wawrzynski said he had, in fact, been "familiar" with Miss Mee.

They discussed the runaway incident Wawrzynski and the SPPD took part in back in 2007 after Jennifer's hiccup star had crashed and burned.

Hunter-Olney objected on the grounds of relevancy.

The judge called for a proffer, so Trevena could ask the question of the detective and the judge could make a call if the question and answer were appropriate for jurors to hear later. That meant the jury would be asked to exit the courtroom—again.

When the proffer concluded, still without the jury present, the judge asked Trevena if he wanted to get the answer Wawrzynski had given into the record with jurors, but Trevena indicated that based on the detective's answer it was not that important, after all.

It was very late in the day. Everyone was tired and sleepy from being cooped up in what was a small, stuffy room.

With the jury happily seated again, Trevena moved on to how Wawrzynski had become the lead in the case.

He said it was his turn.

They discussed what a lead detective actually does.

Wawrzynski explained how his job as lead detective was to keep the case moving, collect data and process items pertaining to the investigation in a detailed manner, within a "fair and reasonable amount of time." He was a working manager.

They moved on to talking about the crime scene and what Wawrzynski had seen while walking through it on that Sunday. Through this line of questioning, Trevena eventually led Wawrzynski to the condom wrapper found at the scene. Trevena wanted to know whose DNA had been found on the wrapper.

Wawrzynski agreed it was Laron's.

This was a contentious issue for Trevena. To him, the idea that Laron's DNA had been found on a condom wrapper found near a victim with his pants partially pulled down might suggest more than a robbery. Trevena proposed it might fall more in line with the first story everyone had told the SPPD—that Laron came upon Jenni and Shannon and he snapped. Who was to say the second story they all told wasn't a cover-up for the first to protect Jenni Charron?

As quickly as Trevena latched onto the condom wrapper thread, he was off it and onto how Wawrzynski had developed suspects in the case.

A lot of this might have come across as redundant because it had been established already by other witnesses and by admitted pieces of evidence. In all fairness to John Trevena, however, he was obligated to go over it again to see if the cop kept to his story and didn't leave anything out. Part of Trevena's strategy here was to plant various seeds he could go back to at some point and explain. For example, Trevena brought out in his questioning that Jennifer Mee didn't have a phone or a computer; yet there were four phones and a computer inside the apartment where she was staying at the time.

"Yes, sir," Wawrzynski confirmed.

When Trevena talked about Jenni Charron's phone in particular, he asked Wawrzynski if he had found it interesting that she would shut her phone off during the course of a murder investigation.

"Absolutely," Wawrzynski said, agreeing.

"Did she ever have an explanation for that?"

"Not to me. No, sir," Wawrzynski answered.

"So, that still, to this day, remains unanswered?"

"Yes, sir."

As Trevena mentioned the word "work" as it pertained to Jenni Charron, ASA LaBruzzo objected, knowing where Trevena was going. Then a sidebar conference was called.

Huddled around the bench with Trevena, the ASA explained to the judge how he believed Trevena was now going to "get into whether or not she's a prostitute."

The judge wanted to know if that was the tree Trevena was itching to climb.

"It is," he said, "and there is evidence, and it's very relevant to our defense. . . ."

Explaining further, Trevena said the point he was trying to make was that Jenni Charron's choice of occupation at the time proved she had money, had several phones associated with her job, and, most important, she had a computer and communicated with potential clients online.

Was Trevena saying that Shannon Griffin was a client of Jenni Charron's, and Laron had caught the two of them?

LaBruzzo piped in and made an excellent point when he told the judge that he could agree all of that was significant in the scope of the trial, but it was something Trevena should focus on asking Jenni Charron herself when she sat on the witness stand and testified.

The judge mentioned how it would be hearsay for the detective to talk about Jenni Charron's alleged call girl status back then, especially seeing that she had no criminal record of prostitution.

Trevena balked at that, saying how he was hoping Wawrzynski could talk about the crime scene and what was found and how it could possibly appear to be a scenario other than a robbery.

"Like what?" the judge asked.

"Well, for example, the fact that she was working as a sex worker would better coincide with the crime scene and what was seen there in terms of his pants down, the condom. I mean, you're asking me, basically, to give [up] my defense."

"No, I'm not," the judge countered. "I'm trying to figure out how this is all relevant and should come into evidence."

"I can promise you I'll tie it in."

"You want to ask him if she's a hooker?" the judge quipped.

"I can ask him a more general question if the court is unhappy with that question—" Trevena said.

"I am!" the judge immediately cut him off.

Finishing up his thought, Trevena said: ". . . as to whether or not [the detective is] familiar with these types of aroma therapy spas, which she claims in the midst she was employed by, that those are typically fronts for prostitution."

"No offense," the judge said, "you better—this is sort of hilarious—you better think about how you answer that question. There are lots of women who do yoga, like me, that—"

This time, Trevena tried to cut her off, saying, "That's—"

But she wouldn't let him, finishing her thought with: ". . . that go to aroma therapy spas. And I can *assure* you, there is no prostitution going on in those."

"Not the type that she was employed by!" Trevena said.

The judge sustained the objection and explained to

Trevena what he could and could not ask the detective regarding Jenni Charron's chosen profession.

When they resumed, Trevena went off on an entirely different track.

CHAPTER 89

IT FELT TO John Trevena that anytime he was gaining the least bit of momentum, the hammer came down as the judge wagged a finger and warned him to watch out, don't go down that road. Here was his most hostile witness to date on the stand, Dave Wawrzynski, and he couldn't question him the way in which he had planned.

So Trevena switched tactics.

He asked Wawrzynski if he had been "aware that Miss Mee had a monthly income."

"Was I? No, sir."

A few questions later, Trevena wanted to know if Wawrzynski felt Jennifer Mee had been cooperative with the investigation.

The cop said she had been.

But Jenni Charron, on the other hand, Trevena asked, she was uncooperative, wasn't she?

Wawrzynski said yes, at first, but then she came around.

Trevena then explained how Jenni was told she was a witness and not a suspect. Then the attorney asked, "Is it suddenly when she realized she was not going to be charged, she became cooperative?"

"I don't know what was in her head," Wawrzynski

said. "I can tell you that during our investigation, at no point did I consider her . . . as a suspect in the investigation."

Trevena focused on Jenni and her potential "participation" in "criminal acts related to this case." As he did this, it felt as though he was attacking everything about her.

Wawrzynski kept telling him he never felt Jenni had committed any serious crimes. He didn't go into detail, but Wawrzynski implied that cops give breaks every day in order to get the bigger catch. You don't bust a dude smoking a joint on the street if he gives up the guy selling pounds of weed out of his home. It's all part of a day in the life of solving crimes.

As they continued, Trevena chipped away at Wawrzynski's leadership skills in this investigation by stating—as a question—how the detective had not known that Jennifer Mee had given that first statement until just the previous year (2012), when Wawrzynski had sat down to give a deposition in the case.

Wawrzynski said that was correct. But there was a lot about the investigation he didn't know. The lead in a case is not privy to every single nuance and beat of a police force as it investigates.

By his determination, Wawrzynski explained, after Trevena got a bit testy asking for a "simple" yes or no in relation to Wawrzynski having failed at some aspects of being the lead detective, "Ultimately the facts that Miss Mee provided me were consistent with other statements I had received which I was not able to disprove."

Trevena moved on to the press conference. Did Wawrzynski brief the chief? Did he participate in preparing the department for that press conference?

Wawrzynski explained that he answered to his immediate supervisor and briefed him about the investigation. What the chief and public relations people from the department did was out of his hands and he had nothing to do with it.

MocoSpace was next.

All the SPPD was able to get out of MocoSpace with a subpoena was "confirmation" that three (Lamont Newton, Shannon Griffin, and Jennifer Mee) of the four had accounts. The website claimed to have nothing more as far as records.

Then came the question, perhaps, many were asking. "Ultimately," Trevena said, "her arrest and the prosecution based on that arrest, you would have to be candid and admit, is based on her statement, not *physical* forensic evidence?"

"Her statement alone?" the detective asked to clarify.

"I won't say her 'statement alone.' I'll say 'testimonial statements'?"

"Based on testimonial, that's the primary. There are some other pieces that are part of that, but a significant portion of it is based upon testimony."

"And if someone had given a false story, had *lied,* that could taint your investigation through no fault of yours?"

Ready for that question, Wawrzynski said, "Which is one of the reasons we try to verify as much as we could through the phone records to confirm that these were the phones that were used to contact each other. Which is why we try to verify through testing of the items *not* attributed to the victim who might possibly own those items to put them at the crime scene, if we could, or at least with items familiar to that."

"Understood," Trevena countered. "But, ultimately, you *weren't* really able to get any reliable forensic data that you could bring into court and show the jury and say, 'See how this connects to Jennifer Mee. We know she sent this text. We know . . .'"

"With texting?" Wawrzynski asked before answering his own question: "No, sir. There are *two* areas where, forensically, she's attached to items."

Trevena said he wanted to talk about that, adding, "Because this *entire* case, if I understand correctly, there is *two* forensic items, and *only* two, that tie to Miss Mee?"

The compelling way Trevena put it called into question the idea that the SPPD had only two forensic items connected to Jennifer—as if there needed to be more than one piece of forensic evidence tying a suspect to a murder. Still, Trevena, such a competent and seasoned defense attorney, was smart to place into question even the forensic evidence the state had against Jennifer Mee.

"Yes, sir," Wawrzynski agreed.

"That would be the fingerprint that was on the driver's license?" Trevena asked.

Wawrzynski nodded and affirmed.

Then Trevena wanted to know if it was possible that the fingerprint could have been "transferred" to the license later on, after the item was taken back to the apartment.

The detective said it was possible.

The other piece of forensic evidence was a tank top found inside the backpack brought to the crime scene by Laron Raiford. Jennifer Mee's DNA was found on that shirt. But, as Trevena concluded, it did not prove anything as far as her being responsible for the murder.

"By itself, no, sir," Wawrzynski said, adding that all of this evidence, combined with the statements they had taken from each suspect and the witness, was what they call "corroborative." It wasn't one piece of the puzzle that made a picture, so to speak, but all of them put together. And even if there was a missing piece here and there, the picture could still come into clear focus.

Trevena tried to trip up the detective by questioning every aspect of his investigation, but Wawrzynski had his answers ready. It was not the first time this detective had been grilled relentlessly on the stand. He expected it here. He understood what Trevena was trying to accomplish, but in the end, as he carefully explained to jurors, as a cop you have to follow the facts as they come to you. A cop should not interject his opinion into a case, or choose a path to go down and put on proverbial blinders. You follow the evidence, as clichéd at it sounded, and you allow it to dictate where a case takes you. Jennifer Mee had brought herself into this case, the others corroborated her independent story, the evidence they gathered backed a lot of it up, and here they were, putting all of that to the ultimate test of a murder trial.

After a back-and-forth between them regarding how many shots were fired and if the number of shots at a scene constituted a robbery or perhaps some other type of crime, Wawrzynski complained about being asked to inject his "opinion" into it, adding how that was something investigators shouldn't do.

"Okay," Trevena said, "you know that Jennifer Mee's first version of events . . . was that Laron Raiford became enraged because he had discovered that Jennifer Charron had had communication with the victim, Shannon Griffin?"

"Yes, sir."

"And that that's why Laron Raiford snapped and filled him with bullets?"

"I've heard that—yes, sir."

"Now, I want you to think carefully while I ask this very *important* question. As we sit here today, you cannot rule out *that* possibility, can you, sir?"

"I cannot. Can I add—can I add something to that?"

"That was my question," Trevena said, with almost an unspoken warning not to add anything to what was just said.

"Yes, sir."

"Now," Trevena said, and then stared down at his notes in silence for quite some time. Then: "May I have a moment, Your Honor?"

There was a long pause in the courtroom as Trevena conferred with his colleagues and Wawrzynski waited for the next question.

When Trevena returned, he said, "Your Honor, I believe that's all I have."

Of course, when ASA Hunter-Olney got up and began her redirect, she offered Wawrzynski that missed opportunity he'd lost with Trevena to clarify something he had wanted to "add."

Smart move.

"There's two parts to that," the detective said. "One is—No one else *ever* repeated that statement. Even her *own* statement after that doesn't equal that first statement. And that second statement that she provided to me is consistent with the other statements that I heard—"

But Trevena objected and the detective stopped.

"Overruled."

Wawrzynski continued without being told: "The second part of that is . . . In the phone records, in looking at Mr. Griffin's telephone, of the phone numbers provided to me by the individuals involved in this investigation, there was *no* phone contact by Miss Charron's phone or Mr. Raiford's phone to Mr. Griffin's phone *prior* to that call we described happening at approximately eight P.M. on the twenty-third of October, all the way up to the sixteenth of October. Before that date period, I don't have those records, but for the period that I requested, there was *no* phone contact in there."

Hunter-Olney asked a few additional questions and indicated that was all she had.

Trevena passed on a recross.

Another day in the books.

CHAPTER 90

THE FOLLOWING MORNING, September 20, began with a surprise. Anticipating the state resting its case, John Trevena submitted a motion for a "judgment of acquittal." It was a formality, in many respects, and all defense lawyers try it (or some version of it) at one time or another during the course of a trial. In that motion, Trevena argued that Detective Wawrzynski had not fully answered his questions and that the state had failed to contradict—"which is their burden"—every "reasonable hypothesis of innocence."

In Trevena's view, a shoddy, slipshod, and speedy investigation, based on a rush to judgment of the defendant because of her celebrity, had brought Jennifer Mee to this point of being tried for first-degree murder, and there was no basis or solid foundation for that prosecution.

"I would respectfully suggest the obligation to not let this case go to jury based upon the testimony you've heard," Trevena asked the judge.

Further along, he talked about a major problem he had with the lack of evidence in the case and how it could not possibly point to Jennifer Mee being involved in the robbery. At best, Jennifer should have been charged with accessory after the fact. But first-degree murder? It was more than a stretch.

The judge was quick with her answer.

Denied.

Move on.

The jury was brought in after a short break.

The state then rested its case against Jennifer Mee.

After asking for and taking a recess, so Trevena could have a conversation with his first defense witness, he called Jenni Charron to the stand. Jenni was reluctant to testify for the defense.

With her head tilted to her left, wearing a brown dress, Jenni was wheeled into the courtroom by ASA LaBruzzo as courtroom spectators all turned to watch.

Yes, wheeled.

Since the last time Jenni had seen Jennifer Mee, Jenni's life had taken somewhat of a downward spiral. In fact, at one time, Jenni was considered a "reluctant witness." Back in August 2013, a month ago, during pretrial hearings in Jennifer Mee's case, Jenni was called to the stand, but she had failed to show up. She had been "avoiding" the pretrial hearings, Trevena had said publicly, because he believed she was "hiding something." Jenni had been so "reluctant" to testify, in fact, the judge had to order an arrest warrant for her during pretrial hearings. She finally showed up after that, with a good reason for not being there previously: Jenni had been in jail on an "order to show cause" charge for not appearing at pretrial hearings before that.

There was a brooding look of melancholy on Jenni's face as she sat in her wheelchair behind the microphone. She'd suffered from Crohn's disease for a while and had also gotten a spinal infection that had paralyzed her from the waist down. Testifying in court, confined to a wheelchair, was certainly not the situation she had envisioned on this day, but here she was, unenthusiastic or not, ready and willing to answer any questions she could.

In Trevena's view, Jenni had changed her story "many times." This was probably the reason why the state had not called her. But the reality of it was that Jenni Charron had lied—telling that same lie they all told—until she realized the others had come clean.

Despite her situation and despondent gaze, Jenni was still a very beautiful woman. Her hair was tied tightly back in a ponytail, which flowed around her right shoulder. She wore a modest amount of makeup, which accentuated perfectly her striking facial features.

The first question Trevena had for Jenni was proffered because of the potential embarrassing and controversial nature of it.

With the jury out of the room, Trevena asked Jenni about her job at the spa during those weeks when they had all lived together and the crime had occurred.

In her answer, Jenni beat around the bush—not truly, in Trevena's opinion, revealing the truth about her work. She called what she did at the time "stress relief."

Trevena responded by asking if she meant "manual stimulation"?

Jenni somewhat agreed.

The state didn't quite get what was going on. The judge didn't, either. It was as if Trevena and Jenni were speaking in a code only they understood.

So Trevena asked his question again, in a different, more straightforward way: "You committed some sex acts in exchange for money while working at the spa?"

Again, Jenni answered in circles, saying, "Well, we did holistic therapy, aroma therapy, stress relief, and stuff like . . . I mean, I don't know exactly. . . ." She stopped herself, clearly unsure how to articulate what she wanted to say.

"Again, you need to . . . like we said, we have to be perfectly honest." Trevena paused, and then came out with it: "Did that include, you know, for better or worse, lack of a term, for example, like a hand job?"

"Well, sometimes. Sometimes it was fetish-based things. Sometimes it was just sitting there talking to someone."

"Would they sometimes want to touch you as well?"

"It depended on the person, or what you were comfortable with, and stuff inside the room."

"Understood," Trevena answered.

ASA LaBruzzo was still unsure of what Jenni was referring to as a job description and what she actually did for her customers. So he asked a series of questions himself, many of which were even more direct, beginning with, "Miss Charron, did you ever manually masturbate an individual while at the spa?"

"I—" she started to say as Trevena interrupted.

"Asked and answered!"

"I think it was more general than that," LaBruzzo pleaded to the judge.

The judge implored Jenni to answer the question.

After LaBruzzo asked again, Jenni said, "I may have."

"'May have,' ma'am?" LaBruzzo said.

"Well, I mean, I had . . . Yeah, I—"

LaBruzzo was getting impatient: "Okay. Had you ever engaged in other sex acts while at the spa—you personally?"

"What are we defining 'sex acts' as?"

"Did you ever engage in sexual intercourse?"

"No. I just did more of the fetish based."

"What do you mean 'fetish based'?"

"Spanking, domination, submission, role-play."

"Everything that you did was consensual, correct?"

"Yes."

"Were you ever charged with a crime related to that?"

"No."

Then LaBruzzo brought up a good point when he asked Jenni to talk about what she did outside the spa. Like, for example, had she engaged in the same work outside of that spa?

"No," she answered.

After a lengthy conversation between Trevena, LaBruzzo, and the judge regarding what could and could not be introduced once the jury was brought back in, the judge said, "I will let you ask something briefly about sex at the workplace based on what you put on the record about the condom. It should be brief.

It should not be the emphasis. . . . All witnesses . . . should be treated with dignity."

With that, Trevena called who would be his first witness for Jennifer Mee's defense, giving Jenni Charron a break.

Dave Wawrzynski walked back into the courtroom.

Trevena asked very few questions, as did the ASA. When Wawrzynski was finished, Trevena sat and went through his notes, preparing for his next witness.

CHAPTER 91

FOR DEFENSE ATTORNEY John Trevena, a rare practical realist when it came to defending his clients, he kept going back to Jenni Charron, the SPPD's investigation, and the state going on a head-hunting expedition, targeting his client. The idea that Jenni could have set up the meeting and met Shannon that night herself, and when Laron found out he flew off into a rage and killed the twenty-two-year-old Walmart employee, was not so far-fetched. The idea of an assignation was not absurd or improbable, given the nature of what Jenni did to earn a living at the time. On top of that, it was the only line of defense with any substance for Jennifer Mee that Trevena had at his disposal.

One of the biggest hurdles Trevena faced with regard to that fight was that when you looked at the statements of Laron, Lamont, and even Jennifer Mee, none of them had involved Jenni planning or executing any part of the crime. If Jenni had been involved

on any level, one would think Lamont and Jennifer
Mee (especially) would have tossed her under a bus.
They hardly knew the woman. There was no loyalty
there. In addition, Laron could not have cared too
much for Jenni's feelings if he was sleeping with other
women, including Jennifer Mee. Why wouldn't any of
them try pinning part of the crime on her?

"By her own statements and her own conduct, Jennifer Charron is definitely a part of this," Trevena
explained to me. "For the life of me, I am never going
to figure out why she was never charged at least—*at
least!*—with accessory after the fact, which is a very
serious felony when the underlying crime is murder."

Jenni Charron had no trouble admitting to being an
accessory after the fact, in her depositions before trial,
to the SPPD, and in interviews with the state. Furthermore, she had cut no deal with the state in exchange
for her testimony against Jennifer Mee. She had never
been offered immunity, at least on paper, or given any
legal protection whatsoever.

Yet, she was still never charged with a crime.

"They cut her a [side] deal for some inexplicable
reason, to this day I do not understand," Trevena said.

Trevena latched onto the idea that when one looked
at this case closely, it became clear that yes, what Jenni
admitted to was bad enough, but there's a fundamental belief there for Trevena that she was involved on a
more deeper level than she had ever admitted to.

"Why didn't the state and investigators say, 'Huh,
maybe she's a co-conspirator'? Why didn't they ask
themselves that question and dig into it?"

A scratching-of-the-head moment for Trevena came
when Jenni was first brought in to the SPPD for questioning on that day she was picked up while walking
with Jennifer Mee. After she said she wanted a lawyer,

the SPPD immediately told her, "You don't need a lawyer."

"Then they get her to talk and tell all these different types of stories. . . . It makes no sense to me," Trevena lamented.

Jenni was twenty-four years old as she sat nervously awaiting John Trevena's first question. She expected a hard-hitting interrogation, some sort of accusatory, finger-pointing query that would put her on the defensive right away. The proffer had given Jenni a solid look into where Trevena wanted to take things.

In his soothing, calm tone, Trevena started by asking Jenni to go through her vitals: where she lived, her boyfriend at the time of the crime, her roommates.

Jurors sat composed, closely listening.

Jenni explained.

"How long had you known Laron Raiford?"

"Maybe a couple of months."

"And were you dating as a couple?"

"Yes."

"And, in fact, you were carrying his child?"

"Yes."

Then, not wasting much time, Trevena got into it.

"At the time, you were employed at a spa facility, correct?"

"Correct."

"And, as part of that employment, not to offend," Trevena said, an embarrassed tone in his voice, "but there were sex acts that would be performed by you in exchange for money?"

"Yes."

"And that provided you a pretty decent living, as I understand it?"

"Yeah," Jenni said, adding, "What I did there with the whole dominatrix and fetish thing paid *extremely* well."

Jenni wore large loop earrings, which dangled from each ear and nearly touched the top of her shoulders. She stared at Trevena mostly, but every once in a while, Jenni took a hasty glance over at Jennifer Mee. She'd dropped her nerves, and yet it was clear she was uncomfortable sitting and answering questions about a life she had left behind long ago.

As her testimony continued, Jenni described what happened that night when she got home from a twelve-hour shift (nine to nine) at the spa. She recalled how they had plans to go see a movie, the odd behavior displayed by all three of her roommates, how Jennifer Mee, strangely, was dressed too nicely to go out to the movies.

Then they moved on to what became a very argumentative subject: Jennifer Mee's monthly government check of "six hundred seventy-fivish dollars," by Jenni's estimate. The question, for one, had to be proffered; but even when the jury was brought back, they talked this issue through so much that one had to guess what the whole point of it was.

Jennifer Mee was on state assistance. Big deal.

By the time they were finished, it became clear that Trevena wanted on record that Jennifer had money of her own and didn't need to rob people in order to survive.

But then neither did Jenni Charron, who made more than twice as much as Jennifer Mee.

With that settled, Jenni talked about what time the movie was set to start, telling jurors it was slated for ten o'clock at night.

Jenni next described how Lamont and Laron took a phone call and they left the apartment shortly after.

"And Miss Mee, at this point in time, was *still* in the apartment?" Trevena asked, and then realized maybe he shouldn't have.

"No, she had left. She left the apartment first and then called the boys, Lamont and Laron, and they left after getting the phone call from her."

And there, in just a few sentences, an image emerged that Trevena didn't need infused into the minds of jurors: *Jennifer Mee leaving, heading out to the location, making contact with Shannon, and then calling in her muscle to roll him.*

"Okay," Trevena said, trying to pull back, "but you *don't* know that was *her* calling?"

"Well, when I seen her number, I gave Laron the phone."

Jenni had just confirmed that Jennifer Mee left the house with Laron's phone and then called Laron on her phone. Phone records backed up the calls, and now a witness put people behind the earpiece of each phone.

Trevena and Jenni discussed whether Jennifer Mee ever mentioned anything about participating in a robbery (before that night).

Jenni said no, she had not. But later, after the crime had been committed, Jenni, of course, heard all about it from Jennifer.

Jenni admitted that she'd seen the .38 revolver in possession of both boys. She told that story of Laron and Lamont coming home one night and waving it around outside on the stoop, claiming Lamont's brother "had got shot at," so they went out and bought a weapon.

Trevena took Jenni back to the night in question, October 23, 2010. He asked the witness again about the movie. After that, he had her explain what happened in those minutes after Laron, Lamont, and Jennifer left the apartment.

Jenni described how, not too long after they had all left, Jennifer came running into the apartment, breathing heavily, saying she had heard gunshots. And Jenni said she immediately went into "rush mode," trying to locate Laron and Lamont.

From there, Jenni went through the entire night: collecting as much evidence as she could from the boys; calling her friend and going over to that uptown apartment; discussing what they would say if the cops came around; wanting to go back to the crime scene to fetch all the items they had left behind. She didn't leave much out and her version came across as sincere and believable. There was an odd likeability about Jenni as she spoke. Her voice was soft and soothing. It sounded pleasant and genuine. While on the stand, she admitted to committing several major felonies herself, without as much as a second thought. These were crimes punishable by serious time in prison. Yet, she laid it all out, unafraid of what perhaps might come of not having secured any deal with the state's attorney's office. In total, the story she told Trevena was on par almost identically with what Jenni had told the police after she had admitted her first story—like the others'—was a lie.

Trevena focused on the conversations they'd had while at Jenni's friend's apartment regarding what they were going to tell police. What hurt Jennifer Mee here was that Jenni could only talk in general terms about what was said because all of it, if she were to

repeat conversations verbatim, would be considered
inadmissible hearsay.

Still, even as Trevena asked Jenni to talk about it in
"subject matter" only, LaBruzzo objected repeatedly,
until the judge told Trevena to move on.

Not getting very far, Trevena asked Jenni if any
promises had been made to her while she was at the
SPPD answering questions.

LaBruzzo objected.

A sidebar conference followed.

They agreed to another proffer.

It got them nowhere. With the jury back, Trevena
asked a question about Jenni being "persuaded" to
give a statement, and she said yes, she might have been.

Then Trevena asked a few more questions that
amounted to details already discussed, and soon he
passed the witness to the state.

During the state's cross-examination, the one item
Jenni mentioned was that she had worked twelve-hour
days at the spa and paid all the bills at the apartment.
The three basically lived off her. The other fact Jenni
shared was that she had no idea where the crime
scene even was, until she saw it on the news after being
"released" from the SPPD.

When they got to the bleach and who actually
poured it on the clothes to wash off any forensic evidence, Jenni could not recall who was responsible.

"And you're not telling this jury that *you* poured
bleach in that bathtub on those clothes, are you?"

"No."

"Jennifer [Mee] poured the bleach on the clothes?"

"I can't say that for a hundred percent."

"Jennifer and Lamont were in the bathroom?" Hunter-Olney asked.

"Yeah."

"You smelled a strong odor of bleach coming from that bathroom?"

"Yes."

"So Jennifer or Lamont poured bleach on the clothes?"

"Laron was in the bathroom at some point, too. I can't—"

"But *you* didn't pour bleach on the clothes?"

"No," Jenni said, then added without being asked: "I may have come up with the idea."

The ASA asked Jenni about her relationship with Laron: "And were you in love with Laron?"

"After a while, yes."

"Were you faithful to Laron?"

"Yes."

"Was Laron faithful to you?"

"No."

Trevena objected under relevancy and ASA Hunter-Olney, after a quick conference with LaBruzzo, indicated she was finished.

CHAPTER 92

THROUGHOUT THE THREE days she sat and watched her daughter's trial, Rachel Robidoux was entirely focused on every word each witness had said.

Rachel tried desperately to stay in the moment. It was the hardest thing she had ever done, Rachel said later: to sit and watch her child slowly drown and not be able to toss her a life preserver.

"Totally surreal."

During what had amounted to almost three years of pretrial hearings, Rachel explained later, "I never once allowed my mind to think about what could be a life sentence," a sentence Jennifer faced if the jury decided on a first-degree murder verdict. Rachel tried to keep her mind on "no more than ten to fifteen years, tops," with the hope that the jury would understand Jennifer's role and come back with a much lesser charge. It only seemed natural for Rachel to see things this way. How could a jury give life to a girl in Jennifer's position, someone who clearly had nothing to do with carrying out the murder? In Rachel's view, her daughter had no more set up Shannon to be murdered than she had known a murder was going to take place.

As Rachel entered the courtroom each day during trial, she told herself that when the time came for jurors to deliberate, they would sit down and realize what Rachel had seen and heard during the course of the testimony and evidence: Jennifer had committed crimes, certainly, but not this horrible crime she was being tried for.

As the afternoon session on September 20, 2013, continued, the court was one step closer to that jury verdict Rachel was now thinking about. John Trevena, after the court took a long break for lunch, told the judge he was prepared to rest his case.

Two witnesses and the defense was done.

With the defense resting, it was time for Jennifer

Mee to stand and answer a few questions from the judge, including, "How far did you go in school?"

"About tenth grade."

"You can read and write, ma'am?"

"For the most part, yes, ma'am."

"Have you had sufficient time to discuss with your lawyer . . . the issue about whether or not you wish to testify?"

"Yes, ma'am."

"Have you also had sufficient time to discuss with your lawyer any request for lesser included offenses?"

"Yes, ma'am."

The judge asked Jennifer to sit down. She then had a lengthy discussion with the lawyers about the charges and how she was going to explain the varying degrees of murder to the jury before sending them off to deliberate: fifteen years for manslaughter was a sentence the judge mentioned as a possibility; thirty years for accessory after the fact; life in prison, of course, for first-degree murder.

The jury had options on the table. They could effectively cut Jennifer Mee a break if they saw fit.

When they were finished discussing the jury's options, the judge asked Jennifer to stand again.

"So as it is, if you were found guilty of first-degree murder, I'd have to give you life in prison. If you were found guilty of accessory after the fact, I could give you up to thirty years. If you were found guilty of manslaughter, I could give you up to fifteen years. Do you understand that?"

"Yes, ma'am."

"Are you in agreement with your lawyers about the lesser included offenses?"

"Yes, ma'am."

After the judge asked a few more questions and received "yes, ma'am" answers from Jennifer, the judge told her, "You may be seated."

CHAPTER 93

A MURDER TRIAL is a lot like a play: the judge is the director, and the sidebars and proffers are the discussions with the crew backstage. There's drama, laughter, tears. There's even joy, as well as anger. In the end, it's a sad affair no matter what, because, within all of that production, the most important reason why they are there to begin with gets lost: the victim. Where was Shannon's voice? Where was that "closure" families seek, but can never find? Here was a young man with an entire life ahead of him whose existence had been snuffed out.

Whether Shannon was going downtown to meet a girl or to buy a bag of weed, it did not matter. The only significant factor in it was that he should be alive today. And jurors, as they sat and listened, looking over at Jennifer Mee every so often, trying to gauge her gaze and figure out where she was coming from, were going to have the opportunity to honor Shannon Griffin by holding one of his killers responsible—that is, *if* they believed the evidence supported the claim made by the state that Jennifer Mee played a part in Shannon's murder.

When it came time for the jury to hear closing statements, a trial that had lasted all of three days felt as though it had gone on forever. Why? Nobody could later figure out. It was just one of those odd things that arises out of the dust of a murder trial.

As the state's closing got under way, one phrase would define the purported future of Jennifer Mee. Christopher LaBruzzo felt he and ASA Hunter-Olney had presented a solid case for guilt. The foundation for that was a tape-recorded conversation, or State's Exhibit 50, of Jennifer calling Rachel from jail on the day she was arrested for murder.

LaBruzzo played that tape for jurors before he began. And it was here, where that phrase would ring throughout the courtroom one more time, and, in the state's view, place the onus of masterminding this crime on one person, in *her* words.

". . . *I set everything up.* . . ."

That was the key "admission" from the telephone call—that one line, according to the state, was all each juror needed to hear to convict.

Putting it into perspective, after the tape played, LaBruzzo addressed jurors, saying, "Ladies and gentlemen, we're here today . . . because Jennifer Mee set everything up. More correctly, she set up Shannon Griffin for a robbery. A robbery which, and as you know in this case, he ultimately was shot four times in the chest in a dark alleyway."

LaBruzzo asked jurors to focus on the two questions the judge had explained and which they *must* answer: Was there a crime committed? And did Jennifer Mee commit that crime?

The verdict could be distilled down to those two factors.

The most damaging statement LaBruzzo could have

made during his entire closing wasn't a point-the-finger moment, accusing Jennifer of being an evil, dark, and twisted sociopath that set out to murder a young man. (She was not that person, and LaBruzzo was smart enough to see it.) It wasn't an accusation by the ASA that Jennifer sat down and constructed this robbery and murder days or weeks in advance. (She certainly had not.) The most powerful statement the ASA made as he spoke loud and clear within the first few minutes of his opening turned out to be how "the court is going to tell you that under Florida's felony murder law, that if you engage in certain crimes, in this case a robbery, and during the commission of that crime, a person is murdered, then you can be *guilty* of murder in the first degree under a felony murder theory. . . . Certain crimes, like robbery, are dangerous enough and have been enumerated by the legislature to include that if you commit a murder in the course of it, you are now *guilty* of murder in the first degree."

Jurors were bound by the law. This was regardless of what they felt or thought about Jennifer Mee, her life, and how much she might have participated in the crime.

From that crucial point, LaBruzzo pivoted every other factor of his closing. He explained the instructions the jury received. He implored jurors to understand that Jennifer "helped" other people commit first-degree murder. He said the state proved this during the trial far beyond any reasonable doubt.

He then answered the question of whether the murder could have been the result of a sexual rendezvous turned deadly—the "Jenni Charron hooking up with Shannon Griffin" theory Trevena had trumpeted throughout the trial.

"There's been some suggestion to you that by the

fact that his pants were down that *that* could, in some way . . . speculate that there may have been some sexual crime going on back there. . . . One, we know that his pockets were emptied. So you have to assume he had something in his pockets that they wanted. People carry their wallet, their keys, in their pocket, and we know that that was taken from him."

Trevena had given it the old college try, but as LaBruzzo summed up the sexual encounter possibility, it felt like a lifeless and weak argument totally devoid of any momentum that it might have gathered heading toward the closings.

"And then there's this condom," LaBruzzo said, continuing to try and answer Trevena's second theory. "And I guess that's the link that there may be a sexual crime occurring back in this area." He then cleared up any misinformation jurors might have had about this evidence, adding, "It's a condom *wrapper.* . . . And we know it has Mr. Laron Raiford's DNA on it. So, what does that tell you? . . . One thing it *can't* tell you is *when* it was put there. It never can and never will. So at some point in time, either that night or at some point previous to that, Mr. Raiford had been in that dark alleyway. Look, it's right around the corner from his house. . . ."

LaBruzzo then furthered his point by stating how Jenni had admitted that Laron was unfaithful—and where would a better place be, LaBruzzo suggested, to cheat on your girlfriend than in the alleyway behind your apartment.

The ASA did not spend much time on this because, in the end, jurors believed one side or the other. There was no gray area there within the Jenni/Shannon sex crime idea.

LaBruzzo hit on the scooter, the phone records, the testimony the state had presented, Jennifer's statements to the police and, finally, the recording. It was all there in that phone call between a mother and her child.

When all was said and done, LaBruzzo explained, the case against Jennifer Mee boiled down to one "principal [main] theory." And that was to "follow the law" as citizens of the community doing your duty as jurors. If jurors simply did that, LaBruzzo was certain, they'd have to come back with a first-degree murder verdict.

He reminded the jury of a very important point that had somehow been overlooked throughout the trial: "It takes *her* to make this happen. . . . She tells you she brought him there."

Was it that simple?

After perhaps carrying on too long, by going through jury instructions more in depth than what was needed, LaBruzzo concluded by saying how Jennifer "benefited from the robbery. She was able to evade detection, at least temporarily, and she's guilty of murder in the first degree. Thank you."

CHAPTER 94

JOHN TREVENA WAS feeling rather ambivalent as he stood to give his closing statement. It had been an uphill battle all the way. Wrapping the case up with a bow was not going to be any easier. Jennifer Mee, Trevena knew, faced a mountain of incriminating evidence if one was to take into account the law and how it pertained to her case. Trevena's hope, of course, was for the jury to see his point that the possibility of Jenni Charron and Shannon Griffin meeting to have sex, and Laron Raiford catching them, was enough to cause reasonable doubt. He felt good about that portion of the case. Jurors had to consider that it could have happened that way.

At least . . . he hoped so.

Trevena began by explaining that the deliberation process had rules that needed to be followed very carefully. There was a burden of proof to consider: reasonable doubt and actual evidence of the crimes being committed by the defendant. Was all of that present in this case? Trevena seemed to ask.

"Miss Mee is not charged with robbery. However, to be guilty of felony murder in Florida, you *must* find that she is guilty of robbery in order to reach a guilty verdict of felony murder. So if you find there is *no* robbery, there can be *no* first-degree murder."

Trevena then broke into a long explanation of reasonable doubt and how it was not just something heard on TV programs. There should be zero reasonable doubt in each juror's mind if the jury reached a verdict of guilty.

He then described the first few witnesses and how their testimony did not do much in making Jennifer Mee guilty of first-degree murder. When he got to Doug Bolden, Trevena elegantly used part of his testimony to point out an inconsistency with the state's charges and the case prosecutors had presented.

"What Mr. Bolden said that was of great importance

is that this was his cousin's *first* vacation, because he had his one-year anniversary at Walmart, who is a drug-free employer—another corroborating factor to his drug-free lifestyle. He had been given the week off and he was going to meet a girl. . . . He had dressed up, was excited, was wearing a lot of cologne. He had said . . . he's going out to see a girl. Nothing about he's going to purchase marijuana—that theory by the state *fails.* . . ."

Continuing, Trevena mentioned all the witnessed and talked a bit about their testimony and how it reflected on Jennifer Mee's innocence. It was rather tedious, but it was something Trevena felt he had to do in order to build upon his points of reasonable doubt and the testimony failing to establish a first-degree murder charge.

Then it was on to the phone call between Jennifer and Rachel—perhaps Trevena's biggest stumbling block.

"The state relies *solely* on the last statement (that prison call). And, unfortunately," Trevena explained passionately, making a solid argument, "she is being pulled away by some jail employee." He said you could hear what was going on in the background, quoting what had been said as "'You need to put the phone down. Come with me.'" Trevena then explained how Jennifer's phone time was up. He argued that had she been able to talk "a little bit longer, we may have had more answers and more explanation as her mother continued to question about what was going on." But she had been "cut off exactly at the point that she said, 'Well, I set everything up.'" He asked jurors to ask themselves what that actually meant. It was out of context, Trevena suggested. One line taken entirely out of a call's framework cannot be enough to convict a young woman of first-degree murder.

Or could it?

"That statement standing alone is *hardly* evidence of murder," Trevena continued. He said that nobody in the courtroom, including the state, was "suggesting that Miss Mee was trying to have . . . this gentleman murdered." He added how it was never part of any "*plan* or *intent*" to see that Shannon Griffin wound up dead.

The interviews with police were next. This was where Trevena saw an opportunity to bring in all sorts of reasonable doubt.

"What was jaw-dropping about that was Detective Wawrzynski, according to him, was completely unaware that Detective Gibson had conducted a *taped* interview of Jennifer Mee just minutes before [he had], and admitted [that] he didn't find out until I confronted him in his deposition almost a year later. He's the *lead* detective. *The. Lead. Detective.*"

Jenni Charron was next.

"But, interestingly, Jennifer Charron, when she took the stand, she seemed really street-smart. She had an answer for almost everything." Trevena talked about how "freely" Jenni "admitted . . . that she engaged in acts to try to cover up what the boys had done." He listed several of the laws she had broken. Then he pointed out, "She invoked her right to a lawyer." He said Jenni "stonewalled" the police. "When you juxtapose the two of them, you have Jennifer Charron—and they are both named Jennifer, oddly enough—and Jennifer Mee. And you have this . . . sex worker, makes good money living her life" and "you have Jennifer Mee, nineteen years old, ninth-grade education, kind of an introvert. . . ."

The implication was that Jennifer Mee was the perfect scapegoat—the ideal stooge to take Jenni's place (and blame) in the crime.

"And then the one (Jenni Charron) that freely admits felonious conduct gets a complete free pass and walks out police station doors!" Trevena explained how he thought it was "remarkable." He said the "whole idea" that the crime was a "setup for a drug deal for marijuana" turned out to be "completely inconsistent with the facts. . . . The victim did *not* use drugs."

Still, Trevena had one question to answer: What was Jennifer referring to in her phone call regarding *"Because I set everything up"*?

He needed to explain that.

"So, what was it that could have been 'set up' by Jennifer Mee when she says, 'I set it up'?" Trevena said, and then paused briefly before answering his own question: "'I set up a meeting with Jennifer Charron'? Miss Charron, attractive young lady, she admitted to you, she's a sex worker, a prostitute."

"I object," LaBruzzo said as Trevena stopped. "This is not facts in evidence."

"Sustained," the judge said with a cautionary glance toward Trevena. "Move on. . . ."

From there, John Trevena took a chance, saying, "To this day, how can you go back and render a verdict of guilty for murder in the first degree? And the lessers that were included, none of those apply—because, again, you *have* to have a *robbery* to get to the felony murder. This isn't a manslaughter case. And the only evidence of an accessory after the fact was a complete confession by Jennifer Charron as to all of that."

It was a bold move, essentially telling jurors not to find Jennifer Mee guilty of manslaughter or accessory after the fact—charges that they could have explored and considered here.

Was Trevena saying all or nothing?

He never indicated—because he was finished.

The state had ASA Hunter-Olney rebut Trevena's closing, but it was more of the same "you should believe us, not him" rhetoric that can get rather desperate-sounding during closings, carrying on far too long.

The judge had her deputy bailiff hand out jury instructions as she read through them. By the time she had finished, it was well after six o'clock at night. The jury needed to eat dinner, the judge explained, as the court considered when the start of official deliberations would begin.

CHAPTER 95

AS THE JURY began deliberating that same night, Rachel Robidoux retired to her hotel room about a mile away from the courthouse to lie down and catch her breath. At any moment, the jury could come back with a decision on her daughter's fate. It was altogether nerve-wracking and disconcerting for Rachel to think about. She had sat in the courtroom for every moment of the trial, unable to help her child. Now all she could do was pace, chain-smoke cigarettes, and think long and hard about all the what-ifs.

Meanwhile, back at the courthouse, after an hour or so behind closed doors, the jury had a few questions. It seemed they were taking the matter of jury duty quite seriously, as they should.

"Please clarify the phrase 'abiding conviction of guilt,'" the foreman, on behalf of the whole jury, requested of the court.

The judge asked John Trevena if he had any suggestions.

"Pull *Webster's*? Google it?"

In the end, the court decided to answer the question by stating that the jury had "all the law they are going to have" within the instructions the court had read through and handed out before deliberations started. If they had questions pertaining to the law, they needed to refer to those instructions.

A second, more technical question came up next. It was in reference to determining if Jennifer Mee was a "principal" in the robbery, and, if so, would that apply?

Trevena thought he had explained this in his closing. You cannot have one without the other. If Jennifer was not part of the robbery, well, how in the heck could she be part of the murder?

And once again, the court told the jury to refer to the instructions.

Jurors went back to work.

CHAPTER 96

RACHEL ROBIDOUX HEARD her phone ringing.

"Yes?" she said eagerly.

"Come back to court," the voice said. It was one of Trevena's colleagues. Word was the jury was apparently ready to announce its verdict. "They could come back [at] any time now."

Rachel was still inside her hotel room. She gathered her things quickly and left.

The jury had spent about four hours deliberating.

Shannon Griffin's mother, Shanna, sat front and center as the courtroom assembled to hear the jury's verdict.

Just before that, John Trevena had stood and announced that he wanted to "move for a mistrial based upon the court's instructions to the jury over" an objection Trevena had raised earlier.

"Very good," the judge said. "Your motion for mistrial is denied. . . ."

It was a formality.

Jennifer Mee sat very still. It was quite obvious she was nervous, with a million and one thoughts soaring through her head.

Judge Nancy Moate Ley wanted to know if everybody was in the courtroom.

Apparently, with that settled, the jury was then brought in.

Judge Ley asked for the jury foreman to stand and hand the verdict to the deputy.

The clerk took it from the deputy and read it into

the record: "'*State of Florida* versus *Jennifer Mee*, murder in the first degree. We, the jury, find as follows as to the defendant in this case. The defendant is *guilty* of murder in the first degree as charged.'"

A deep, collective gasp could be felt more than heard.

It was the worst-possible outcome for Jennifer Mee, who began crying almost immediately. And the one person Jennifer had leaned on throughout, the one person she had been through everything in her life with, the one person she relied on for support more than any other human being, as Jennifer turned to look for her mother, Rachel Robidoux was not yet there.

"It took me about fifteen minutes to get back and I was . . . too late," Rachel said later, nearly in tears herself recalling the moment her daughter was found guilty of first-degree murder and she was not there to cushion the fall.

Thus, a panel of seven women and five men had found Jennifer Mee guilty. The jurors were now being polled as Jennifer could be heard heavily breathing, nearly hyperventilating, crying loudly.

Shannon's mother cried, too, as did Doug Bolden.

There were no winners here.

John Trevena was not at all surprised. And yet anytime a client is found guilty, especially with the stakes as high as they were on this day, Trevena felt hurt and frustrated To him, it had been a witch hunt from day one. Here it was the state had offered a deal to the admitted *shooter* and not once did it take seriously a deal that Jennifer could consider.

Jennifer Mee now faced sentencing.

The judge wasted little time: "All right. The jury, having found you guilty of murder in the first degree,

Miss Mee, I will adjudicate you guilty and sentence you to life in prison without parole. . . . You have thirty days to appeal."

What many found to be an indication of how emotionally taxing it had been in such a short time of just three days of testimony, four jurors cried as the verdict was read into the record and Jennifer Mee was told the remainder of her life—which, by average, would amount to sixty years or more—would be spent behind bars.

"I lost it," Rachel said after arriving and feeling the weight of the world pressurizing that small courtroom, emotions raw, whispers abounding. She walked in and knew right away. No one had to tell her.

As everyone left the courthouse, the media descended upon Rachel and the lawyers, demanding comments.

"How are you feeling?" someone asked Rachel as she walked quickly away from the courthouse.

"How do they *think* I'm feeling?" Rachel responded.

Later, the mother of convicted murderer Jennifer Mee said: "It was one of the worst days of my life. I didn't want to live anymore. The pain was so bad. As a mother, it's your job to protect your children, and yet there was no way I could. I wanted to hold her, tell [her] I loved her, and everything would be okay."

Leaving the courtroom, Jennifer Mee could barely walk on her own accord.

"I had never seen a jury openly weeping as they are giving their verdict," Trevena commented.

CHAPTER 97

THREE WEEKS AFTER the verdict, John Trevena's law firm filed a surprise motion seeking a second trial based on "new evidence," which had, according to Trevena, surfaced shortly after the trial concluded.

That evidence, the motion claimed, came from an online comment posted to the *Tampa Bay Times'* website. On the site, a woman who identified herself as "Rosalea Hughes" posted a comment under a story about none other than Jenni Charron. The motion claimed Rosalea Hughes wrote: *Miss Charron went around telling people that she'd "had her boyfriend killed."*

It was a rather revealing comment.

If true, of course.

Shockingly, the judge ordered a hearing.

"We simply don't believe that the state met its burden," Trevena told the court during that October 2013 hearing. "She certainly should not be serving a life sentence for what conduct they have alleged."

Trevena's co-counsel Bryant Camareno offered "printouts of [that] e-mail exchange he had with the commenter . . . Rosalea Hughes about the possible involvement of Jennifer Charron" in the murder of Shannon Griffin.

LaBruzzo and Hunter-Olney countered by stating that a "fourth person's involvement in Griffin's death wouldn't have affected Mee's case and that the allegations raised by her lawyers are hearsay, anyway."

All spot-on.

"It is speculative at best," ASA Hunter-Olney told the court.

Again, a very accurate statement. Taking it even further, one had to ask: was the court now inclined to listen to Internet trolls commenting on the outcome of cases?

"Her statements to the police and to her mom show there was a plan," LaBruzzo said, feeling as though he'd explained this rather perfectly during trial. The jury believed him by returning a guilty verdict. "Her statement showing that she, in fact, set it all up is an important part of this."

After the proceeding, Trevena said he did not "believe Judge Ley would grant the motion" because she would essentially have to reverse herself. "And I don't see that occurring."

And he was right.

It didn't happen.

As for the commenter Rosalea Hughes, Trevena said they investigated further, "but it went nowhere."

No surprise, in December, after a brief trial and three-and-a-half hours of deliberation, Lamont Newton was found guilty of first-degree murder and sentenced to life in prison without the possibility of parole.

The saga, for now, was over. All three involved in the death of Shannon Andre Griffin would serve life behind bars.

CHAPTER 98

JOHN TREVENA HAD said just before the judge sentenced Jennifer Mee that he was not going to take on her appeal. Jennifer would have to get a public defender. In the end, however, on July 28, 2014, Trevena filed it himself.

Some later accused Trevena of failing to bring in several significant issues about Jennifer Mee's life that might have helped her win over a few jurors, such as Jennifer's claim of being raped, her Tourette diagnosis, her low IQ. These all seemed to be strong mitigating factors that could have helped explain some of her behavior and maybe lessen her charges and sentence.

"The problem with all of that is that you cannot bring it in," Trevena explained to me. "The way the law is in Florida, there can be no mitigation."

There are mandatory laws in Florida with regard to sentencing and the guidelines that judges use for sentencing. In most states, the time to bring in all of that information about Jennifer's life would have been during the sentencing phase of Jennifer's trial after a guilty verdict, whereby the lawyer argues on behalf of his client for a lesser sentence based upon certain "mitigating" factors. In many of these instances, the lawyers bring in witnesses to testify on behalf of the defendant, and family members and friends can write letters to the judge asking for leniency.

"She's convicted. It's life without parole. End of story," Trevena explained. "Normally, I would use all of those witnesses on my sentencing argument, but they're not going to be any help in a murder case [in Florida]. I could put them on, but it would all be futile. There is no way the judge could impart anything other than life in prison."

Interestingly enough, John Trevena said Jennifer Mee never told him about being raped. My mention of it to him was the "first time" he had ever heard about it.

The appeal Trevena filed with the court runs fifty pages. It is a brilliant piece of appellate work by an extremely competent, passionate, and caring lawyer. In short, one of Trevena's major points of debate is this salient idea: *[The court] erred in failing to grant a judgment of acquittal, as the state presented insufficient evidence to show that [Jennifer] intended to participate in the underlying attempted robbery.*

It is a strong opinion, made by an experienced lawyer.

The second issue revolves around the notion: *[The court] reversibly erred in denying [Jennifer's] request to provide the "independent act" jury instruction where there was evidence to support the instruction.*

He was blaming the judge here—an unfortunate way of trying to get Jennifer a new trial, which lawyers in Trevena's position use all the time.

Next, Trevena appealed where the court erred once more: *[It permitted] a law enforcement officer to testify that [Jennifer's] statement was consistent with other statements he heard.*

In other words, Dave Wawrzynski put blinders on and didn't take into account that Jennifer and Jenni and Laron and Lamont all told the same story at first; he only viewed their second story as valid. Trevena was insinuating that the SPPD kept searching for the narrative it wanted and did not stop until it got all of the suspects to give them that official, incriminating story.

Finally, Trevena said in his appeal, *[the trial court] abused its discretion by excluding on hearsay grounds testimony showing that one of the witnesses had discussed "cover stories" with co-defendants and that she made inconsistent statements to law enforcement officers concerning the incident.*

And thus, it was back to the Jenni Charron argument for Trevena.

In total, Trevena requested that the appellate court "vacate" Jennifer's conviction and sentence and "remand" her to trial court with "directions to discharge her."

"The way it is here in Florida," Trevena said of the appellate court, "if they feel that the defendant deserves a break, then great, they suddenly find one and it gets reversed. If they think the defendant deserves what they got, or they don't want to deal with the media fallout from a decision, then no matter how strong the issue, nothing will happen."

In June 2015, Jennifer's case was heard by the Court of Appeals. Without any explanation or written opinion whatsoever as to why or how the judges came to a conclusion, the appeal was denied.

Trevena was incensed. "For us it is a slap in the face to be given . . . no explanation." In some thirty years of practicing law, he added, "I have never seen a case that has gone south like this . . ."

Pinellas Pasco State Attorney Bernie McCabe seemed to take a shot at Jennifer after the verdict was announced. "It is a tragic case but there is nothing unique about it except that she appeared on television with hiccups . . ."

Trevena said he was determined to get Jennifer's out of jail, concluding, ". . . We are now investigating new evidence in the case that will hopefully support a motion for post conviction relief," Trevena said. "We will continue the fight for her exoneration and release."

EPILOGUE

LOOKING AT THIS case, studying all aspects of it for over a year, it's easy to see how Jennifer Mee bought into the myth and disillusionment that a "celebrity"—a Dance Mom, Teen Mom, wealthy duck call inventor(s), Real Housewife, tattoo artist, Big Brother, Master Chef, Gold Digger, king crab fisherman, hot rod mechanic, antique hunter, pawnshop owner, etc.—that was created by what is a short-attention-span, merciless, pop culture–driven, i-everything society, becomes something more than he or she was before being plucked out of obscurity and put on display without any direction. The idea, essentially, that being on television can change one's life is a fantasy. Celebrity used to be earned. It was special. Real life has become a carnival, and certain "freaks" of society are the main attraction. Reality television is a vacuum; its "stars" sucked up into a black hole and disposed of when ratings fall. I find it appalling, actually.

Jennifer "Hiccup Girl" Mee was stripped of her dignity and privacy by a common ailment that turned her into a household nickname. She and her parents, in part, allowed some of that to happen. But, in truth, Rachel reached out to a newspaper in desperation, hoping to get her daughter the help she needed. That led to a firestorm of coverage—Rachel could have never seen coming—precipitated by a celebrity-driven cult of media today that determine what is and is not so-called "news."

Now Jennifer is a convicted murderer. She did that herself. A twenty-two-year-old man, a good human being with a future ahead of him, was killed for *nothing*—three youngsters in their early twenties locked up for the remainder of their lives.

That, alone, is the *only* reality here.

I wrote to Jennifer Mee in 2013 asking if she would be willing to talk about her case. I was interested in Jennifer's case for a number of reasons, mainly to take a look at the rise and fall of an Internet/reality/pop culture celebrity and how we as a society treat disposable celebrities. I wanted to chronicle how those celebrities react to the instant fame, and then afterward, where their lives go, and how they manage the crash. (Go back and look at my dedication in this book—that list, within this context, becomes remarkable.)

I reckon a comparison can be made to some lottery winners. We've all seen the reports of rags to riches: Someone hits Lotto. They immerse themselves in the lap of luxury and then go down in a ball of flames from all the debt they've amassed. Their lives turn out ten times worse than before it had all started.

I wanted to know how Jennifer Mee had gone from the Hiccup Girl to convicted murderer. What happened in between? And what did the backstory of her life encompass? Was she, in fact, guilty as charged?

Jennifer didn't write back to me right away. Her parents called. We had long chats. They spoke from their hearts, believing that Jennifer was not guilty and that she'd been drawn into something she had very little to no part in.

"Jennifer is no killer," Rachel and Chris told me.

I agreed—she was not like the sociopaths I generally write about.

At the time I spoke to Rachel and Chris after sending that first letter, I was skeptical. I had not seen much of the evidence and had not yet read through Jennifer's trial or interviewed many of the players. I was going with my gut. I am familiar with Florida law. Florida is not a state where you want to be around anyone who has killed another human being for any reason. A small role in a crime that results in a murder can, as you have just read, put you in prison forever.

After a long discussion and an agreement that Rachel and Chris would open up their lives to me and provide me with unfettered access to Jennifer and the case records, including medical records and everything in between, I agreed to go into the case with an open mind—as I try to do with every case. I promised to listen to what they had to say and look for those holes in the investigation and prosecution of Jennifer Mee that Rachel and Chris were certain I would find.

"This will not be your typical true-crime book," I told Rachel Robidoux, speaking of my vision for the book I wanted to write about Jennifer Mee and her ordeal. What I meant was, I would approach it differently: from a perspective of knowing that Jennifer Mee was unlike the typical female psychopaths I write about.

"That's all we ask," Rachel said.

"I cannot promise anything, however," I told Rachel. "I am going to report what I find."

She accepted that.

In the end, I met those promises.

I feel sorry for Jennifer Mee and her family. I wanted to find a loophole for Jennifer. I wanted to uncover a glitch somewhere that told me and them that she had been wrongly convicted. I do not believe Jennifer is a vicious killer who set out to lure Shannon Griffin to that house so her boyfriend and his BFF could rob and then kill him. I also don't believe she knew about the murder or that there was a murder planned, to begin with. But all three committed robbery, and a murder occurred during the course of that crime. There can be no denying those *facts*. Nothing can change what happened. The law in Florida is the law. The evidence, furthermore, points unequivocally to the three charged in the case. Jennifer Mee herself admitted to her mother later, while Rachel and the family visited her in prison, that she set up the robbery. That's all we need to know. There was never any evidence linking Jenni Charron to any part of this crime besides the cover-up afterward. (Yes, that was a serious crime in and of itself, but not part of the murder.) I do not believe for a moment that Jenni Charron and Shannon Griffin set up a sexual rendezvous and Laron walked in on it. There is zero evidence to support that claim. A condom wrapper with Laron's fingerprints found near the scene is hardly enough to suggest anything of the sort.

It was difficult to get Jennifer to write to me. As you've read, her answers in the letters she finally wrote were rather terse and sometimes hard to follow. (I always sent her specific, direct questions.) As we wound down our interviews, I sent Jennifer a list of final questions. By this time, I had made it clear to the family that things I was uncovering were not necessarily going to help Jennifer. Before sending this list of final questions, I told Rachel: "You're not going to like everything in this book."

Some of the questions I wrote to Jennifer included: *Maybe the most important question of all: What happened the*

*night Shannon Griffin was killed? Begin as early as waking
up that morning and continue until you call your mom from
jail the following night. Take as much space as you need. Details are very important. Did you know Laron and Lamont
had a gun? Did you know they owned a gun? Did you know
they brought the gun with them? Did you ever hear Laron or
Lamont talk about killing Shannon? Where was Jennifer
Charron that day/night?*

I also encouraged Jennifer to talk about the Hic-
Cup deal, if she ever faked the hiccups for attention,
how much money she was paid in total for anything
having to do with the hiccups, if she was ever mad at
Rachel for taking any of the money she made from the
hiccups (something I was told), and about Debbie
Lane and that hypnotherapy session.

It took months. I thought she would not write back.
So I e-mailed Rachel: *She hasn't gone into detail about the
crime—but I need that from her now. I need her version of
what happened. She's told it to the police. I thought she was
participating [in this book]?*

I'll let her know, Rachel wrote back. *I wasn't aware she
had gone into detail about [the] crime. I think she is worried
that it may hurt her case too bad [and] she didn't think that
way in the beginning.*

Now, *at this point, she* doesn't *want to talk about the
case!?* I e-mailed back to Rachel. I was totally taken
aback. All throughout the process of interviewing
Rachel, Chris, two of Jennifer's sisters, and Jennifer
herself, I had been given what I thought was full
access—or, rather, as complete as I could get. Here
came the hardballs from my pitching rotation, and
now Jennifer wasn't willing to take a swing. She'd

spoken to everyone about her case—the entire world, in fact. I wanted it from her, myself.

After all she has said? I wrote to Rachel. *They are very important questions.*

She told me she doesn't feel comfortable talking about [the] case with possible appeals, Rachel answered.

I had set a date (September 30, 2014) as a cutoff point for any information the family wanted to share with or send me—including Jennifer. I had sent Jennifer a package of several self-addressed, stamped envelopes, along with enough paper to write to me anytime she wanted. Jennifer had requested this because she did not have any stamps or money for paper, I was told.

In late October, I finally received a letter from Jennifer. She acknowledged that I had asked her those hardball questions.

I'm not tryen 2 avoid answern your questions about my case, she wrote in her broken, childlike, street language.

She went on to say it was a "hard subject" for her to talk about: *As when I had the hiccups, I never once did it 4 the media attention.*

She went on for only one page, and I am going to include her misspellings and strange syntax here, verbatim, the way in which it was written to me. She avoided my questions. Instead, Jennifer once again played the victim. She wanted readers to know she had joined a faith-based group in prison and is forced to watch inmates "sexten on each other" and "peopel be cutten on other peopel." She said she hadn't gotten into any trouble while behind bars and was working on her GED. Her wish was for the "world" to see her as "not the person they clamed me to be."

Yeah, I've fucked up in life, but I'm only humman, Jennifer wrote.

"Fucked up"?

She is a convicted *murderer.* That is more than "fucking up."

Once again, it's clear that Jennifer Mee doesn't truly understand that she lured a man behind a vacant home, where he was ambushed and murdered. She, effectively, by law, took a life. Yet, she constantly and consistently places herself in the role of the victim.

I kept asking Rachel to get me the state police reports for the alleged rape case, offering to pay any costs associated with obtaining them. Rachel told me the police had been called at the time of the incident. That meant there would have to be a report. I could not send a Freedom of Information Act request myself—or I would have—because of certain issues. And it was never prosecuted. I'd never get those reports without years of bureaucratic red tape and lawyers. But the mother of the "victim" in the case would certainly have the best chance to get her hands on them.

As of this writing (September 2015), almost a year after asking and asking and asking, I do not have the reports. Do they exist? I have never seen them. Thus, the rape allegations from Ashley, Jennifer, and the family are based solely on their tesimonials.

I grew fond of Rachel. She has never been given the benefit of the doubt; she has always been judged, by the public and by the media. Several people told me Rachel and Chris were money-grubbing scoundrels, who used Jennifer. Not true. Not one bit. Rachel or Chris never asked me for money, while some others in this case did. Rachel shared deep, dark secrets with me, which I did not write about. I greatly respect that trust. I wanted so much to find something that proved Jennifer was not involved. But it just wasn't there. Jennifer broke the law. She was prosecuted to the fullest for that. Was she overcharged and used as an example because of her quasi-celebrity? We could argue that all day long and never come to a conclusion.

Anyone familiar with my work knows that I try to place the victim of murder first and foremost. My goal—always!—is to tell the complete story of the victim and bring him or her back into the headline of the case, where his or her place rightly belongs. This case was especially tough in that regard. I reached out to Doug Bolden several times with no response. I left four messages for the victims' advocate representing Shannon and his family. No one ever called me back.

ACKNOWLEDGMENTS

MY READERS ARE always the hardest to thank—because nothing I can say will extend to each the gratitude I feel in my heart for returning, book after book.

Kensington Publishing Corp. and Michaela Hamilton are, by far, the only publisher and editor in the business for me at this time in my career. We've worked on over twenty books together now. I am entirely grateful for their support.

I also would like to give my sincere appreciation to everyone at Investigation Discovery and Beyond Productions for being responsible for my television career. We have some things in the cooker now that I am really excited about!

For my entertainment lawyer/business manager, Matthew Valentinas, a continued thanks.

I would also like to thank Deb Allen, Jasmine Fox, Donna Dudek, and Dave Lane from Jupiter Entertainment. They helped me out tremendously with research for this book.

I interviewed scores of people for this book, conducting well over one hundred interviews with those sources. They know who they are and I thank each and every source that took the time to talk to me. John Trevena was open and honest, and I have a tremendous amount of respect for him. Betty Long, supervisor, Records and Identification Division, St. Petersburg Police Department, was incredibly helpful.

Rachel Robidoux made herself available to me anytime I needed, and I thank her immensely for her time and honesty. I have a place in my heart for Rachel that I cannot explain. She has been through so much in her life, beyond the hiccups and the murder her daughter was involved in. I don't know how many other people could ever manage what Rachel has and come out of it.

Jennifer Mee is still, in my mind, a paradox. I need to say a thank-you to her because she did help; but, on the other hand, I do not believe she was as totally honest and open with me as she could (or should) have been. Prison will destroy this fragile soul and my hope is that she can get out of prison and get involved in some other type of program. However, I also realize that is highly unlikely and that Jennifer has a debt to pay society for what she did.

Here's what needs to be said: When you are involved in taking someone's life, you can never take it back. As much as you wish like hell you had made better decisions, there are no do-overs in murder. Jennifer never planned on that man being slain. But he was. And she was part of it. That can—and will—never change.

The last word of this book should be that a good man, Shannon Andre Griffin, is dead and is greatly missed by his family.

NOTES

1. This quote was excerpted from http://criminal.laws.com/criminal-news/reputable-criminal-defense-attorney-john-trevena-talks-crime-and-punishment-37015.html

2. According to the National Library of Medicine, "Gilles de la Tourette syndrome is a condition that causes a person to make repeated, quick movements or sounds that they cannot control. These movements or sounds are called tics. . . ." http://www.ncbi.nlm.nih.gov/pubmedhealth/PMH0001744/

3. Jennifer was clear that her attackers were not family members. They cannot be named, because no charges were brought against them.

4. I need to make a point here about Jennifer and her comments. Some of her comments—such as the way they are sourced here—were written to me in letters we exchanged for the book. In lieu of stuffing and stifling the narrative with misspelled words, bad grammar, and my corrections (there would be many instances), I've opted to correct the words without notation, without changing the context or meaning of her prose. I have also included them as conversation rather than as

italicized letters/notes. That said, however, Jennifer's writing allows us to look deeply at her education and learning disabilities. For example, in the passage quoted above, she misspelled simple words like "awsome" and "growen." She would often misspell "try." Misspellings like this are littered all over her writings and it tells me that she truly suffers from learning disabilities and/or little education.

5. I asked Rachel to call the state police and order the police report from the day the police showed up at the house and took a statement from Jennifer, Rachel, and other family members. Generally, I do this myself with a Freedom of Information Act request, but since Jennifer was a minor at the time and the case against her attackers was never prosecuted, I could not get the report. As of this writing, I do not have any report detailing these allegations; all of the information stems from Rachel, Chris, Jennifer, and her sister. Personally, I have no reason not to believe Jennifer.

6. This passage is from WebMD (http://www.webmd.com/digestive-disorders/hiccups-chronic), where you can find an abundance of information about the hiccups.

7. I would encourage readers to Google this video and have a look. It's worth watching to see how genuine Jennifer's torment was during this period of her life, not to mention how bad you will feel for her as you sit and watch this girl suffer from what can be a life-altering, irritating, and painful condition.

8. I asked Rachel to produce medical reports regarding Jennifer's Tourette condition and the hiccups. As a journalist, I cannot gain access to these reports by myself. And she did mail me some documentation

proving that Jennifer's condition had been diagnosed and treated by medical professionals.

9. When asked, Rachel did not recall saying this.

10. Michele says her records indicate this FedEx package was sent to Rachel overnight.

11. The Mayo Clinic classifies hiccupping as a "simple tic" associated with Tourette's.

12. To be clear, although the family wishes to keep it a private matter, the "dark family scandal" referred to here is *not* the alleged sexual assault Jennifer went through as a child. It is an entirely different matter.

13. See a complete diagram and key of this crime scene in the photo section.

Don't miss the next stunning real-life thriller by
M. William Phelps

If You Only Knew

Coming from Kensington Publishing Corp.
in Fall 2016

Keep reading to enjoy a preview excerpt . . .

CHAPTER 1

SOME THINGS ARE not what they appear to be at first glance. Take, for example, the quiet stillness of the night inside her patrol car, interrupted only by the crackling static of a police scanner every so often. It was that sound, rolling over her relaxed breathing and the occasional shuffle and leathery crunch of her well-oiled duty belt, that had misled Patrol Officer Lynn Giorgi into thinking it just might be a slow night, devoid of any major public evils.

Officer Giorgi had worked for the City of Grand Rapids, Michigan, before becoming a police officer in Troy, about a 150-mile drive east, two years prior. Troy is sandwiched between slices of Lake Michigan, Lake Huron, Lake St. Clair, and Lake Erie. Troy is, essentially, part of the metro Detroit region, within Oakland County. A family-oriented city, one of the largest in the state, Troy bills itself as the "most dynamic and livable" metropolitan area in the "Wolverine State." It's the schools, everyone says, that attract the yuppies and hipsters to settle down with their privileged kids and live the good life in suburbia.

As Officer Giorgi patrolled through downtown during the early-morning hours of August 12, 2000, near the halfway point of her midnight-to-eight shift, the otherwise quiet radio in her cruiser buzzed with a voice. It was dispatch: "Man down . . . not breathing . . ."

A second request then came in for an ambulance.

CPR run, Giorgi thought.

Some poor bastard probably had a heart attack and was fighting for his life.

Up until then, it had been an inconsequential night in Troy. It generally was.

As Giorgi hit the lights on her patrol car and took off toward Grenadier Drive, a rather swanky end of town, she expected to arrive at the scene and find a man she needed to perform first aid upon. In two years with the Troy Police Department (TPD), Giorgi had answered maybe ten of these same calls.

As Giorgi pulled into the driveway at four twenty-five in the morning, her colleague, friend, and fellow officer, Pete Dungjen, pulled in right behind her. The single-family home, with four bedrooms and three-and-a-half baths, at about three thousand square feet, was spacious and kept meticulously. The area had a reputation for building half-million-dollar homes. Not necessarily the ultrarich, but most of the people in this neighborhood did not have to worry about money.

Giorgi went directly into her trunk and took out the first aid CPR kit and ran toward the front door.

When she reached the stoop, the door opened. There were two females, Giorgi later said, standing in the foyer, waiting on the TPD to arrive. Both women seemed "calm," but also were in great need of someone to help the victim inside the house.

One of the women, whom Giorgi would later come to know as Billie Jean Rogers, said, "He's in there—in the kitchen." Billie Jean pointed the cop in the right direction.

Billie Jean was the man's wife.

Inside the kitchen, Giorgi's training kicked into action. On the floor was a man "in his fifties," she later guessed (he was much older), lying on his back, on the floor. There was a chair turned over on its side next to him. Without any other information provided, it seemed to Giorgi that the man had grabbed for the backrest of the chair on his way down to the floor, flipping the thing over as he hit the floor.

Donald Rogers was actually seventy-four years old. Billie Jean's husband was a local business owner who had made quite a bit of money manufacturing a line of automotive assembly tools. In the "car capital of the world," Don Rogers and his business partner, Don Kather, had started the business together back in 1977. Kather actually bought Don out in 1990, but Don had still invested in the company and went into the office every day, helping to keep it afloat after the car industry boom left only ashes in its wake.

Kather had gotten together with Don Rogers the day before, August 11, as they did daily, to meet for lunch. Rogers looked and sounded good, Kather later said. Rogers was "very frugal" with his spending habits, Don Kather explained, which became somewhat of a component of his life. He had plenty of money, yet he never went on vacations or bought luxurious items or drove glamorous cars. Same as when he went out to eat, Don chose middle-of-the road restaurants, always forgoing the four-star hot spots. He lived life simply. And yet, there was one thing Don never skimped on—

something he spared no expense at and did every day: drink.

Billie Jean was quite the polar opposite when it came to spending money—most of which was Don's.

"Well, if she saw something she liked," her daughter later said, "she would just buy it." Billie Jean had no real "concept of money," the daughter added. "She saw money as fun. . . . That [was] what it was for, in her mind." More than that, she was a "very poor money manager."

Billie Jean had lived both sides of the coin. In Tennessee, where she grew up with seven siblings, she was "dirt poor." There was not even running water in the house; they literally lived hand to mouth. Hand-me-downs and handouts were a way of life.

As Officer Giorgi prepared to work on Don, Billie Jean Rogers, Don's wife for a second time—they had married once, divorced, and then remarried—stood over her, explaining what she thought had happened.

"He's been drinking—he has a problem with alcohol," Billie Jean said. "He's a chronic alcoholic." Then, oddly enough, Billie Jean added, "He suffers from rectal bleeds."

The drinking had, apparently, gotten so out of hand, she was saying, Don often bled all over the place from his rectum.

Giorgi noticed that Don Rogers had very slight bruising on his face and one small abrasion on his upper lip. But one would expect some mild scruffs and scrapes on a guy who had supposedly passed out drunk and had fallen on the floor. Suffice it to say, he probably fell into that chair that was on its side lying next to him. In fact, he probably made a habit of falling down and into things, if he drank as much as his wife claimed.

Giorgi had to move the chair so she could kneel next to Don and begin to work on him.

Acclimating himself to the situation, trying to figure out the best way to help Don Rogers, Officer Dungjen walked up and knelt on one knee next to Giorgi. By now, Billie Jean was a bit more antsy, but not at all frantic or exceedingly concerned, both officers noticed. The way she acted, this fall seemed perhaps to be a common thing around the house: Don tying one on and then passing out on the floor.

Dungjen touched Don Rogers.

"He's cold," Dungjen said to Giorgi. "Rigidity has set in."

Giorgi didn't have to check for a pulse. She knew.

Don Rogers wasn't passed out this time.

He was dead.

CHAPTER 2

THE OTHER WOMAN, standing next to Billie Jean Rogers as law enforcement backup was called in to determine what happened to Don Rogers, and if the scene warranted further investigation, was thirty-two-year-old Vonlee Nicole Titlow. She went by Vonlee alone. Born in Maryville, Tennessee, a deep southern town at the foothills of the Smokey Mountains, Vonlee had lived in Nashville and in Denver, and had a penthouse in Chicago at one time. Vonlee's aunt, Billie

Jean, her mother's sister, had invited Vonlee to stay with her and Don in Troy, and Vonlee had been living at the house for the past few months. While the age difference spanned decades, Billie Jean and Vonlee shared a common love of going out and partying at the local casinos in Detroit. Whereas Billie Jean was more focused on gambling, Vonlee was a nightlife gal, dancing and drinking, working the rooms. She'd been an exotic dancer and had run an escort service in Denver and Chicago, making upward of—Vonlee later claimed—$20,000 a week. Back then, Vonlee later said, she was dating a few different men at the same time.

"I took care of them," she claimed. Meaning, she paid for their lifestyle and living accommodations. "It was kind of like a power thing. Kind of fun . . . You know, I loved those guys."

Moving to Chicago from Denver in 1999, Vonlee was effectively running from the escort lifestyle in Denver, while still dabbling in it to make some money in Chicago. But she wanted the simple life now. From the early 1990s until that move to Chicago, Vonlee had been running from herself, essentially. She'd gotten caught up in a life of booze, men, clubs, cars, and clothes. All material things. By the time she made it to Chicago, Vonlee had a life waiting for her, if she wanted it. A man she had been dating signed over the deed to a house that she could live in free of rent. All she had to do was be there for him when he needed her. The man wanted to take care of Vonlee. "A lot of men did this throughout the years," Vonlee told me later. However, as Vonlee thought about it, she was nobody's possession—nobody's "thing" to have when he wanted. Whereas it might have been something she went for during her younger years, not anymore.

Vonlee was now in her thirties. She needed to focus on herself and what *she* wanted.

"It's on the counter," she said one night when that man came home.

"What?"

"The deed. I signed it back over to you—I'm going home to Tennessee."

By now, Vonlee had been to rehab, a familiar face in AA meetings around Chicago. She wanted out of the big city, away from that fast-paced nightlife she had taken part in through much of her twenties. Back in Tennessee, she took a job at the local Waffle House and went back to living with her grandmother, Annis Lee, the woman who had raised her.

"I was giving her twenty or thirty dollars a day for rent," Vonlee said.

Life was simple. She was around family. The smell of that Tennessee air—there was nothing like it, she felt. She embraced the downhome, simple folks she interacted with every day, the sheer snail's pace of life itself. She'd take her nephews fishing. She'd go for drives in the country to see friends. She'd attend barbeques the relatives spent all day preparing, and would enjoy Sunday dinners after church services.

"I was extremely happy," Vonlee recalled.

But then something happened.

"Aunt Billie Jean shows up. . . ."

Vonlee was actually working when Billie Jean walked into the restaurant, sat down, and called her over. Vonlee hadn't seen her in over a decade. She'd spoken to her, but that was it. Now her aunt sat in front of her during the spring or early summer of 2000, surprising

Vonlee with the visit, making a proposition Vonlee had a hard time turning her back on.

As Vonlee approached the table, shocked to see her aunt there all the way from Troy, she noticed Billie Jean was laughing.

"A waitress," Billie Jean said in a mocking tone, talking down to Vonlee. "You're a waitress in this dive? I cannot *believe* you took to waiting on tables, Vonlee."

Vonlee wanted to curl up in a ball right there. She felt belittled and a total failure.

"Sit down," Billie Jean said. It sounded as though she had an offer to make.

"What are you doing here?" Vonlee asked. She was looking back toward the kitchen and register. She didn't want her boss to see her sitting in a booth with a customer.

"Look, honey, you don't have any drinking problem. What are you running from?" Vonlee and Billie Jean, living somewhat close to each other in the upper Midwest, had communicated, and Billie Jean knew about Vonlee's journey into recovery. In some ways, there was a bit of envy on the older woman's part. She valued Vonlee's no-holds-bar attitude, not giving two shakes about what people said or thought about her. Billie Jean wanted to be her own person, same as Vonlee. She knew the more she hung around Vonlee, the more of a free spirit she would become.

As for Vonlee, she certainly had the pizzazz, flare, and fortitude, along with the clichéd, sassy Southern charm of a luxurious, expensive call girl. She looked the part with her long, muscular, and yet feminine legs, her bleached-blond hair down to her shoulders, and her curvaceous, womanly figure. And if you were to ask Vonlee, she had no trouble taking clients on by herself when her girls couldn't handle the influx of calls or the specialized requests from such a high-powered clientele.

But that was another time, another life. She was back home now in Tennessee and pretty content living a simple life.

During those preceding months leading up to the early morning Don Rogers was found dead inside the kitchen of his home, however, Vonlee was determined to spend her free time seeing old friends and spending time with her rather large family. Chicago and the escort business were rather old and worn. And Billie Jean, who claimed she was back to visit family, insisted that Vonlee come back to Michigan at once with her and live inside the home Billie Jean shared with Don. Billie Jean told Vonlee that a restaurant, waiting tables, was not the place she wanted to see her niece. It was degrading.

Vonlee considered the question: *Should I go back? It isn't Chicago. It's Troy, Michigan. What kind of trouble is in Troy?*

"You don't have no dranking problem, Vonlee," Billie Jean said, that southern accent unmistakable. She was leaning over the table, almost whispering. "You just need to buy bigger bottles and drank it slow all day long." The aunt laughed at her own wit.

Vonlee suddenly pondered the idea. *Maybe I don't.*

"Let's you and me get out of here," Billie Jean said. "I got money."

"Where?"

Harrah's, Billie Jean suggested.

July Fourth weekend was a day away.

"In North Carolina?" Vonlee asked.

"Yes."

Vonlee took off her apron, tossed it into the kitchen,

and headed out the door. She would pack something while Billie Jean waited in the car. Like Thelma and Louise, she and Billie Jean would head out to Harrah's Cherokee Casino in Cherokee, North Carolina, to party it up for the weekend. Any sobriety Vonlee had earned, she had just given away.

It was a spur-of-the-moment decision that would change Vonlee's life forever.

CHAPTER 3

OFFICER GIORGI GATHERED Vonlee and Billie Jean in the den of the house and began to assess Don's medical history, trying to figure out what might have happened. With no outward signs of trauma, no injuries that Officers Giorgi or Dungjen could see, the "alcoholism" bell Billie Jean had rung when the officers showed up now seemed most plausible. Giorgi wondered if this was the root cause of Don's demise. Hell, in just the short time she'd been a patrol officer, Giorgi had seen death come to people in both the most mundane and unimaginable ways.

Billie Jean was not at all surprised by Don's death. Or, rather, she didn't come across that way to Giorgi and Dungjen. She went through all of the ailments Don suffered from beyond being what Billie Jean described as a chronic drinker who would guzzle goblets full of vodka as if it were water.

"He'd take one of those mason jars and fill it up,"

Vonlee explained. "Then down it. I had seen him do it more than once."

Dungjen and Giorgi got together and decided their next move.

"We should probably call for the detective on duty and an ME," Giorgi offered.

It was a formality, both cops considered, a not-so-routine part of their day, but an obligation, nonetheless. They did not suspect foul play, but that was, of course, not their call to make. First responders showed up, evaluated the scene, did what they could to help, asked some questions, and then called in the investigators, if they believed a case warranted their time.

Giorgi covered Don with a yellow blanket and then sat with Vonlee and Billie Jean in the den. She wanted to ask a few more questions and hopefully help to figure out what had happened. The mood in the house was subdued, despite however anxious Vonlee, who later admitted to being totally inebriated during this time, seemed. Billie Jean appeared composed, with a handle on things.

"Understanding," one of the first responders called it later, referring to Billie Jean's demeanor.

Although, perhaps, alarmed that her husband was on the floor of their kitchen, dead, Billie Jean's behavior, at least initially, seemed appropriate to the circumstances.

Vonlee, on the other hand, was acting "surprising and out of place, considering the situation," that same first responder recalled. She was "resisting" the questions posed by both officers.

"Vonlee and I went to the casino," Billie Jean told Giorgi. "We were gone for a few hours—Donald did not want to go."

In a statement Billie Jean later handwrote that night, she talked about leaving for the casino at nine-thirty or ten-thirty at night, and coming home at four-fifteen in the morning, at which time she and Vonlee then called 911.

Billie Jean was "pretty calm" and "very quiet," Giorgi observed. "Didn't really speak unless I asked her questions."

Billie Jean also paced at times and chain-smoked cigarettes.

Probably nerves. Her husband was dead.

Giorgi walked back over to Don Rogers and thought about the scene a bit more, trying to picture what might have happened. Don was lying directly next to the kitchen table. He was on his back, with his legs crossed at the ankles. His arms were outstretched in kind of a Jesus-on-the-Cross position. This didn't raise any red flags, specifically, but the more they looked at it, the way in which Don's body lay seemed almost staged. Feeling this, the intuitive officer considered that she ought to look even closer. They had to wait for the detective and medical examiner, anyway. What would it hurt?

His legs are crossed at his ankles? Giorgi kept going back to this fact. It seemed odd, taking into account that Don might have fallen from the chair. How many people fall out of a chair and wind up on the ground, faceup, their legs crossed?

"It looked kind of unusual," Giorgi later explained. "It appeared that he had fallen out of his chair, and looking . . . It just seemed unlikely that you could fall from somewhere and end up with your legs perfectly crossed at the ankles."

Maybe it happened as one of the women tried reviving him? Maybe they had done this inadvertently?

Both said no.

Giorgi walked over to Billie Jean and asked several more questions. The officer was more direct and accusatory in her tone this time around. Maybe she didn't mean to be, but that was how it came out.

Vonlee stood by and appeared agitated with the officer. She viewed the situation as the officer attacking Billie Jean.

"You-all just need to leave her alone right now," Vonlee snapped at one point. Vonlee didn't think Billie Jean needed to be treated in this way—at least not right after her husband had died. "Why do you have to ask her all of these questions *now*?"

Vonlee, with her sassy Southern attitude and noticeable accent, was "very excitable and very loud . . . and very protective of [Billie Jean]," Giorgi noted later.

"Why are you being so rude?" Vonlee then asked the officer. "You must be a cold person to be asking all of these questions."

Giorgi and Dungjen tried to explain that they were just doing their jobs, but Vonlee wasn't having any of it. She didn't want her aunt subjected to such harsh treatment while her uncle was lying dead on the floor in the kitchen. It could all wait, Vonlee seemed to be suggesting.

"Look, this is a process," Giorgi explained, trying to put out a brush fire now gathering fuel, "and we've called in a detective and the medical examiner. . . . These are necessary questions we need answers to. I need to write a report."

Giorgi asked Billie Jean and Vonlee if they could sit, calm down, and perhaps write out for her what happened that night, what they did, and what they came home to. Details would be important. Would they mind writing a statement?

Neither indicated any interest in doing this.

Giorgi changed her tactic, as she often did in situations when people became stressed. She, instead, asked questions that did not pertain to the situation. Questions with answers they did not need to think about. How old are you? Where'd you grow up? Where do you work? Things of that nature.

That tactic did not work, either. Vonlee hemmed and hawed about how the cops were being unsympathetic to Billie Jean and the notion that Don was dead.

Giorgi continued to insist that both females needed to sit down and write out a statement she could include in her report.

"Oh, well, okay then . . . ," Vonlee said.

She began writing. But as she did, Vonlee quickly put the pen down and stated, "You know what, I am not doing this right now!" She was angry. Vonlee had secrets. Big ones. She had a lot to hide.

"Miss Titlow, these are things we need to know," Giorgi said again, more pleasantly than she had been in her previous tone.

Vonlee refused.

Billie Jean walked over and Giorgi asked about Don having any prior medical conditions—if either woman could shed any light on that.

"One time he passed out in the bathroom upstairs and hit his head on the tub," Billie Jean said. "He was bleeding and I wanted to call 911, but he told me not to."

The officers decided to check out the rest of the house. Since Vonlee and Billie Jean said they had just walked in and found him, it was possible that someone else had come by. But the only unlocked door into the entire house was the pedestrian door from the kitchen into the garage.

"That's how we came in," Billie Jean said when one of the cops pointed it out. "We used the garage door opener to open the garage and then came in through that door."

None of the windows or any of the other doors in the house were unlocked or seemed broken into. Even in the basement, Giorgi noticed when she went downstairs to look around, those windows seemed to be fine. No glass was broken. Nothing was out of place. All of the windows were locked.

Giorgi went into the family room, which had a fully stocked bar. She noticed not one bottle was open or even out. Everything appeared to be in its place on the shelves. But when she walked over to the pantry area of the house, just beyond the kitchen, not far from Don's body, there were several large bottles—"gallon size"—of vodka. But upon a careful examination of those, none of them had been opened, either.

Giorgi found Billie Jean. "Listen," she asked, "you said he once blacked out and hit his head."

"Yes," Billie Jean answered.

"Let's take a walk upstairs to check and see if anything like that might have happened again."

They went upstairs and walked through all of the bedrooms and the bathrooms.

Nothing seemed out of place.

When they got back downstairs, Billie Jean showed Giorgi one of the living-room chairs with blood on it. The blood was crusty and dried up.

"That's from Don's rectal bleeding."

It was the only spot in the entire house where they could locate any blood.

Giorgi was stumped. And yet, with all the talk going on inside the house, including the questions Vonlee and Billie Jean had asked, the one inquiry neither had made was rather telling in and of itself: *"What might have happened to Don?"* Neither Billie Jean nor Vonlee seemed to be interested in the opinions of the two officers.

"Can't we do this tomorrow?" Vonlee asked one of the officers. She was tired of all the questions. Accusations, as Vonlee saw them. She was mainly worried about Billie Jean, Vonlee said, not about herself.

"She was just sitting, at one point, smoking cigarettes and staring," Vonlee later said of Billie Jean.

What the hell? Vonlee wondered.

"I thought she was maybe ready to snap. I had never seen that look on her face before—it was eerie."